IMAGES
of America

THE STEWARTVILLE AREA

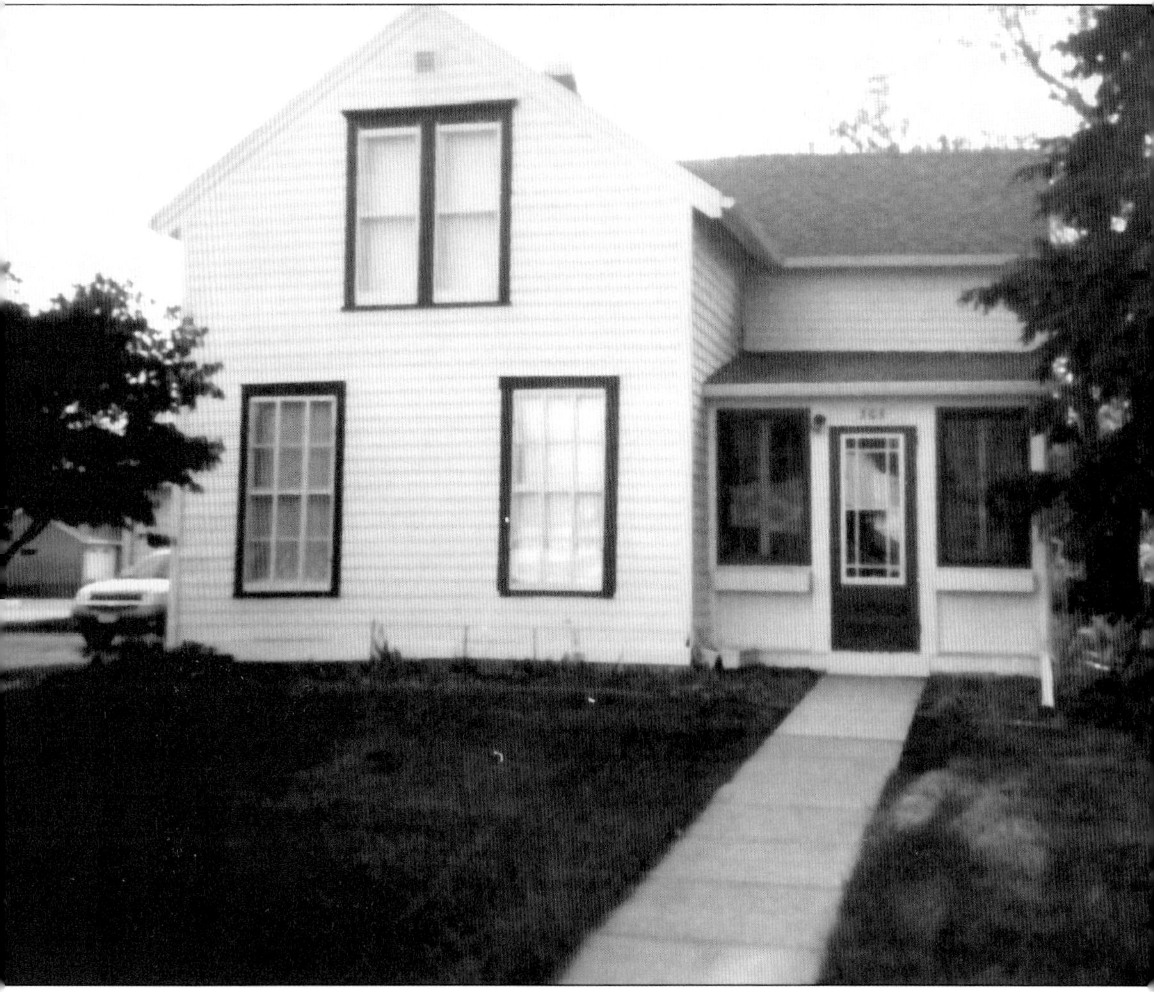

Richard W. Sears's birthplace is the hub of the Stewartville Area Historical Society. The society was formed the year the house was acquired in 1993. Through many donations, society fund-raisers, and grants, the house was paid for in less than three years. The catalog entrepreneur would be proud to see the results of the ongoing restoration by society members and volunteers. The house is part of Sears's Great American Home program, which helps keep this home painted, with the help of the local fire department. The mission of the society is to be a depository and an interpreter of the area's history. It is open every second and fourth Sunday during the summer months or by appointment. (Courtesy of the Stewartville Area Historical Society.)

On the cover: The Ringling Brothers Circus attracted unusual interest when it made its stop in Rochester on Friday, July 26, 1912. A three-mile parade contained specimens of strange animal life that were new to American zoos. Audiences were entertained by 375 of the greatest European circus artists and three herds of trained elephants. The great feature of the show was the newly added spectacle "Joan of Arc." About 10 people who had purchased tickets to Rochester to attend the circus were disappointed as the train was packed, so there was no room for them. About 60 cars passed through the village on their way to the circus and are lined up on the west side of North Main Street in the cover picture. (Courtesy of the Stewartville Area Historical Society.)

IMAGES
of America

THE STEWARTVILLE AREA

Stewartville Area Historical Society

ARCADIA
PUBLISHING

ISBN 978-0-7385-6000-7

Published by Arcadia Publishing
Charleston SC, Chicago IL, Portsmouth NH, San Francisco CA

Printed in the United States of America

Library of Congress Control Number: 2009923291

For all general information contact Arcadia Publishing at:
Telephone 843-853-2070
Fax 843-853-0044
E-mail sales@arcadiapublishing.com
For customer service and orders:
Toll-Free 1-888-313-2665

Visit us on the Internet at www.arcadiapublishing.com

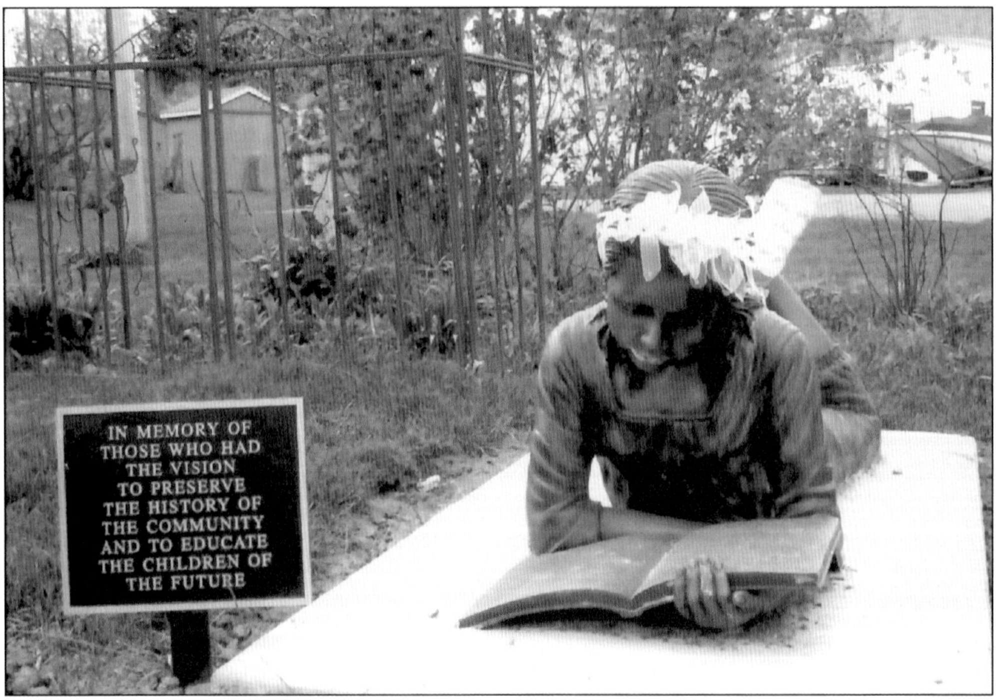

This book is dedicated to "those who had the vision to preserve the history of the community and to educate the children of the future." (Courtesy of Eleanor Crane.)

Contents

Acknowledgments 6

Introduction 7

1. Early Residents 9
2. Towns and Townships 23
3. Education 45
4. Main Street 57
5. Lake Florence 79
6. Agriculture 91
7. Historic Places 99
8. People 113
9. Important Events 123

Index 127

Acknowledgments

In 1993, the board of trustees (Buck Fredricksen, Doris Jensen, Carol King, Carl Oehlke, Luella Severson, and Aggie Splittstoesser from the Stewartville Area Historical Society) stood in front of 305 North Main Street, the former residence of John Lins. The home, the birthplace of Richard W. Sears, was turned into a museum after being purchased from Ed and Dorothy Lins-Hanson.

Thanks to the rich historical writings of area authors, we had the following resources to draw out the stories of the people who settled here: *Stewartville Story*, *Pleasant Grove*, *Early Days of Stewartville*, *Merchant to Millions*, and the *Stewartville Times/Stewartville Star*. The Stewartville Area Historical Society (SAHS) used its photograph archives donated through the last 16 years by area families to help make this book a reality.

A special thank-you to those people who spent countless hours collecting, organizing, and writing about each of the photographs shared by our community's families. The Stewartville Public Library lent its resources and scanner for all the photographs in this book. The Olmsted County Historical Society (OCHS) allowed us to use some of the photographs of Stewartville from its collection.

INTRODUCTION

The Stewartville Area is a pictorial walk back through time as the area and the state celebrated their sesquicentennial years.

Glacial action and the drainage of the vast Lake Agassiz carved the face of the land that became Minnesota. The channels of the Mississippi and Minnesota Rivers along with their tributary streams, including the Root River, cut paths through the landscape. The Root River is a translation from the Native American word *hokah*, meaning "root." The footprints of the mastodon, the Native Americans, and the pioneers have left traces affecting the lives of the people who live in this area today.

The Minnesota territorial legislature, on October 27, 1849, created Wabasha County, of which Olmsted was a part. But it was not until February 1855 that Olmsted County was official, and the townships were organized in 1858 and beyond. Settlers came into the area as early as 1855. The first five settlers in the Stewartville area were Truman Wooldridge, Jabez Clemens, William Sargeant, Luther Barrows, and Reuben Austin. The pioneers were drawn to the fertile soil, the stands of timber with abundant wildlife, the springs for drinking water, and the river as a power source. A culturally diverse group of people settled and celebrated their traditions.

The pioneers' legacy can be found in famous sons from the Stewartville area. Nicholas Brewer, a famous painter who wrote his autobiography *Trails of a Paintbrush*, was from the High Forest area. John Goode, a famous author, cartographer, and scientist, was born in Stewartville on November 21, 1862. Goode became an international authority of geography. He completed his revised edition of the school atlas in 1932 and had connections with Rand McNally. Stewartville is the birthplace of Richard W. Sears, cofounder of Sears, Roebuck and Company. The birthplace home is now a museum serving the Stewartville Area Historical Society.

The Root River valley continues to draw people to its shores. Whether one is looking for arrowheads or remnants of the Dubuque Stagecoach Trail, is a model train enthusiast or enjoying the Racine Antique Threshing Weekend in July, is searching for family history or following the trails of Native Americans or Laura Ingalls Wilder, the footprints of the past, present, and future trails cross here.

One

EARLY RESIDENTS

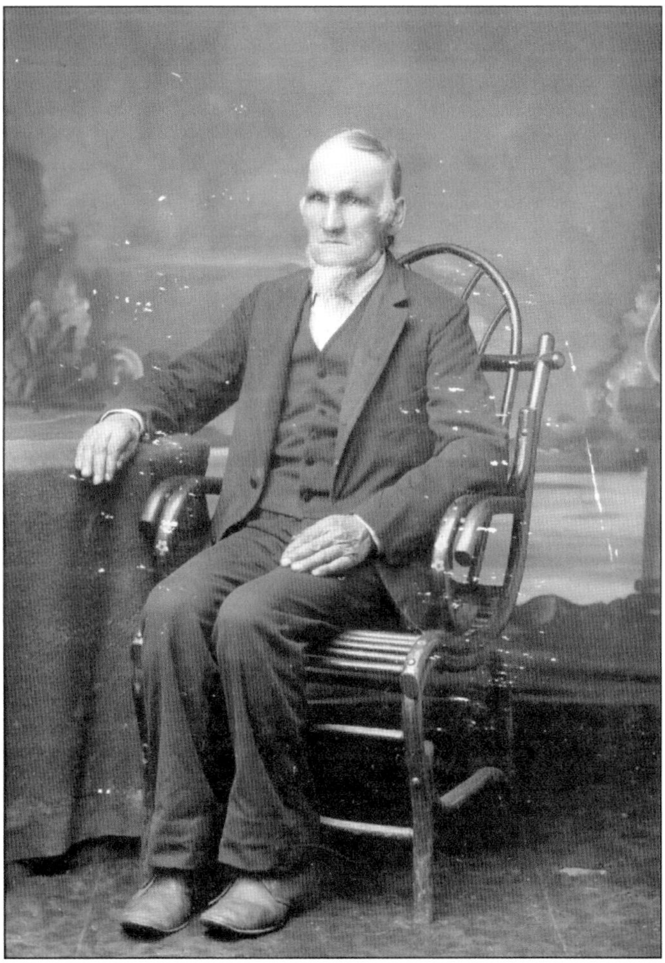

William R. Tubbs was born on January 25, 1824, in Ohio. A Mexican War veteran, Tubbs immigrated to California during the gold rush. During this trip, he met and married Sophia Smith before returning west of Stewartville in 1856. He later purchased land in the heart of the village, and incoming settlers lodged with the family. Tubbs built a chair-manufacturing business and a general store and served as postmaster before his death in 1897. (Courtesy of Buck Fredricksen.)

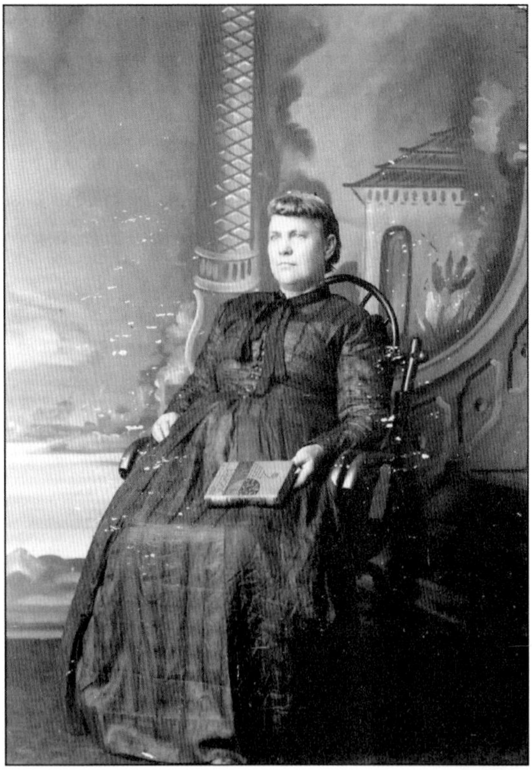

Sophia (Smith) Tubbs met and married William R. Tubbs in Salt Lake City, Utah. They lived in Iowa and Wisconsin before settling in the Stewartville area. It was said that Sophia had considerable amounts of jewelry, but she sold it to buy windows and doors for her new home. This pioneer couple had nine children who grew up, married, and built homes around Stewartville. Sophia died on April 11, 1904. (Courtesy of Buck Fredricksen.)

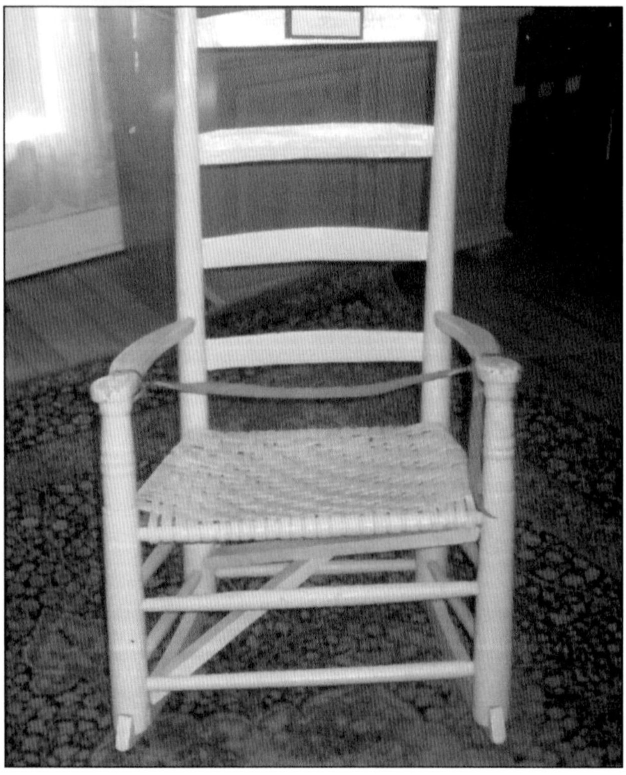

Chair making was William R. Tubbs's sideline business. He had a turning lathe run by foot power and turned out a light substantial chair. Several are in the community (barring the seat) intact. This chair was donated to the historical society by Elinor Lamb. (Courtesy of the SAHS.)

Merritt Tubbs was a son of early settler William R. Tubbs. Merritt worked in his father's chair-manufacturing business. The chairs, made of wood from the virgin forests in the Stewartville area, are still prized by the people who have them. (Courtesy of Buck Fredricksen.)

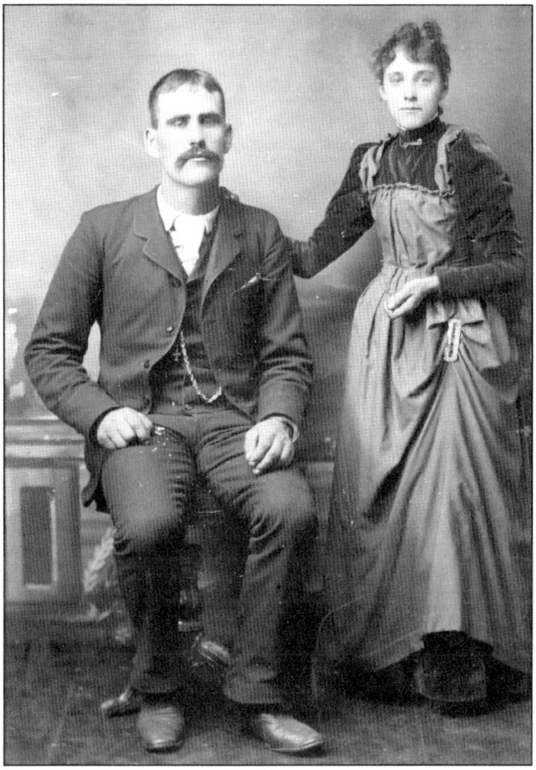

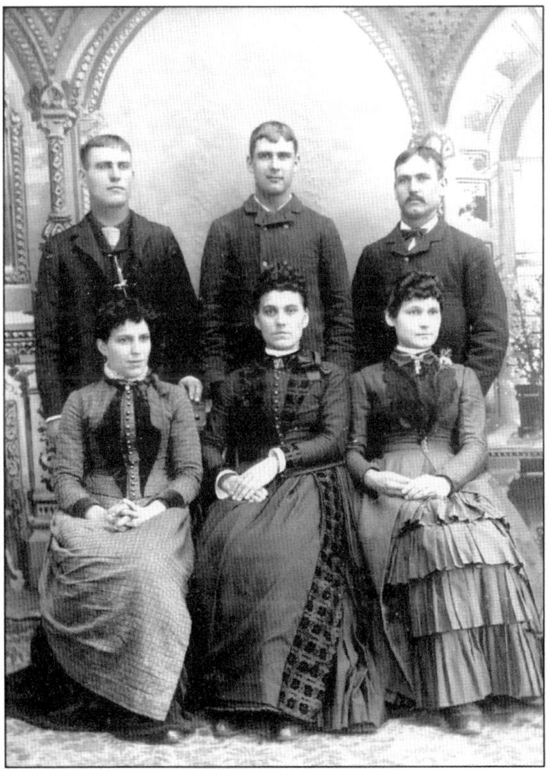

In this Tubbs family group photograph are, from left to right, (first row) unidentified, Sophia Tubbs, and Ida May Tubbs, wife of John F. Owen; (second row) Lester G. Tubbs, Charles S. Tubbs, and Merritt Tubbs. (Courtesy of Buck Fredricksen.)

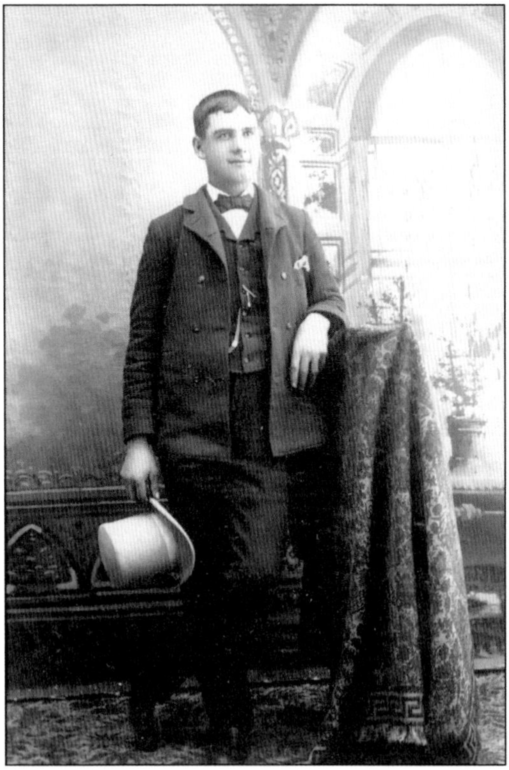

Lester G. Tubbs was the youngest son of William R. Tubbs. Lester loved nature, so he planted trees and landscaped to add beauty to Stewartville. (Courtesy of Buck Fredricksen.)

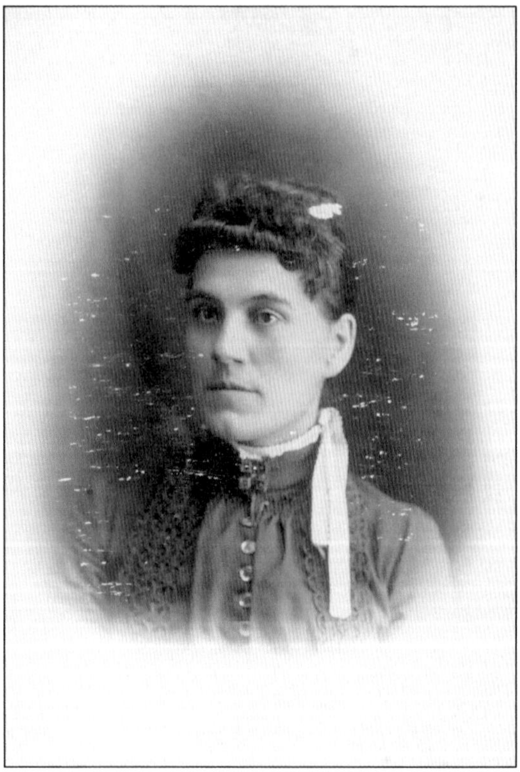

Ida May (Tubbs) Owen, wife of John F. Owen, was a homemaker. John erected the first hotel especially made for transients, roomers, and boarders in 1890. As the railroad came to Stewartville, the workers were glad to have lodging at the Owen House. Ida May and John were the parents of three daughters: Lissie, Olive (Predmore), and Gladys. (Courtesy of Buck Fredricksen.)

Stewartville is the namesake of Charles Stewart, who was born on June 12, 1816, in York, Livingston County, New York. In 1840, Charles married Margaret Macnab, who died 11 years later following the birth of a daughter. Grieving the loss of his wife, Charles left Helen with her maternal grandparents and headed west. Charles arrived in High Forest, Minnesota Territory, and joined in partnership with William Russell running a mill. (Courtesy of the SAHS.)

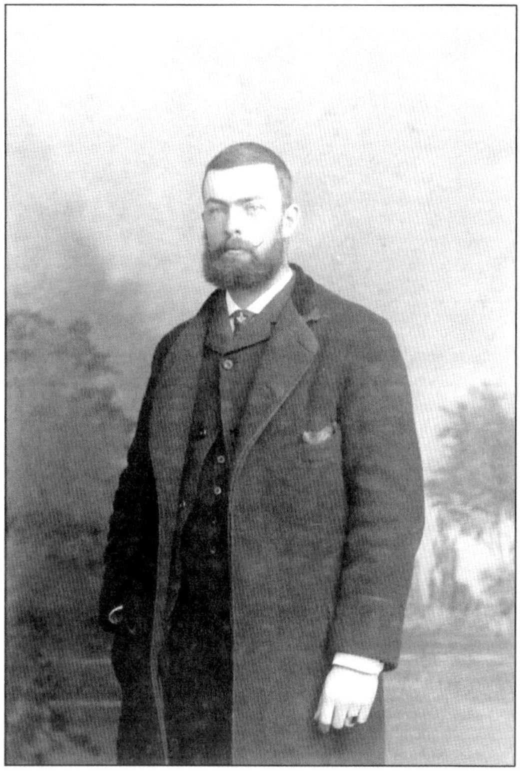

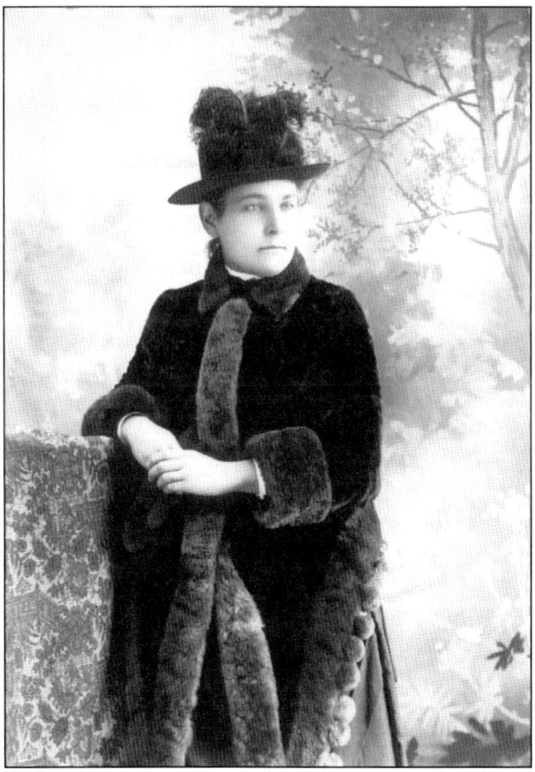

Charles returned to New York and married Ellen Douglas. He hoped to bring his new wife and daughter, Helen, back to Minnesota. The grandparents refused to have Helen raised in a wild western country. During Charles's second marriage, son Charles Neil Stewart was born on May 31, 1858. In 1862, Charles returned to New York and brought his 12-year-old daughter back to Minnesota. A lawsuit resulted, but custody was granted to Charles. (Courtesy of the SAHS.)

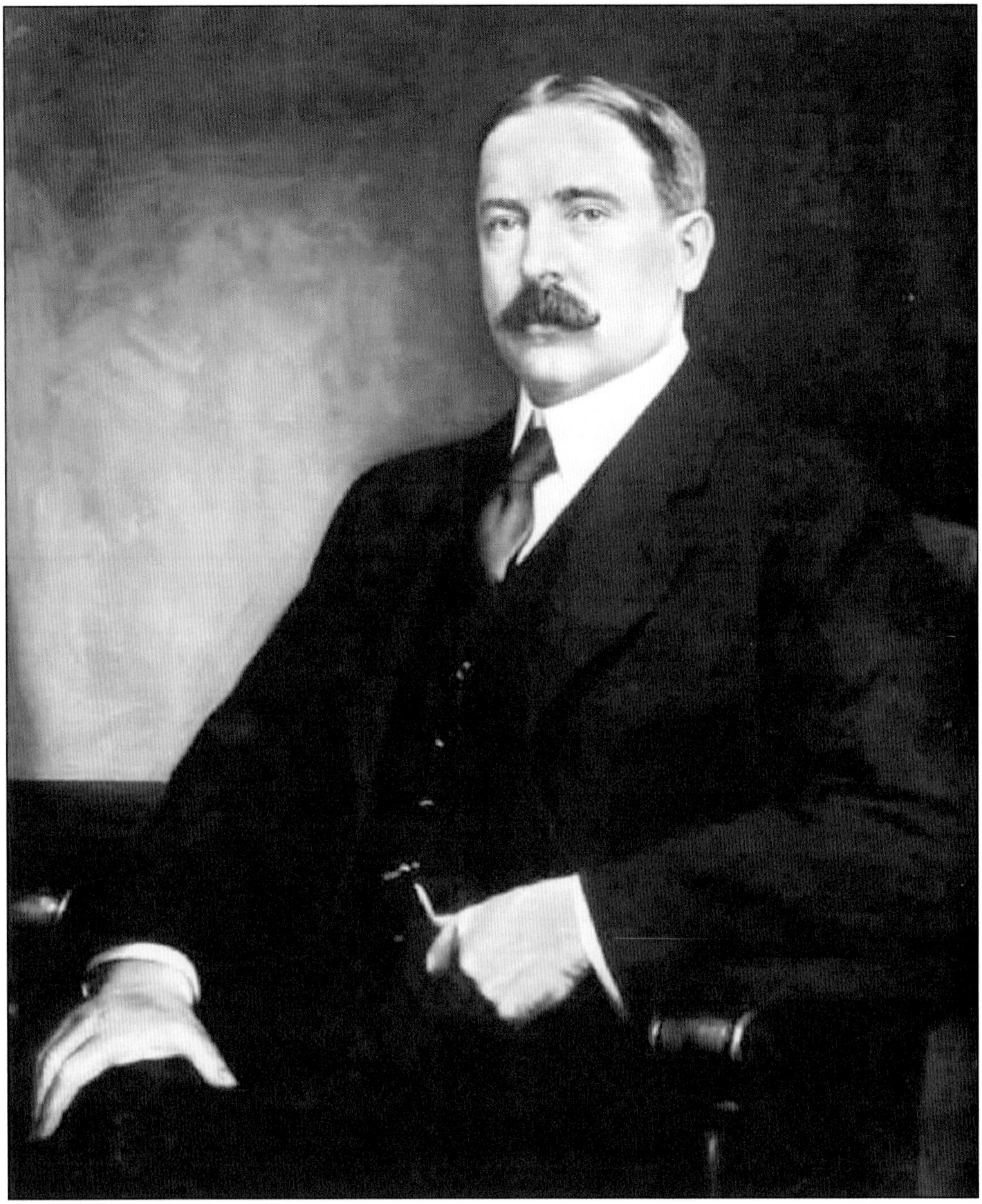

Richard W. Sears, known the world over as the cofounder of the famous mail-order house, was born on December 7, 1863, in Stewartville. His father, James W. Sears, a local blacksmith and wagon maker, married High Forest pioneer Eliza Burton. The Sears family lived in Stewartville for six years before moving to Spring Valley, where Richard attended elementary school and one year of high school. When Richard was 16 years old, his father died and he was left with the responsibility of supporting his mother and two younger sisters. Richard learned telegraphy and became a station agent at North Branch and then North Redwood. A local jeweler did not want a shipment of watches and wanted them returned to Chicago. Richard purchased the watches, sold them, and netted a profit of $5,000. Richard went into business for himself in Minneapolis and later relocated to Chicago. He hired Alvah Roebuck to fix the watches he sold. In 1893, the corporate name for the firm was Sears, Roebuck and Company. (Courtesy of the SAHS.)

On December 19, 1880, W. E. Smith married Edna Staples, daughter of a High Forest township early settler. Her wedding dress is on display at the Stewartville Area Historical Society's museum. The couple had two daughters: Bertha Kuehntopp (wife of Eugene H. Kuehntopp) and Beatrice Mills (wife of Alonzo D. Mills). W. E. Smith established a store and made horse nets and hammocks. Edna also helped in the weaving of these articles. (Courtesy of the SAHS.)

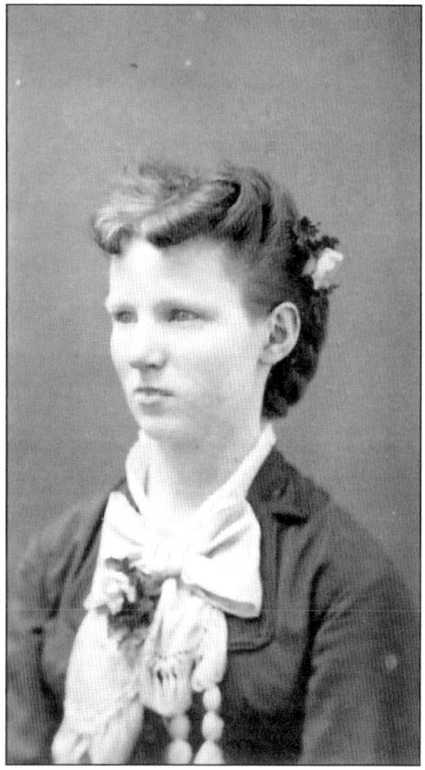

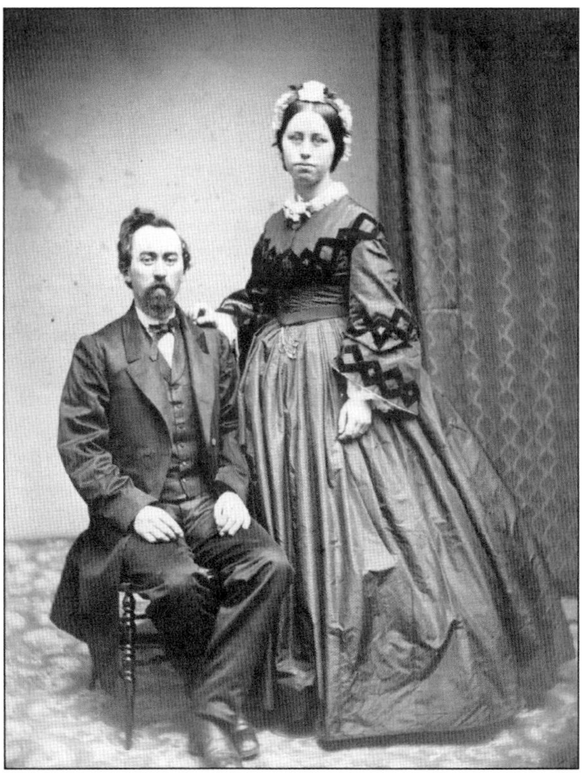

This notation was taken from the bill of their auction: "Nathan and Mercy Benedict, having sold their farm, late residence in Sennett, four miles east of Auburn, and one mile north of the Skancatelas Road, had a public auction on Wednesday, February 19, 1868. Terms–Sums of $10 and under-cash and over $10 one year's credit with good approved notes with interest, payable at the Auburn Savings Bank." Nathan and Mercy Benedict moved and settled in Stewartville. (Courtesy of the SAHS.)

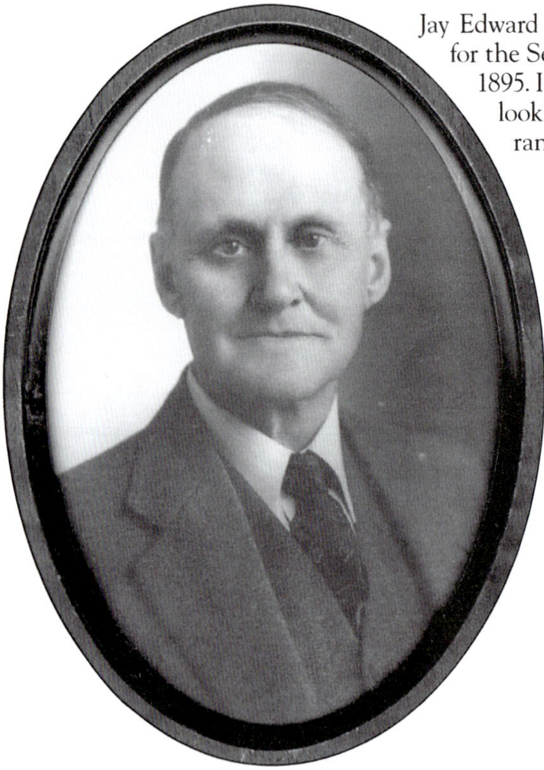

Jay Edward (J. E.) Benedict was the assistant cashier for the Security Bank of Stewartville, established in 1895. In 1896, J. E. Benedict went to South Dakota looking after business connected with a big ranch near Pierre. (Courtesy of the SAHS.)

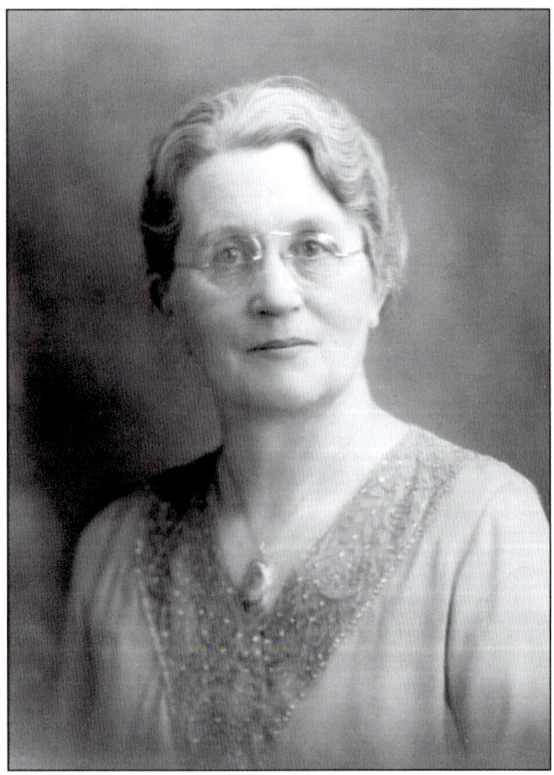

Ida Ann (Stevenson) Benedict, second wife of J. E. Benedict, prior to her marriage in 1918, taught in the Minneapolis school system. Ida was active in Stewartville's civic and educational circles. She served on the school board and was active in local, county, and state clubs. She helped organize the Olmsted County Historical Society. (Courtesy of the SAHS.)

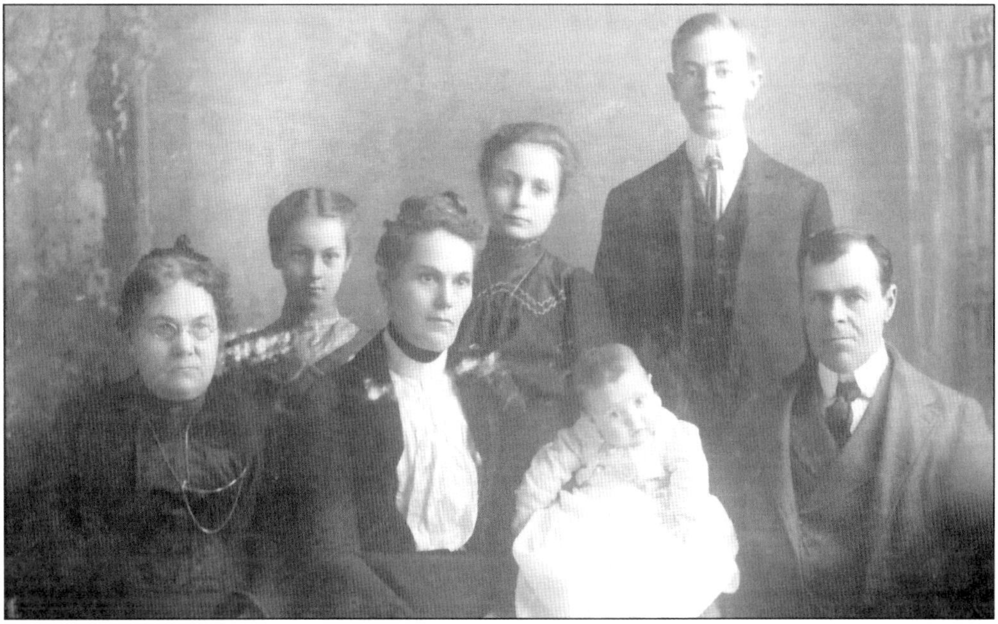

Fred and Alice (Siman) Tews made certain the Tews Hotel ranked among the very best. It was a family-run business. The children waited on tables, weeded the garden, made beds, washed kerosene lamp chimneys, milked the two cows, and embroidered the pillow covers. They ran the hotel until 1947, when it was sold to Mr. and Mrs. Ralph Hoeft. From left to right are Ann (Smart) Siman, Irene Tews, Alice (Siman) Tews, Bess Tews, baby Helen Tews, Avery Tews, and Fred Tews. (Courtesy of the SAHS.)

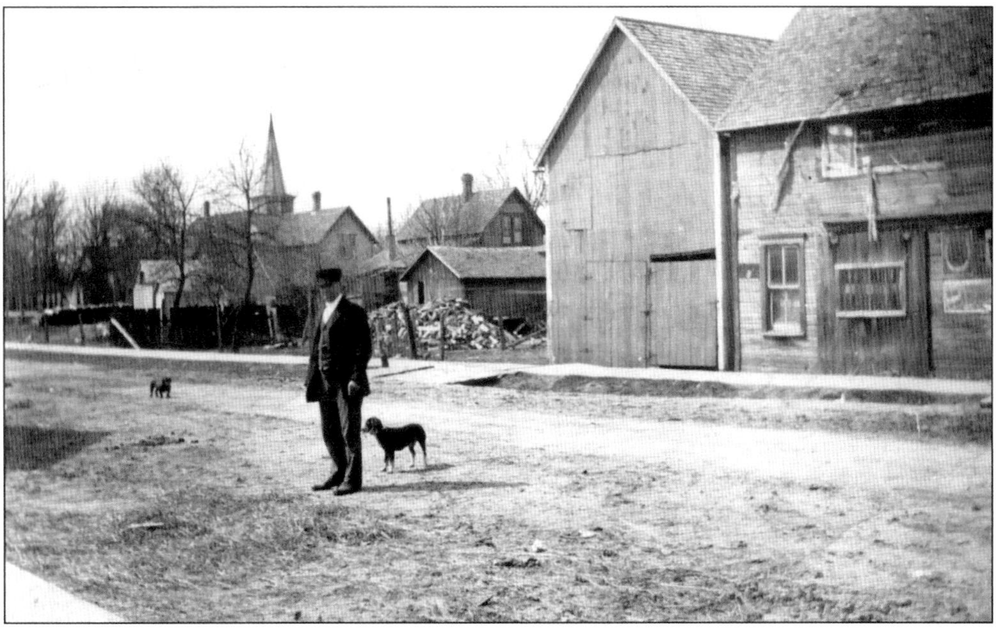

On March 1, 1900, Fred and Alice (Siman) Tews came from Easton to Stewartville and purchased the hotel from O. G. and Anna Mack. Business increased and Fred erected a three-story brick building. Meals were served every day from 1900 to 1941, when the dining room was closed. The family operated the hotel for 47 years. (Courtesy of the SAHS.)

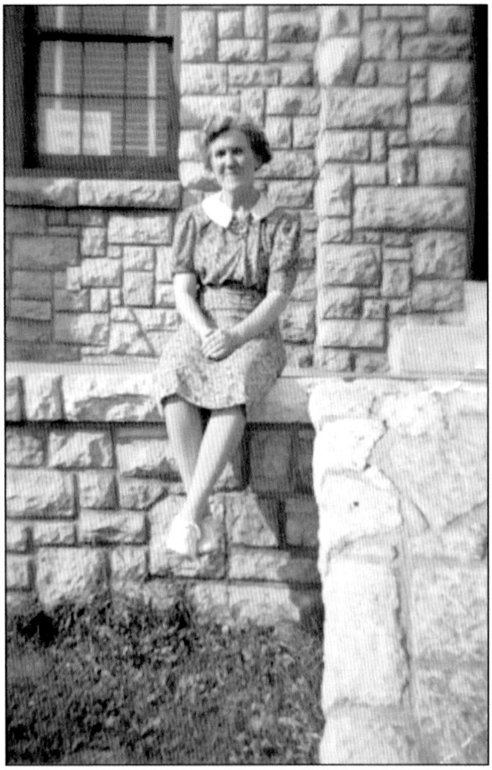

Cecelia Gray, wife of B. F. Gray, was appointed the first librarian, and meetings were held at her home until the community building was ready. All books were cataloged and carded by her at her residence. When the council granted the library board permission to use one of the rooms at the new building, the books were moved to the new location. Cecelia continued as librarian until she moved to Rochester. She was paid $15 per month for her services. (Courtesy of the Gray family.)

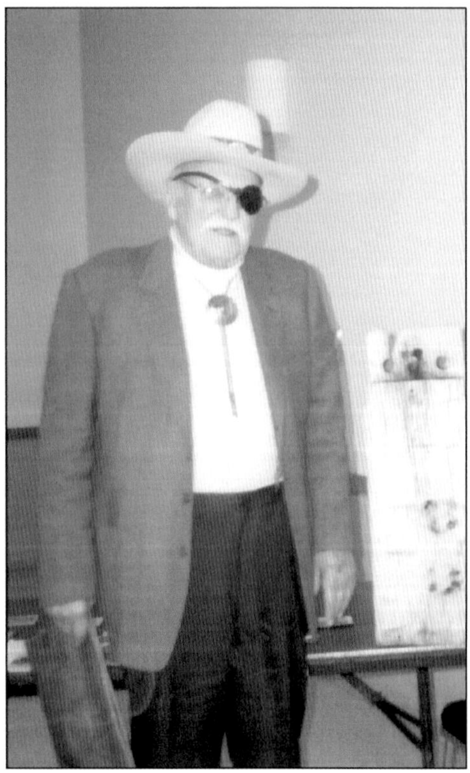

Hersh Hoaglan was a nephew to John M. Cussons, who ran the Cussons mill in Stewartville. Hoaglan is standing beside a beam piece from the mill. He gave a talk about the Cussonses and the mill at the annual meeting of the historical society. (Courtesy of the SAHS.)

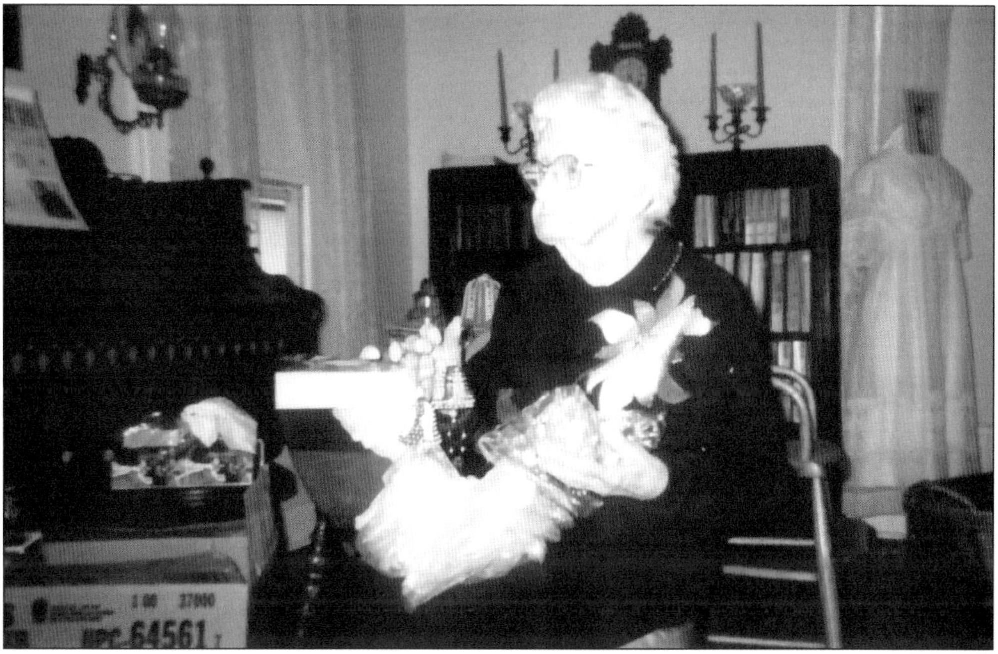

Marion Light was a descendant of Truman Wooldridge, who was one of the five original settlers of Stewartville. In this picture, Light is helping to decorate the Christmas tree with ornaments hand made by her over the years. These ornaments can be seen each year at the Christmas open house on the first Sunday in December. (Courtesy of the SAHS.)

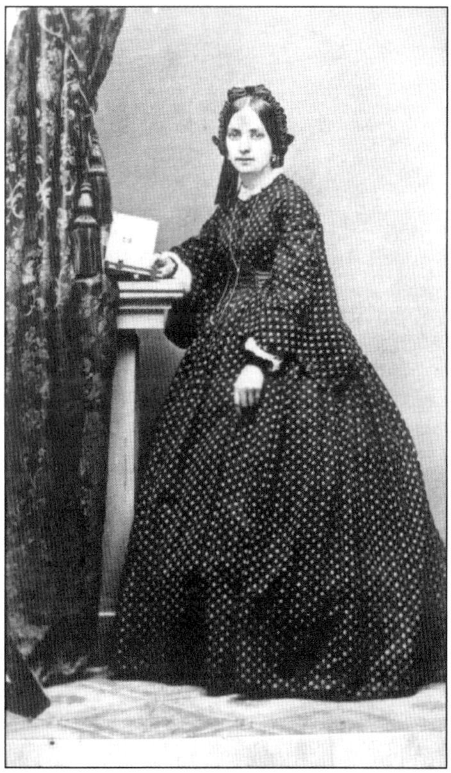

Mary Elizabeth Tattersall was the daughter of Capt. William K. Tattersall, an Englishman from New York City. William built the Tattersall House, a three-story hotel in High Forest on the Dubuque Stagecoach Trail. (Courtesy of Gordon Stiles.)

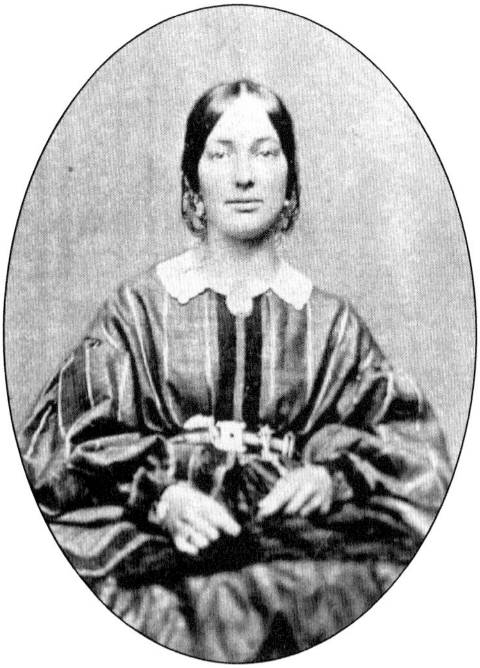

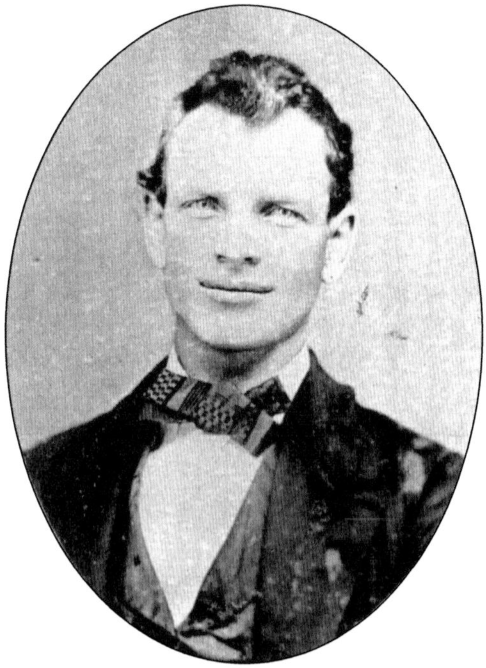

On November 7, 1861, Mary Elizabeth Tattersall married James L. Rockwell. James's father ran the Rockwell Blacksmith Shop on the corner of Stoddard and Sherwin Streets of the High Forest town square. (Courtesy of Gordon Stiles.)

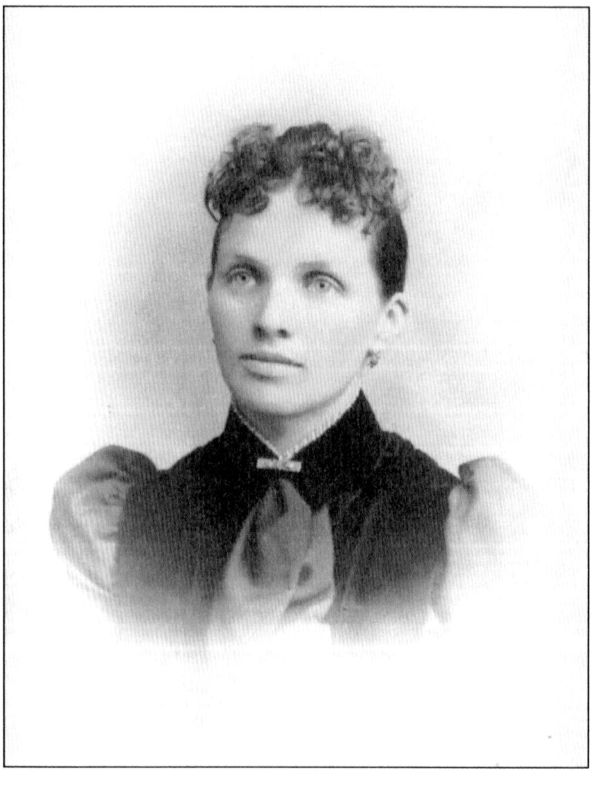

Cornelia Elizabeth (Lizzie) Chaffee was the daughter of James L. Rockwell and Mary Elizabeth (Tattersall) Rockwell. (Courtesy of Gordon Stiles.)

Gibson A. Chaffee married Cornelia Elizabeth Rockwell. (Courtesy of Gordon Stiles.)

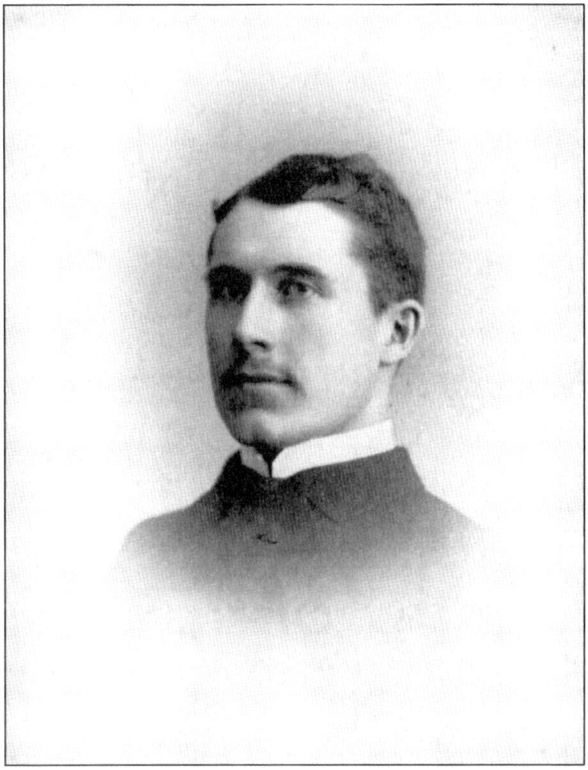

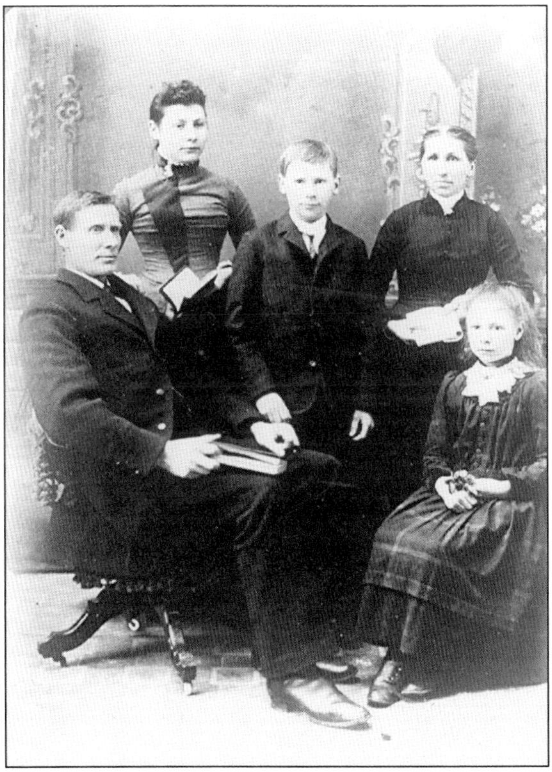

Wilhelm A. F. Wegenke Sr. was born in Posen, Germany. He married Karolina (Mietzner) Ebemberg. This couple had a daughter named Anna Marie. (Courtesy of Ardis Copple.)

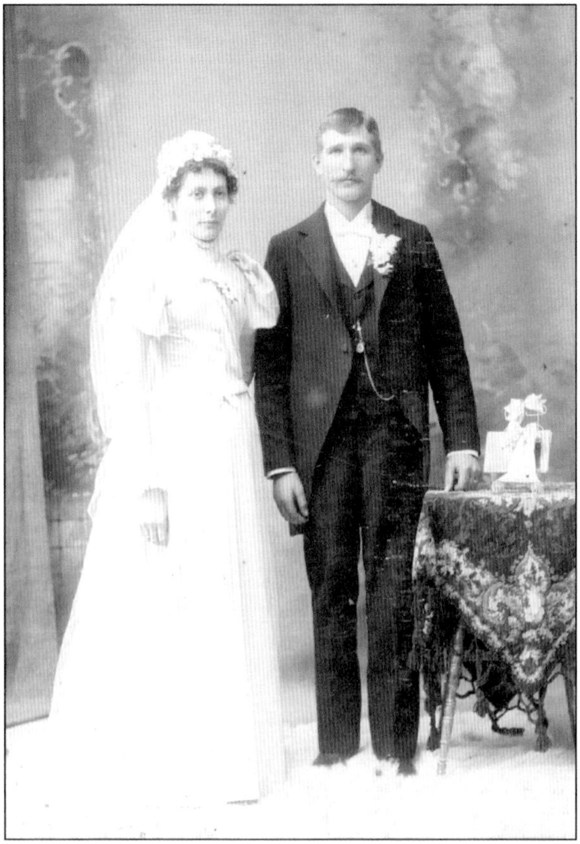

Anna Marie Wegenke married John F. W. Rausch on January 1, 1898. They lived in the Pleasant Valley/Potsdam area and farmed. The couple had six children. (Courtesy of Ardis Copple.)

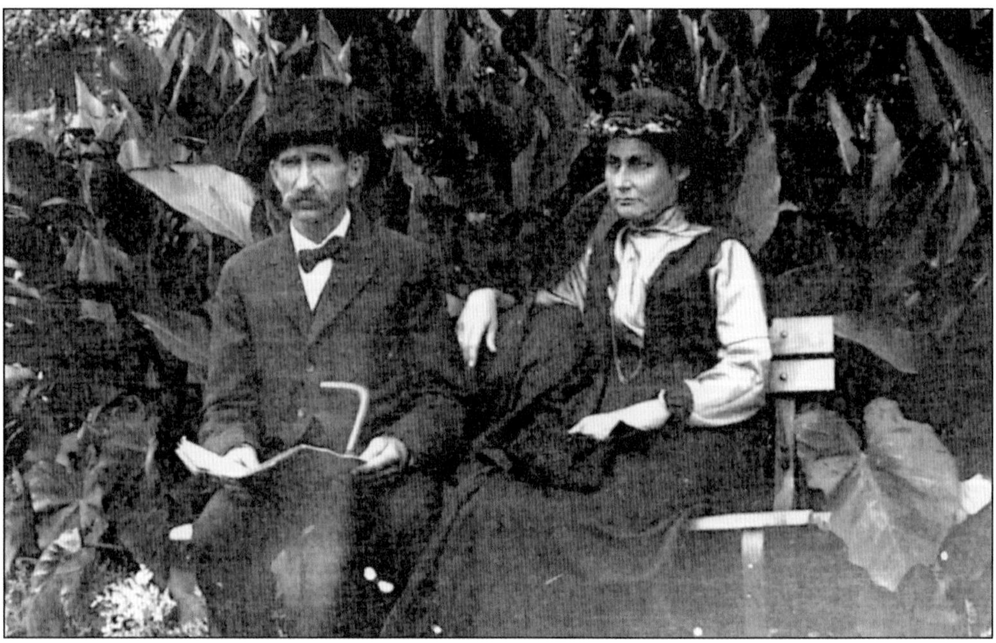

This is a picture of John F. W. and Anna Marie Rausch enjoying themselves on a trip to Florida. (Courtesy of Ardis Copple.)

Two

Towns and Townships

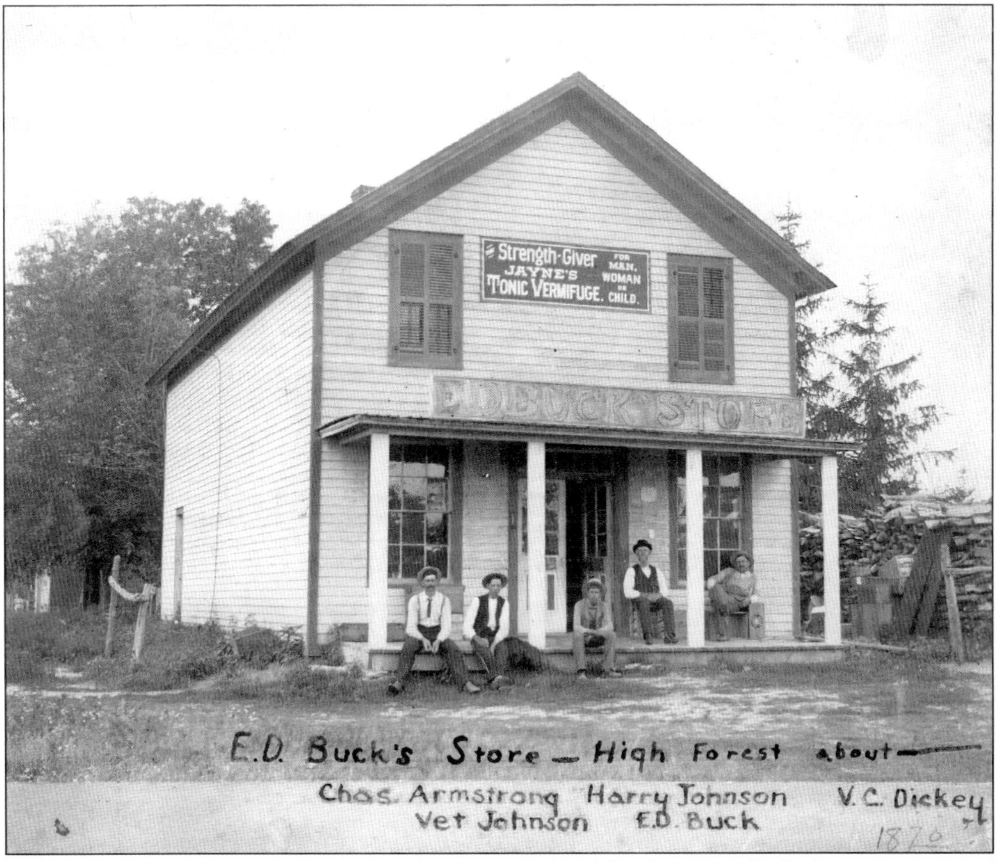

The mercantile business began in High Forest in the fall of 1855. A little later, George and Edward Buck and others came with general merchandise. Edward became owner of his store and is here on the front porch in 1870, pictured with Charles Armstrong, Harry Johnson, Vet Johnson, and Verge Dickey. (Courtesy of the OCHS.)

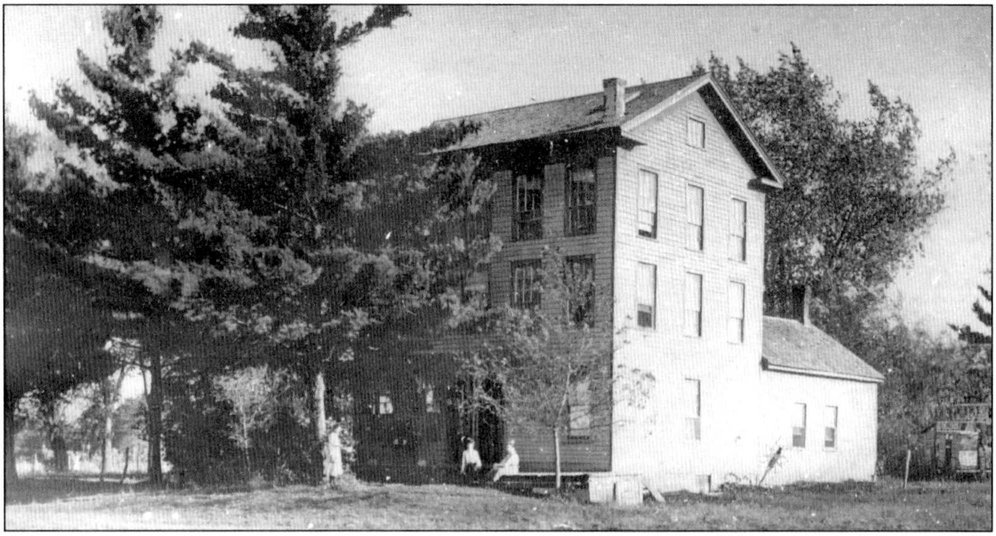

In the spring of 1856, Capt. William K. Tattersall, an Englishman from New York City, came to High Forest. In that year, he built a three-story hotel, the Tattersall House, of which he was the proprietor until about 1880. It was the best hotel in the county outside Rochester, serving the pioneer hotel trade for many years. The Tattersall House, on its opening, attracted statewide attention in the press, and it became the center of travel in the region and a stage stop for the coaches from Marion and Rochester. The old inn stood staunchly; its oak and walnut timbers from the High Forest woods were still sound in March 1945, when the building was finally torn down. (Courtesy of the OCHS.)

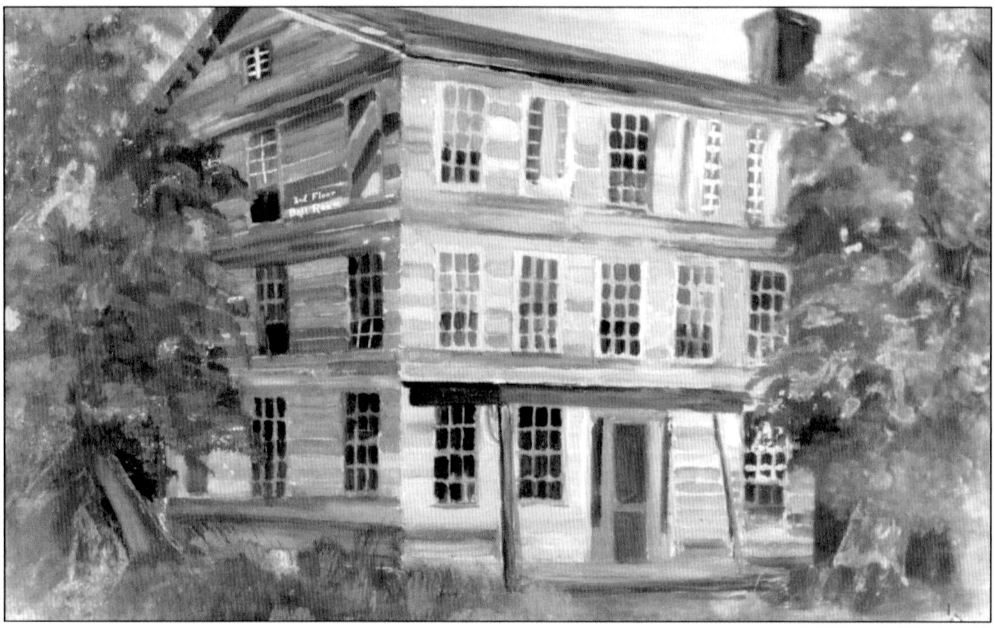

This watercolor picture of the Tattersall House was painted by Robert Griffin of Stewartville on June 21, 1941. A portion of the building was used as a home during the last several years of its 89-year existence. Tattersall was captain of Company H, 6th Minnesota Regiment, serving until the end of the Civil War. Then he served as sergeant of arms of the state senate during 1869–1870. He died at High Forest in 1893. (Courtesy of the OCHS.)

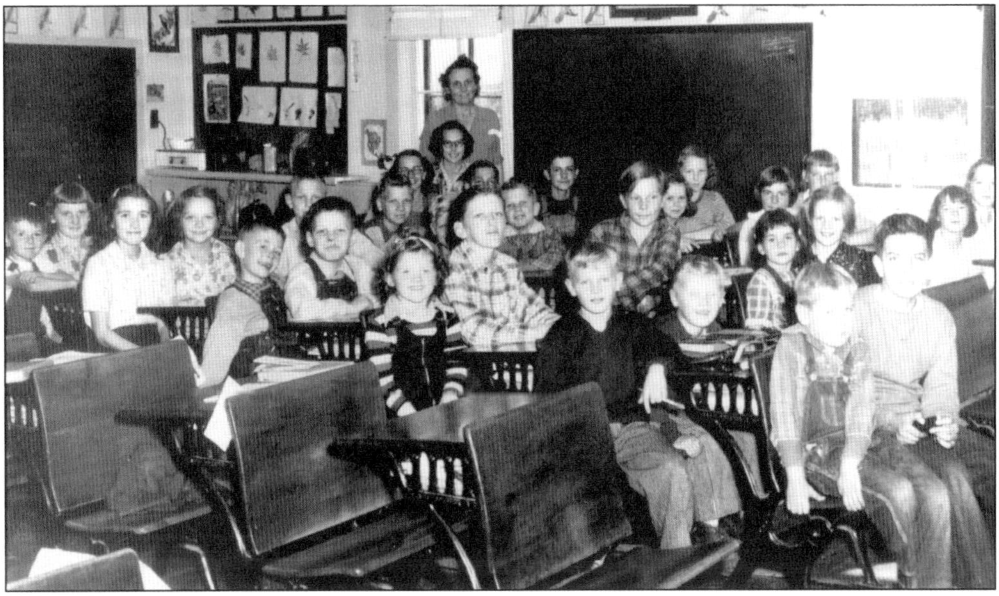

A High Forest School class is seen here. From the front of room to the back are Ron Henry, Jim Prokasky, Katherine Swanson, Frank Reese, Myrtle Stiles, Edith Stiles, Dorie Henry, Shirley Lenn, Russell Ames, Janet Nord, Patrick Nord, Darrell Reese, Marilyn Foler, Wayne Briese, Glenis Betcher, Nancy Briese, Alden Stiles, Gordon Stiles, Don Born, Carol Girton, Joan Shober, Cora Hodge, David Oeltjen Rollie, Bill Briese, Joseph Moe, Donald Foler, Ardeen Moe, Norman Moe, and teacher Helen Carroll. (Courtesy of Elsa Paulsen.)

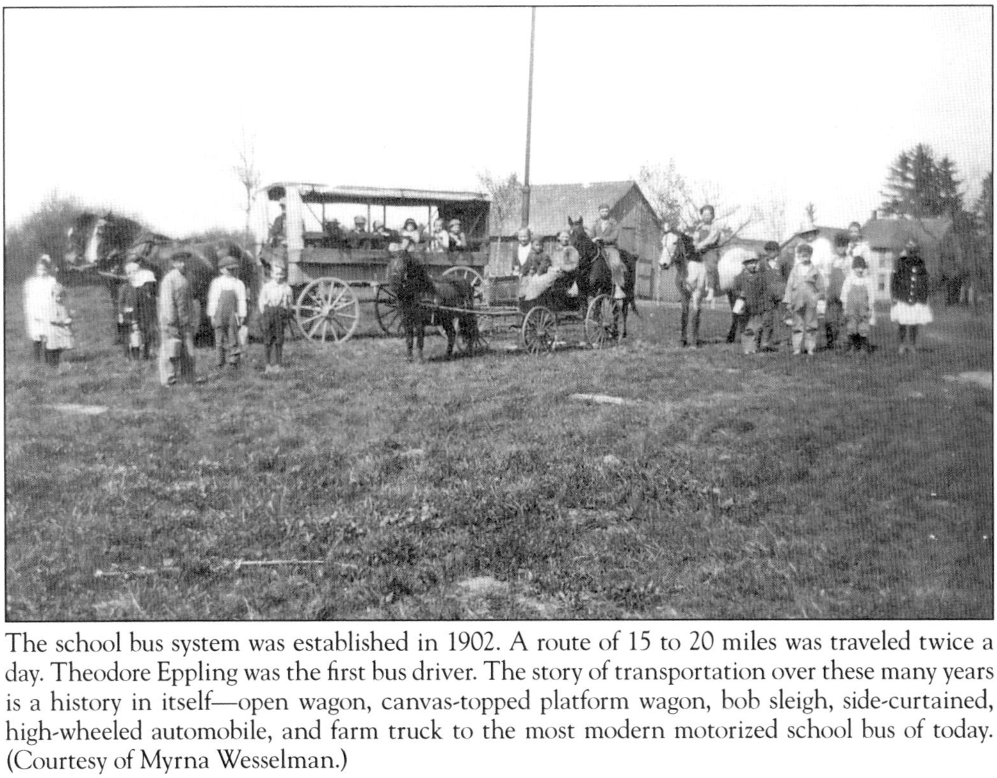

The school bus system was established in 1902. A route of 15 to 20 miles was traveled twice a day. Theodore Eppling was the first bus driver. The story of transportation over these many years is a history in itself—open wagon, canvas-topped platform wagon, bob sleigh, side-curtained, high-wheeled automobile, and farm truck to the most modern motorized school bus of today. (Courtesy of Myrna Wesselman.)

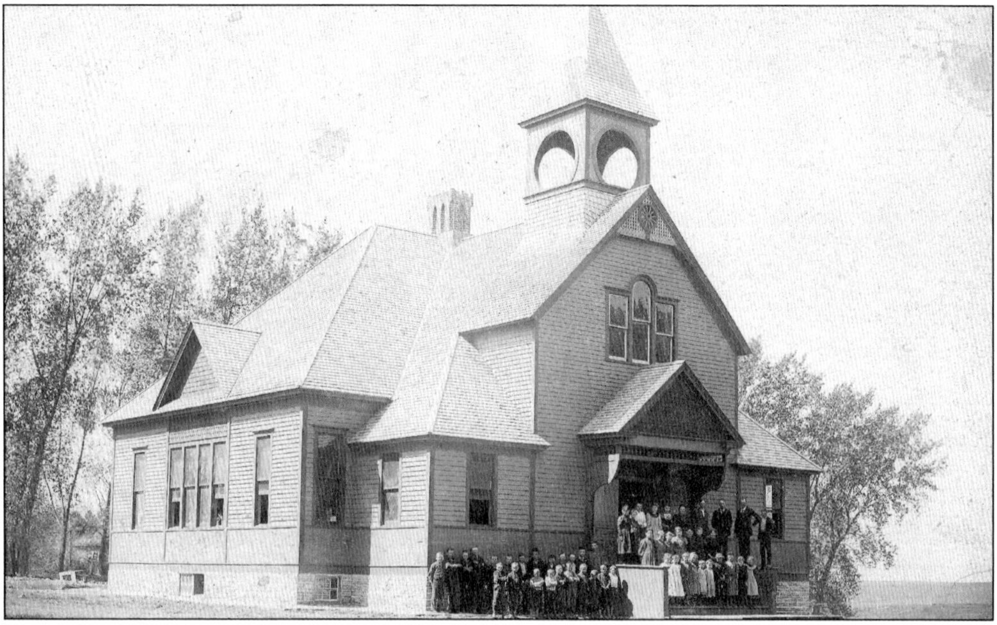

In 1903, a large ground-floor framed schoolhouse was erected. This was reportedly the largest and most modern school building outside the city of Rochester. It had two large assembly rooms, two large petitioned coatrooms, two large entries, two entrance stairs, and a well-shelved library. H. E. Wolfe and James Chapman were the first teachers. Pupils averaged from 18 to 32 in each room. (Courtesy of Myrna Wesselman.)

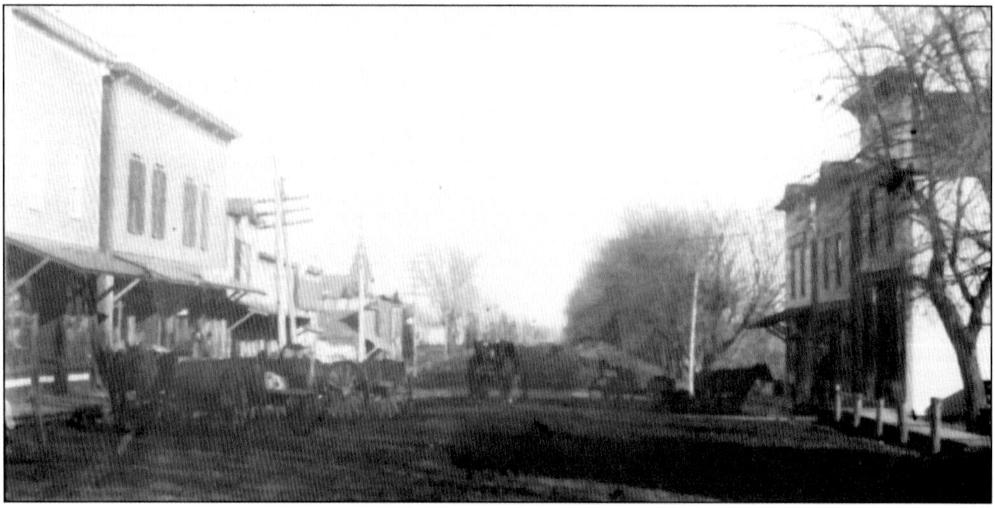

The Racine area was part of the "neutral ground," as it was called by the U.S. government. During 1853–1854, the settlers from the eastern states came into the area by the hundreds on horseback, on foot, and with wagons. For a cash income, they depended on their crops of wheat, which in the 1850s were marketed at Winona. A railroad was built from Winona to Rochester in the 1860s and thus became a marketplace for wheat. Later the railroad came to Grand Meadow/ Spring Valley, and in 1890, it came to Racine. S. J. and A. O. Sanborn, whose land was occupied by the railroad, platted the village of Racine on October 3, 1890. This picture was taken around the dawn of the 20th century before a disastrous fire destroyed three businesses on the south side in 1908. (Courtesy of the Thompson/Betcher family.)

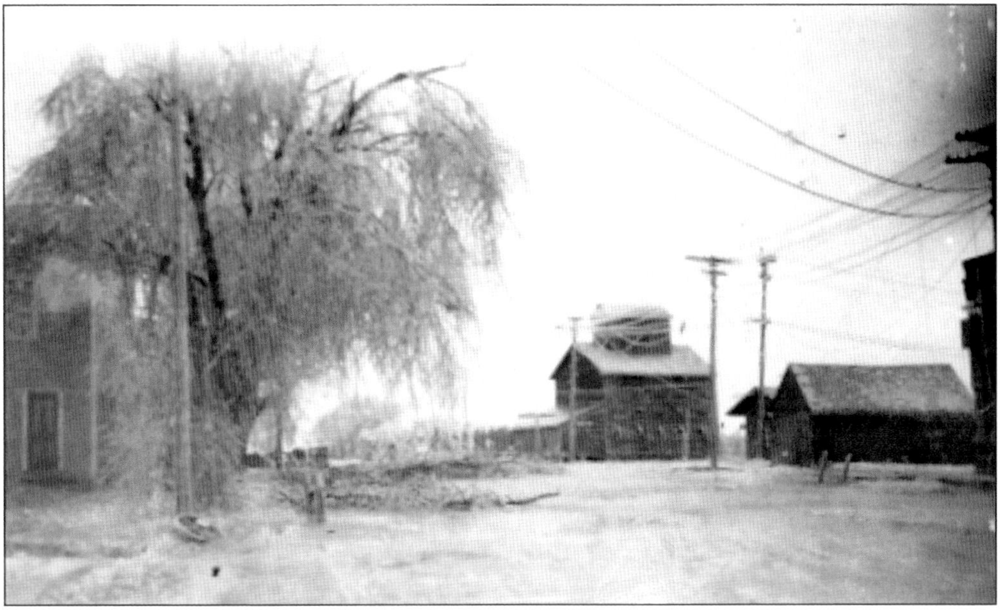

The first elevator in Racine was built by the Lacrosse Grain Company. The manager was D. A. McKee, who held this position for many years. Later the Stevenson Grain Company bought this elevator. Shortly after the building of the first elevator, the Cargill Grain Company built a large elevator, which was managed by O. W. Jones for many years. Later S. J. Sanborn and Wade Bailey were managers. This elevator was closed and the building sold in 1928. (Courtesy of the Thompson/Betcher family.)

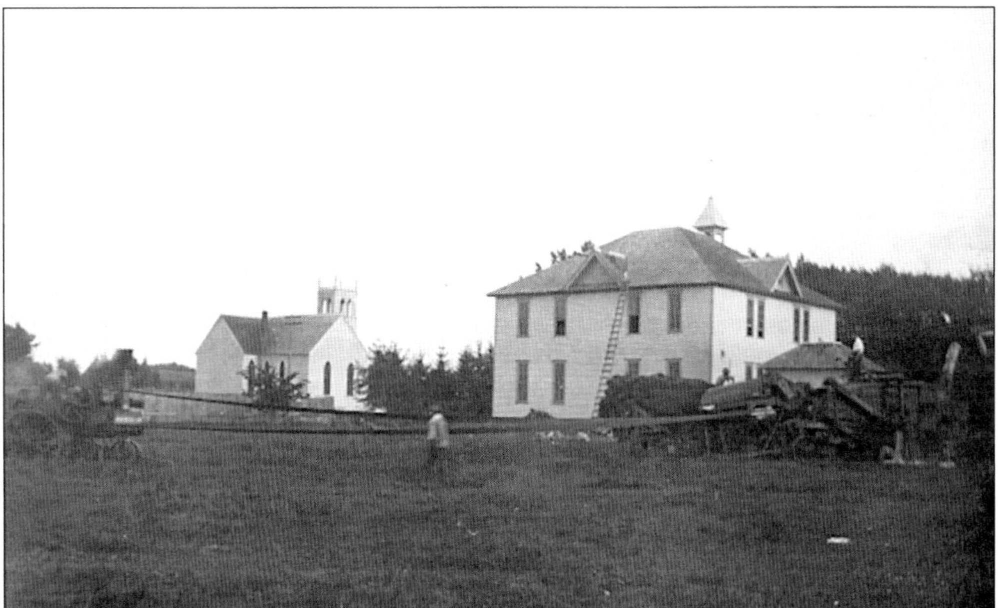

This is the Racine Church and School. It is pictured as it was in 1914. After the railroad came to Racine, the population of the village increased and this building was erected. At one time, two years of high school were given. Later the high school students went to Stewartville. (Courtesy of the Thompson/Betcher family.)

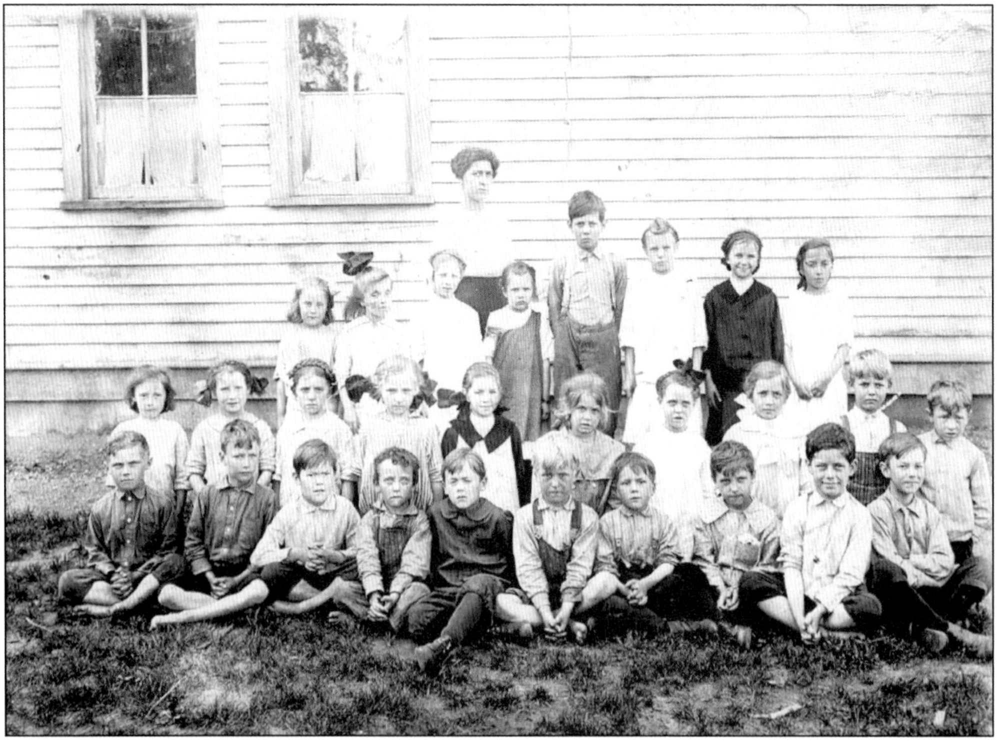

Matie Pulford was the teacher of fourth grade in the Racine schools. Pictured are the students from first, second, third, and fourth grades. (Courtesy of the Thompson/Betcher family.)

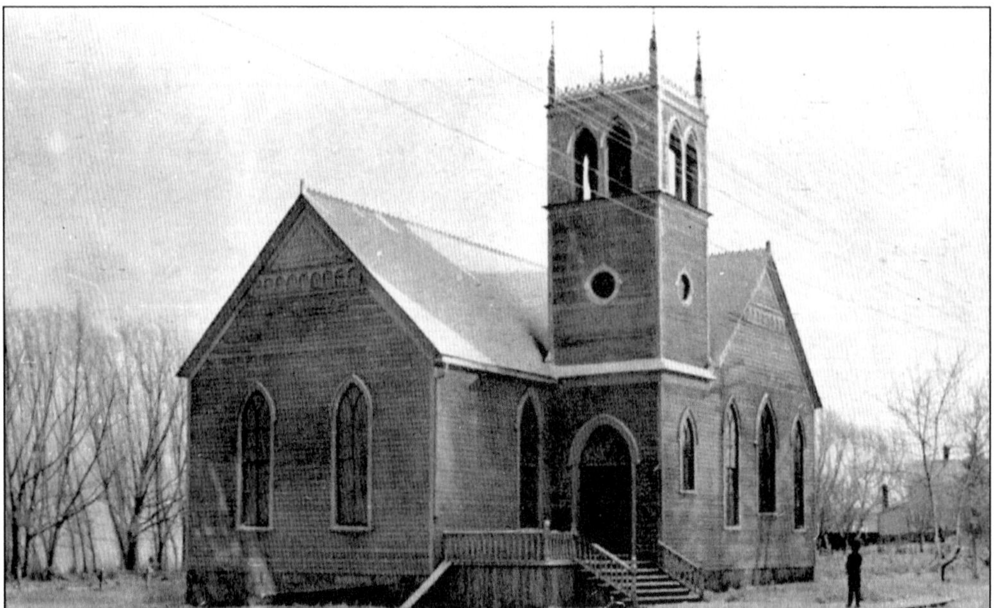

Racine Methodist Church, built in 1892, is located on the corner of Main Street and Oak Avenue. It has seen many renovations and additions, using portions of churches from the Baptists and Congregationalists. (Courtesy of Madelyn Betcher.)

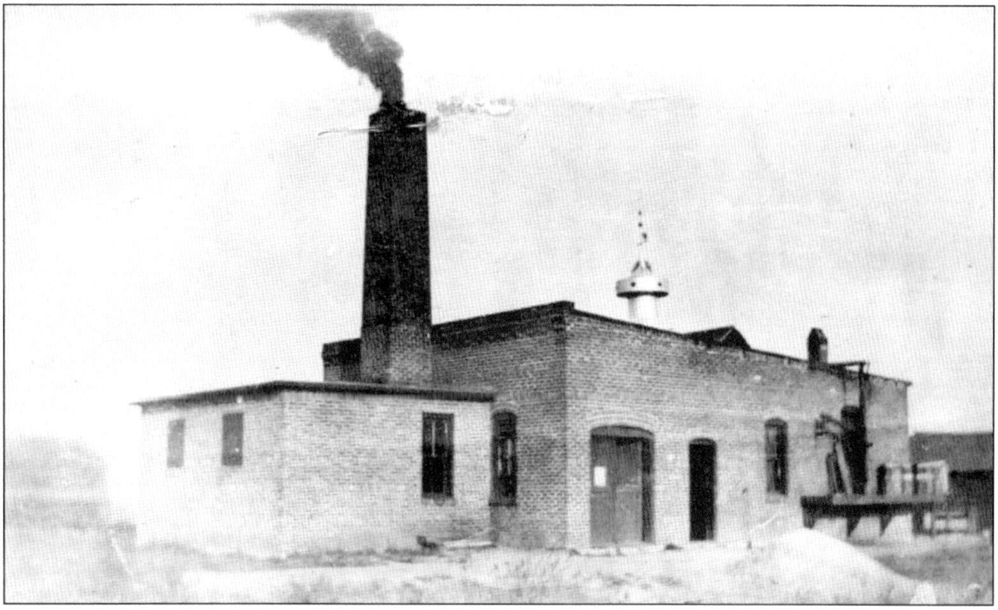

In 1893, plans were made to build a creamery. Shares were sold at $100 to 50 stockholders. R. Shrigley was the butter maker. About 1905, the creamery was destroyed by fire but promptly rebuilt. Ed Koebke was a butter maker for many years. Around the early 1970s, the creamery was reorganized as a cooperative. Julius Johnson was the butter maker at that time. (Courtesy of the Thompson/Betcher family.)

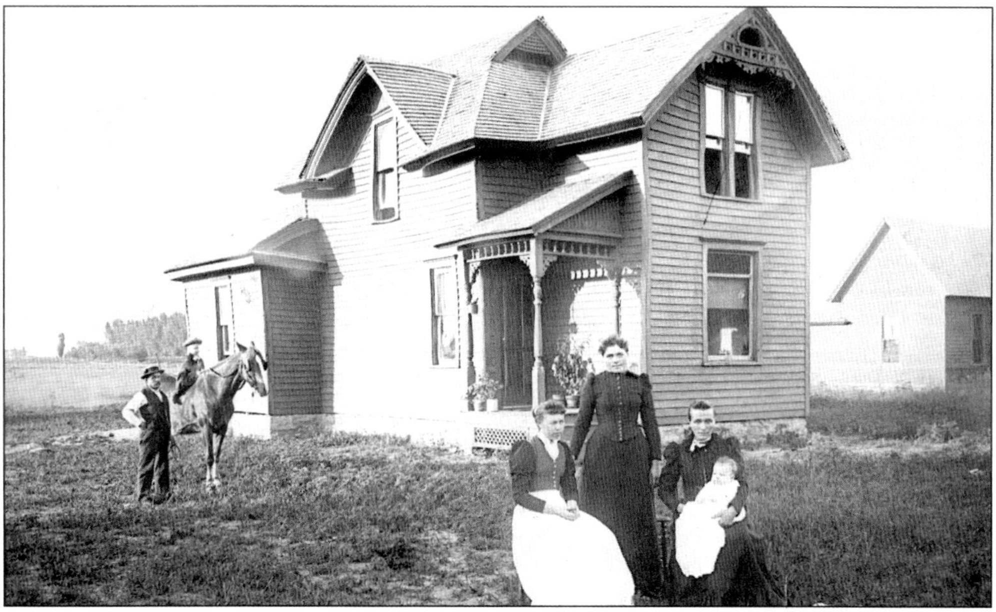

The creamery house in Racine was built by Hans Christofferson, who was a blacksmith in the area. It was on the west side of the creamery. Caroline Christofferson, Hans's wife, was the town's midwife. In the picture are, from left to right, Hans Christofferson with his son Clarence on the horse, Sylvia (Weeks) Berg, ? Kvall, and Caroline Christofferson, holding her son Torval. Another son, Halbert, was a distinguished professor of mathematics at an Ohio college. He later married Ruth Ringey of Stewartville. (Courtesy of the Thompson/Betcher family.)

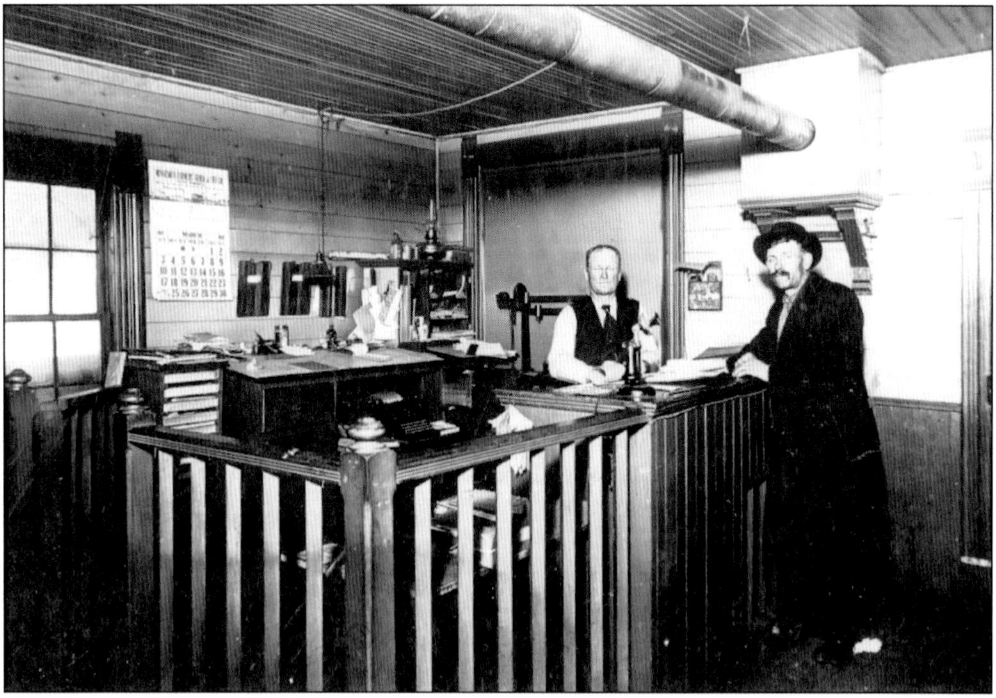

Here is the Racine Lumber Yard as it was in 1912. Eli Leonard started the lumber business in 1892. He soon sold to James A. Smith Lumber Company of Osage, Iowa. About 1912, the whole plant was rebuilt so that all the stock could be kept under cover. In 1942, the Hayes Lucas Lumber Company of Winona bought it and was still owner in the 1970s. (Courtesy of the Thompson/Betcher family.)

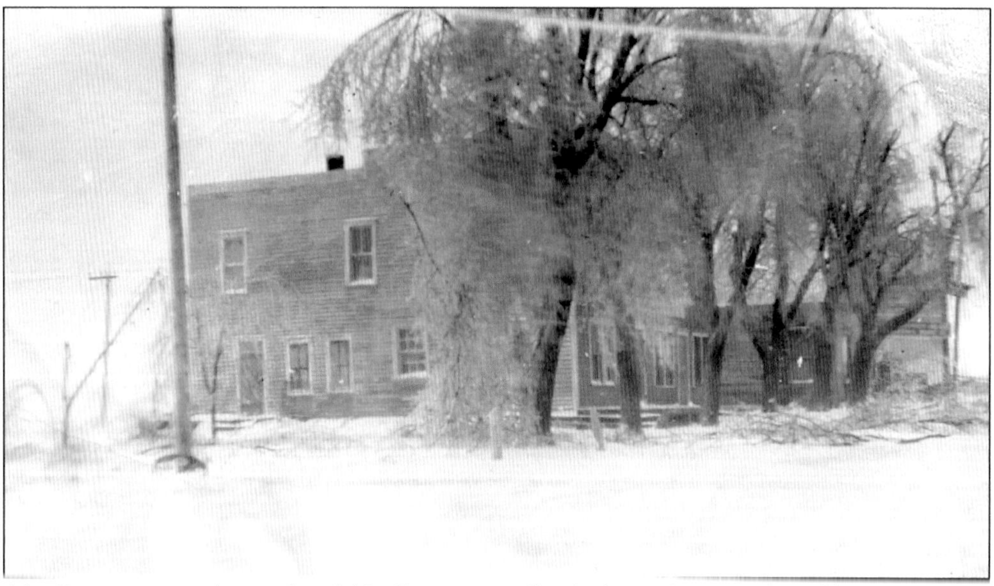

Alec Brown operated a new hotel (the Racine Hotel), which was later purchased by a Mr. Briggs. Sarah Clements was the owner of the Commercial Hotel in 1905. The register had names from the chautauqua troupes that visited Racine over the years. (Courtesy of the Thompson/Betcher family.)

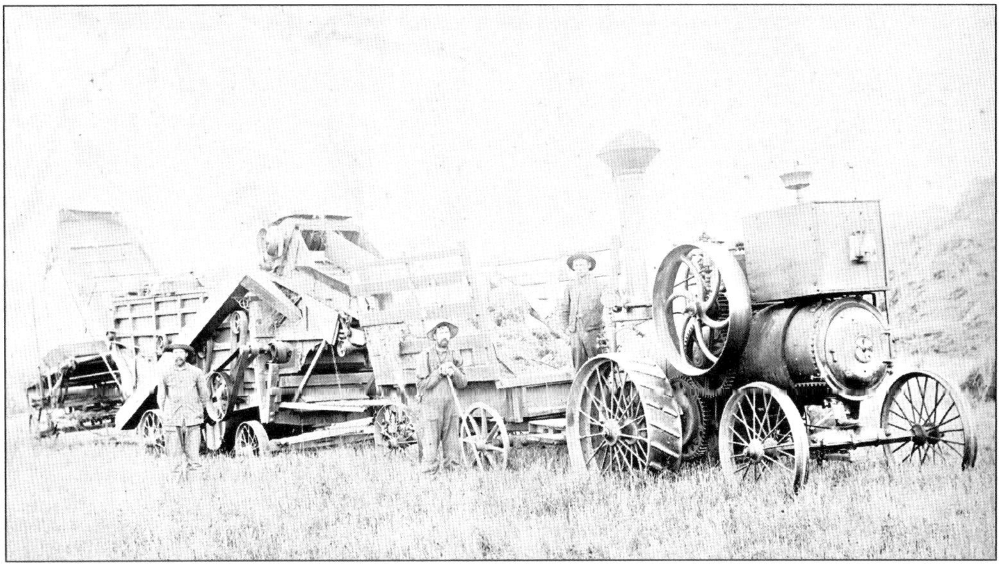

Pictured here are threshing machines in 1898. In the late 19th century, the traveling threshing machines were a colorful spectacle. Farmers piled their dried sheaves of wheat in huge stacks and awaited the machines, drawn either by teams of horses or a steam engine. Neighbors helped one another with the threshing. This is a harvest near Bear Creek by the Allen Dalen Threshing Company with a Northwest steam engine and an Avery Yellow Fellow separator. In the picture are, from left to right, Allen Dalen, Henry Simonson, and Ole Thompson. (Courtesy of the Thompson/Betcher family.)

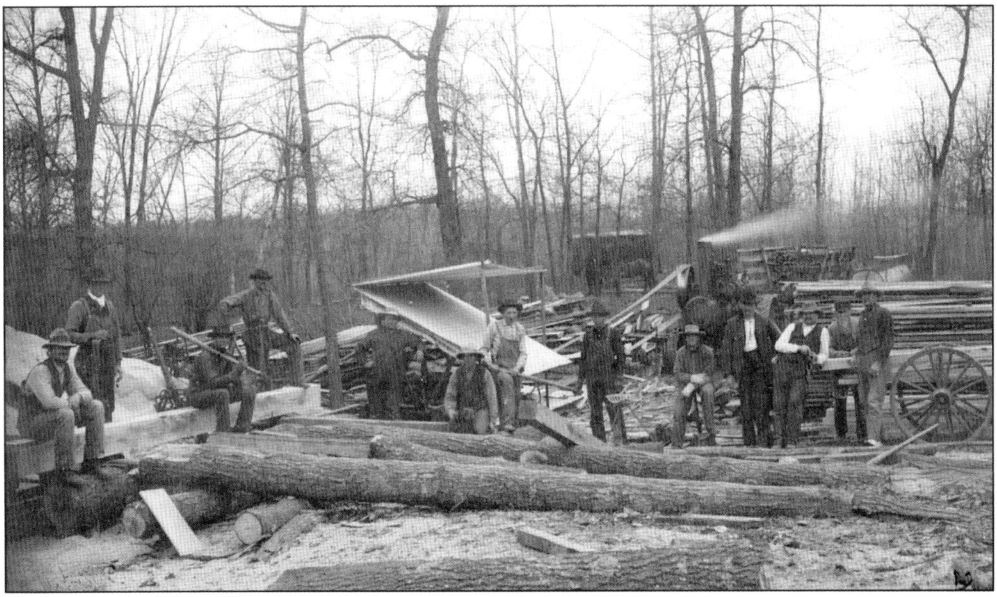

Here is the sawmill in 1920. Ole Thompson had a sawmill operation east of Racine. Logs were sawed into planks for use in building homes, barns, and businesses. The Racine area keeps this tradition alive with the annual Antique Power Association held in the third week of July. This picture on the Bill Jensen farm shows Jim Thompson, Martin Thompson, Jesse Klemmer, William Meschke, Ole Thompson, "the Swede," Dennis Maloney, High Boyer, and a Mr. Warren. (Courtesy of the Thompson/Betcher family.)

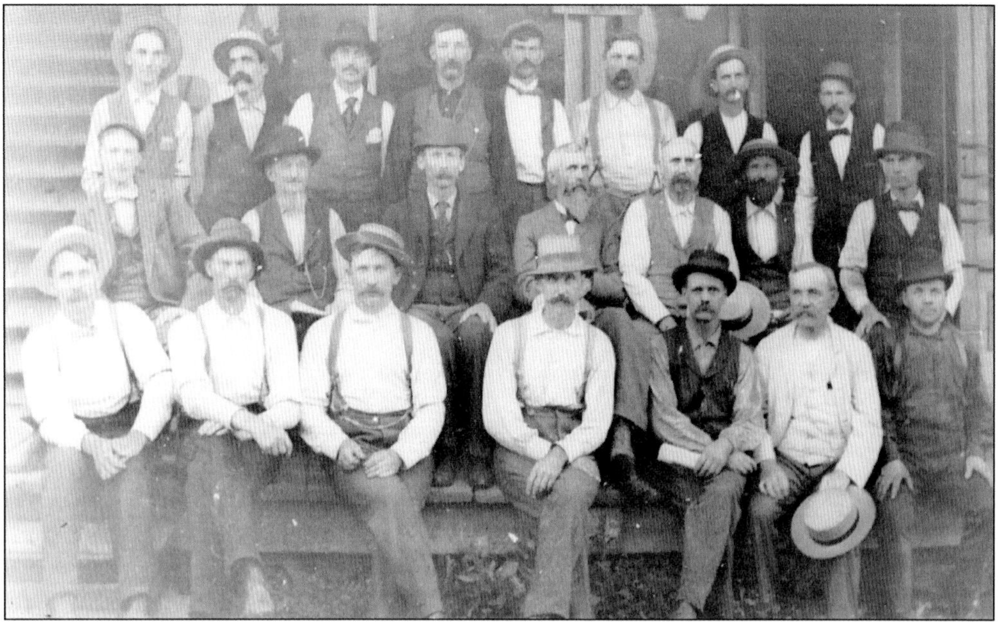

Pictured here are Racine businessmen in 1895. From left to right are (first row) A. Longnecher, A. Brown, C. Schwarz, F. Gahringer, M. Farnsworth, ? Emerson, and H. Christofferson; (second row) J. Martin, O. B. Morse, Robert Eichorn, Dr. Albert Plummer, S. J. Sanborn, and Lawrence and John Foley; (third row) Jay Patterson, R. Schrigley, A. F. Stiles, S. Utzinger, D. McKee, O. W. Jones, ? Schermerhorn, and B. Northrup. (Courtesy of the Thompson/Betcher family.)

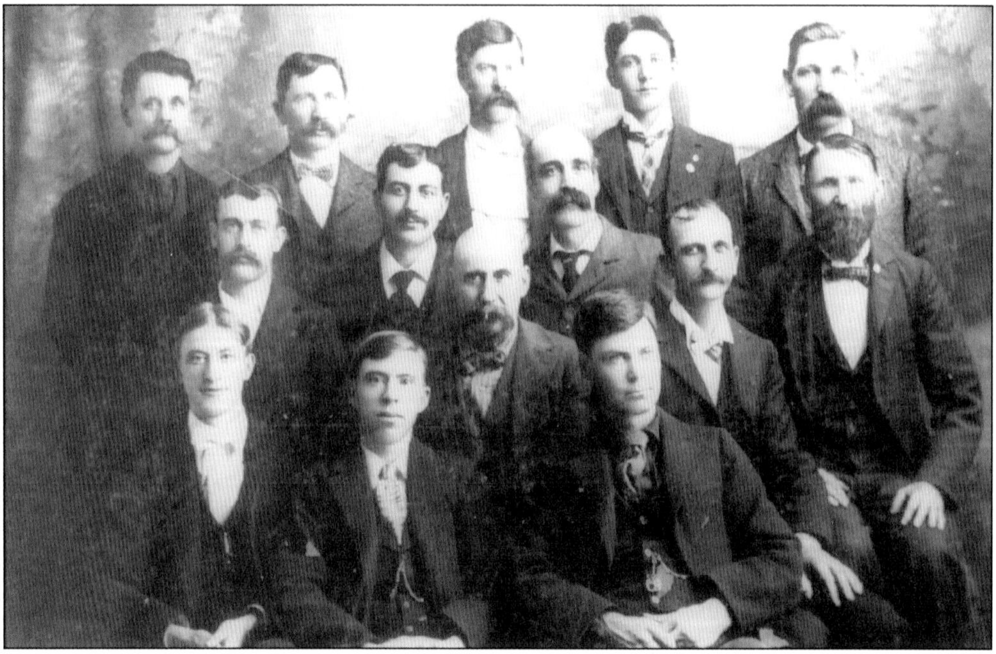

Here can be seen Racine businessmen in 1905. From left to right are (first row) Jimmy Martin, Pete Weeks, C. J. Sanborn, John Foley, and William Schermerhorn; (second row) John Lyman, Alvah Stiles, R. D. Schrigley, and ? Andrews; (third row) F. E. Farnsworth, Chris Schwarz, Elic Brown, Jay Patterson, and O. W. Jones. (Courtesy of the Thompson/Betcher family.)

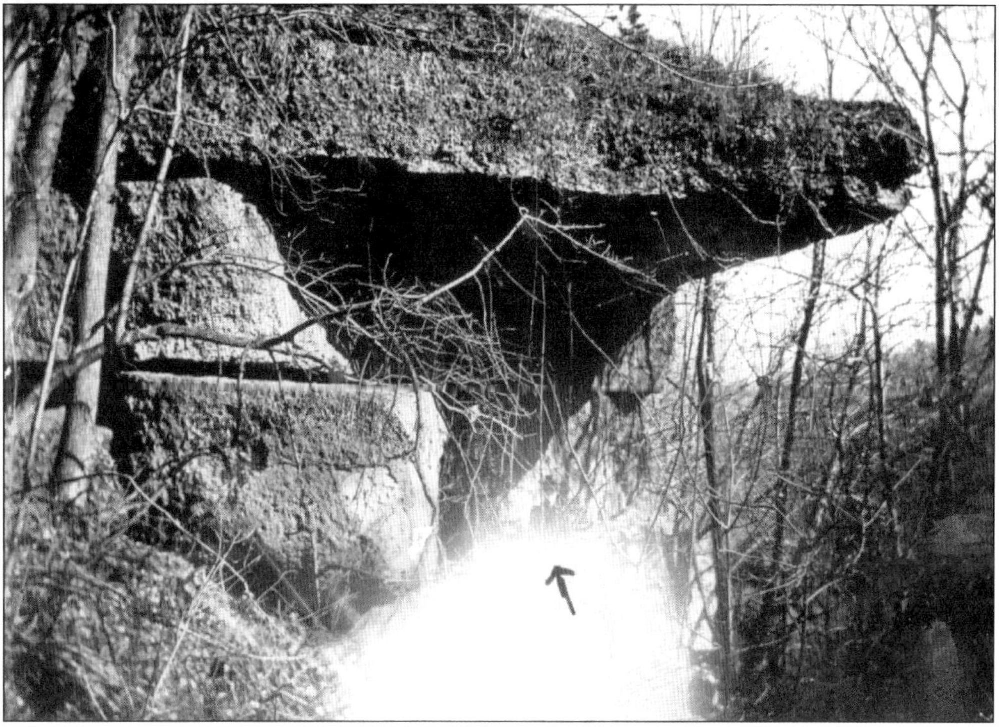

Rock Dell township is so named because of the rock ravine that winds a picturesque course of one and a half miles between banks that in places are sharp cliffs of limestone. Between these banks lies a stream fed by live springs. This rock formation is on the Marcus Wing farm at Rock Dell. Ida Wing, age eight, daughter of Marcus, stands under the ledge. (Courtesy of the OCHS.)

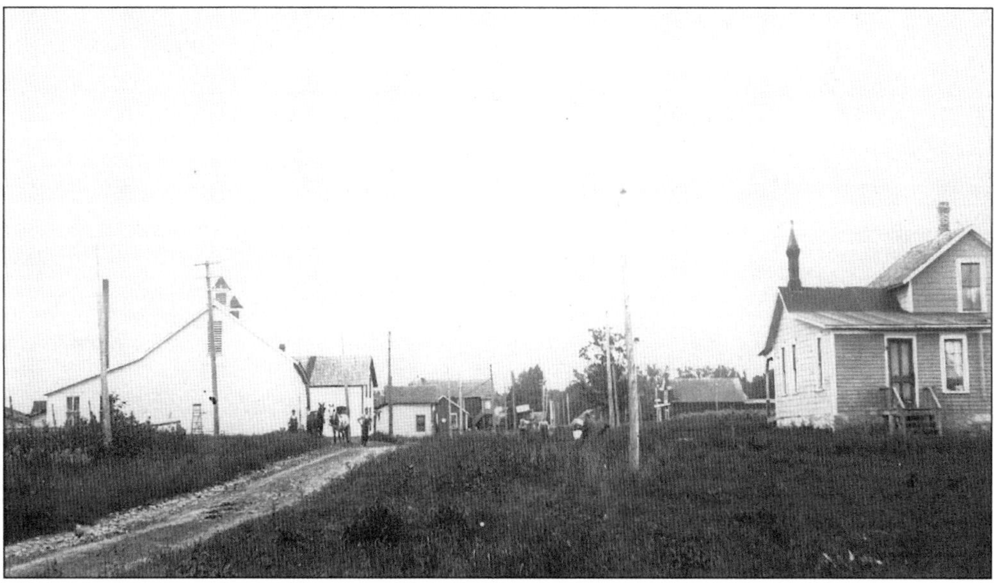

Pictured here is Rock Dell Broadway. From front to back, on the left, the buildings are a creamery, an old house where dances were sometimes held, a telephone building, and the town hall. (Courtesy of the OCHS.)

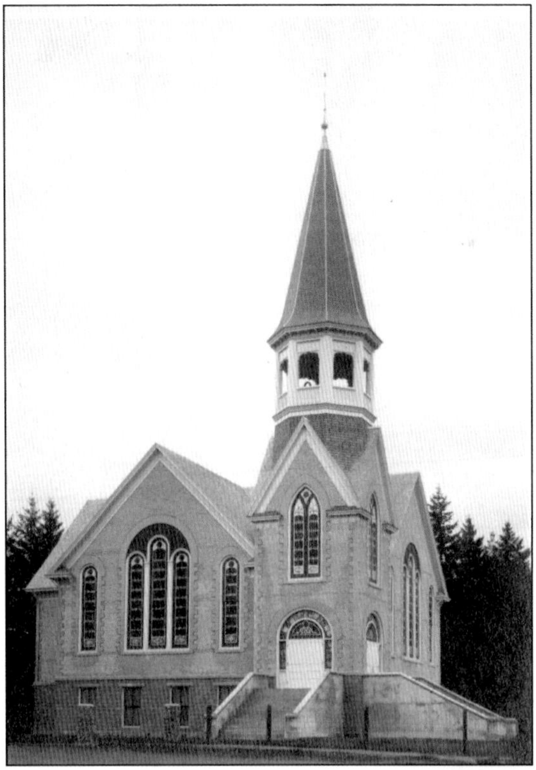

The religious need of the group of predominantly Norwegian Lutheran people was fulfilled when St. Olaf's Norwegian Evangelical Lutheran congregation was organized in 1856 by Rev. C. L. Clausen of St. Ansgar, Iowa. For the next two years, the congregation was served by visiting pastors, and the places of worship consisted of schoolhouses and farmhouses. (Courtesy of the OCHS.)

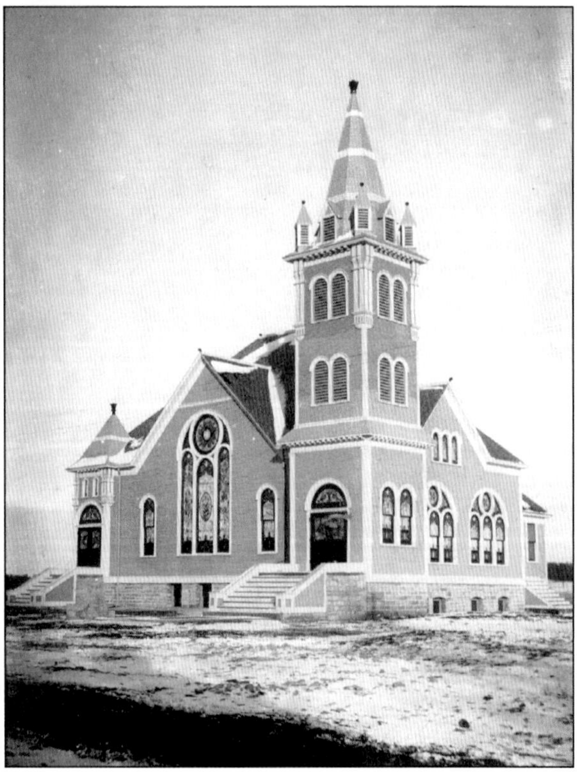

In 1863, it was decided that the members from the western part of the congregation would build their own church but still exist with the east church as one corporation. Then in 1873, it was decided to form two separate congregations, East St. Olaf and West St. Olaf, rather than remain as one corporation. The new stone church was completed in 1875 and dedicated that same year. (Courtesy of the OCHS.)

Rev. J. A. Thorson of Rock Dell began coming to Stewartville twice a month on Sunday evenings to preach. The church bell was purchased later by the Zion Lutherans after the church union in 1917. (Courtesy of the OCHS.)

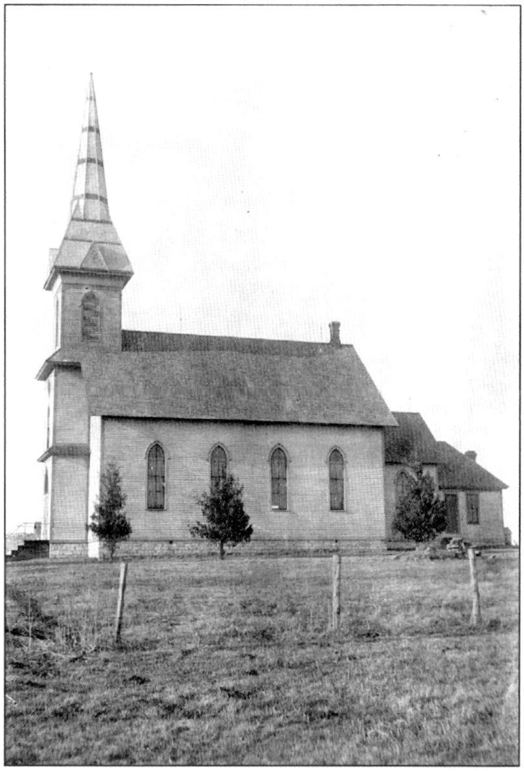

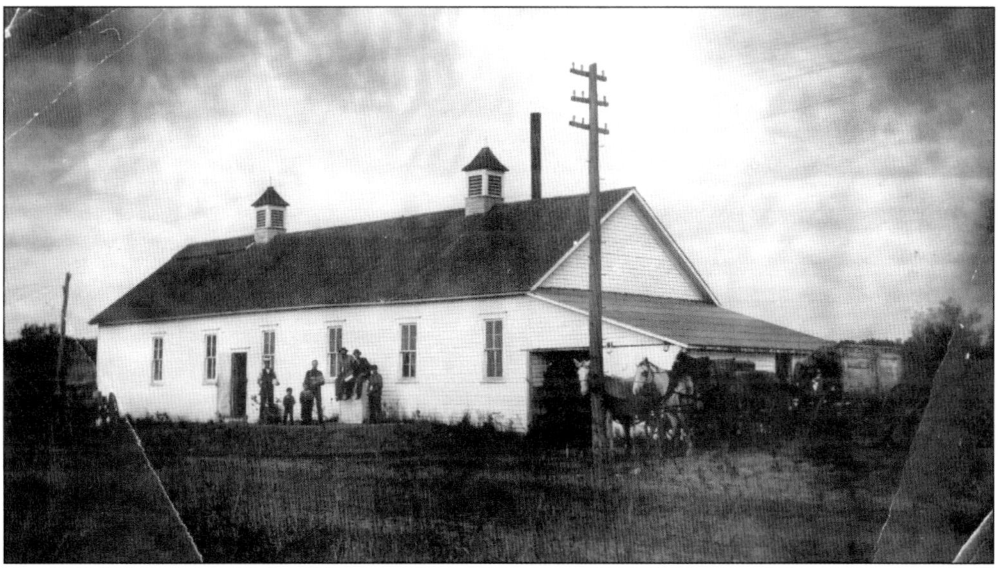

Pictured here is Rock Dell Creamery. When two competing creameries, Marvin at Rochester and Morse at Stewartville, reached a gentleman's agreement back in 1886 that each would respect the other's territory, the farmers at Rock Dell, Salem, Canisteo, and Vernon townships knew that they would be the ones to pay for this withdrawal of competition in the way of lower prices received for cream. As a result, some of the leaders in the area began talking about a cooperative creamery, a venture hitherto untried and unknown in this section of the country. (Courtesy of the OCHS.)

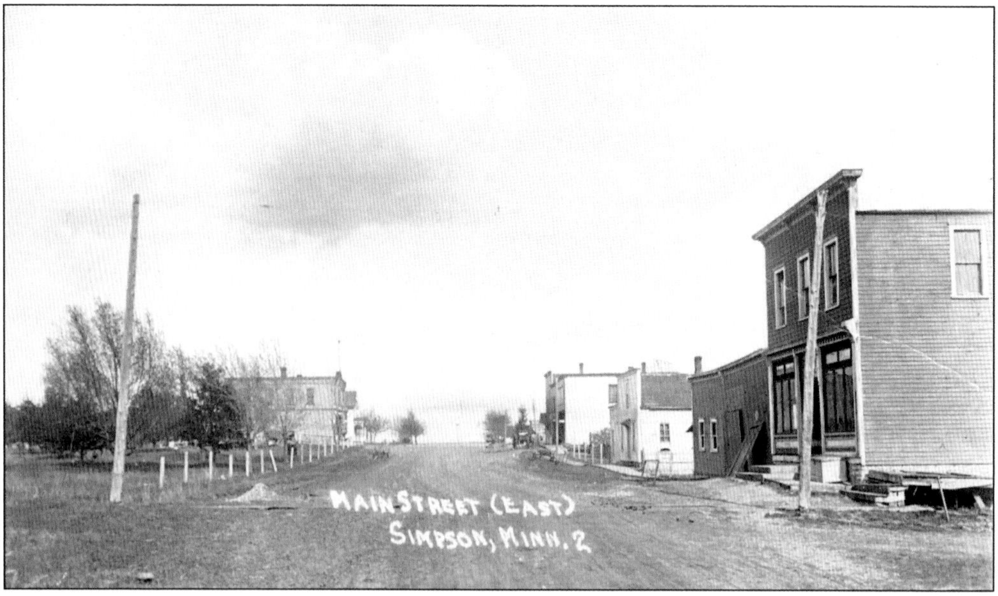

Simpson's main street can be seen here. Church Street is seen looking west from Brown Street. From left to right on the right side of street are a hotel, the Brown office building (doctors, dentists, and the Brown machinery and twine office), Geer Store, vacant lots, Brown Hardware, a meat market, and Tyler Store with a community hall above. The Chicago Great Western Railroad tracks can also be seen. (Courtesy of John King.)

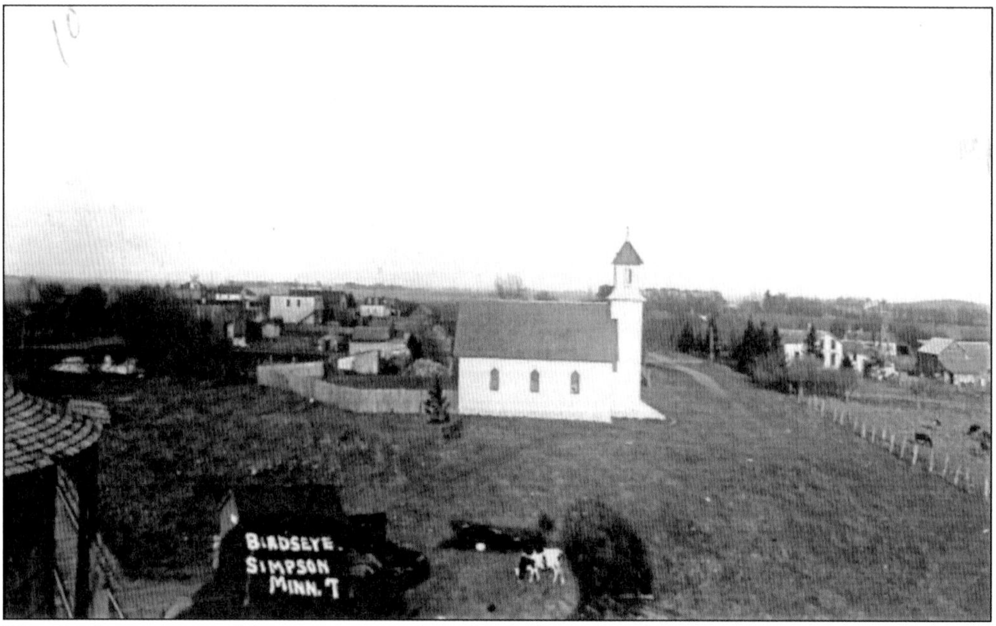

This bird's-eye view of Simpson was taken from the railroad water tower, from west to east. On the far right is the Stephen H. Brown farm residence, and in the center foreground are the Disciples of Christ church. To the left are the timber section, Tyler-Brown buildings, and Geer Store, and the rooftop over the Tyler-Brown buildings is the Whitney Block. (Courtesy of Elsa Paulsen.)

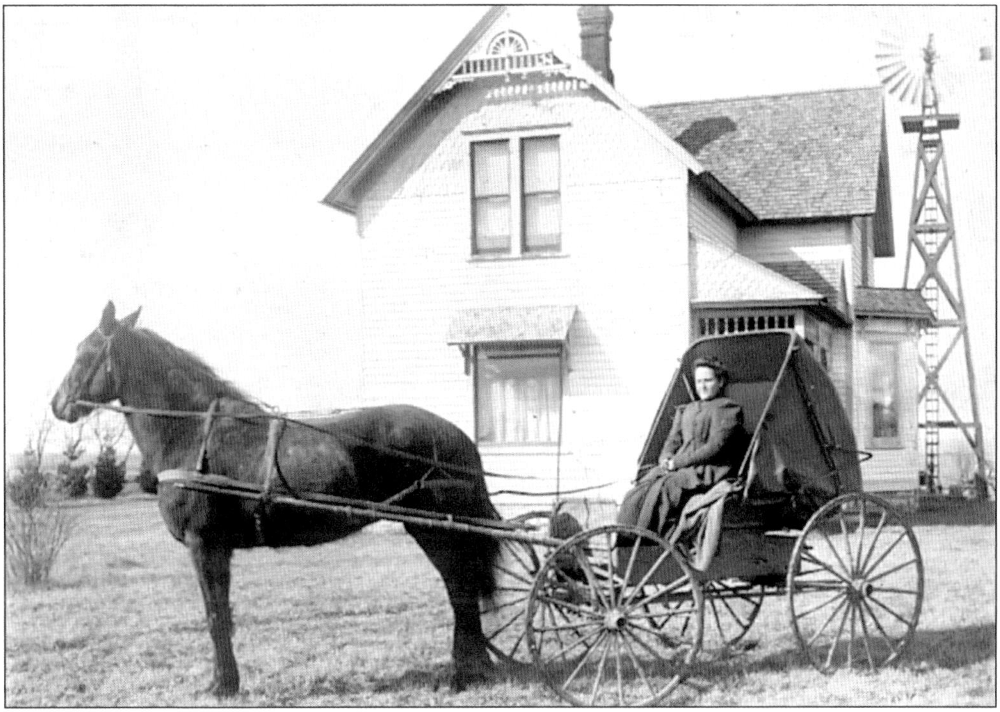

Electra Bostwick of Simpson is riding in a fancy, one-horse carriage. Notice the Queen Anne–style farmhouse behind her and the windmill on the right. (Courtesy of Elsa Paulsen.)

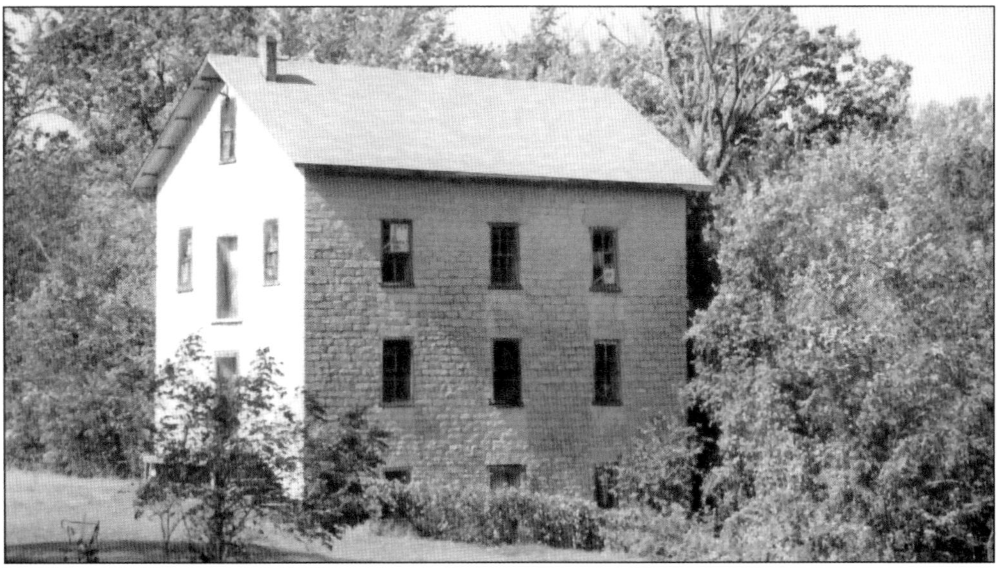

In 1868, Matthew Fugle purchased land where the Territorial Road forded the Root River and erected a flour mill of native stone. Farmers from Byron, Grand Meadow, High Forest, and Stewartville waited in turn for the fine flour and livestock feeds. Closed during World War I, it was later reopened by Jeremiah Chase for feed grinding, which was continued until 1938. This mill and the picnic grounds to the east along the rock cliffs are intricately woven into the lives of the local residents. In 1954, the mill was converted into a museum by Joseph Chase. (Courtesy of Myrna Wesselman.)

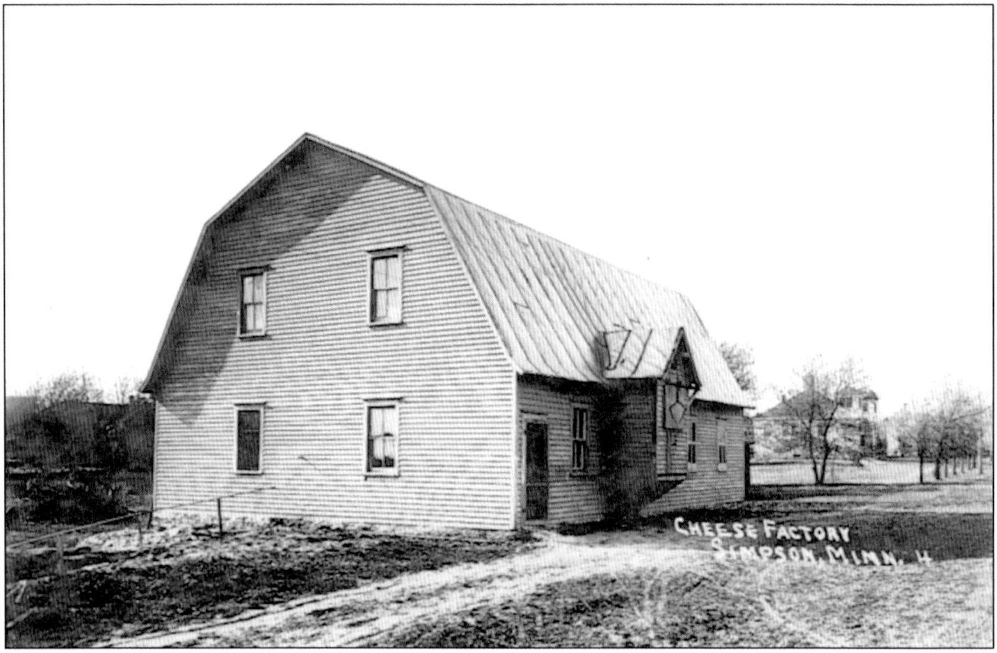

Pictured here is the Simpson cheese factory. South of the school block and at the extreme southeast corner outside the original plat of the village, a privately owned cheese factory was erected. Destroyed by fire, rebuilt, and again burned, this progressive industry in a productive dairy community was of financial interest to the village and rural patrons. (Courtesy of Elsa Paulsen.)

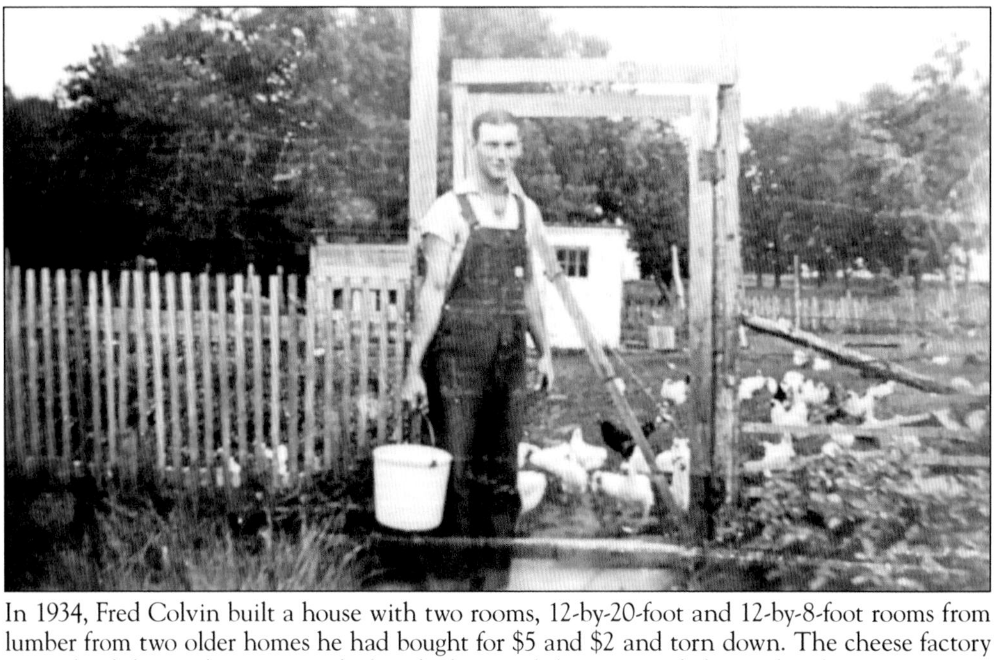

In 1934, Fred Colvin built a house with two rooms, 12-by-20-foot and 12-by-8-foot rooms from lumber from two older homes he had bought for $5 and $2 and torn down. The cheese factory sat on land that Colvin is using for his chicken yard. (Courtesy of Elsa Paulsen.)

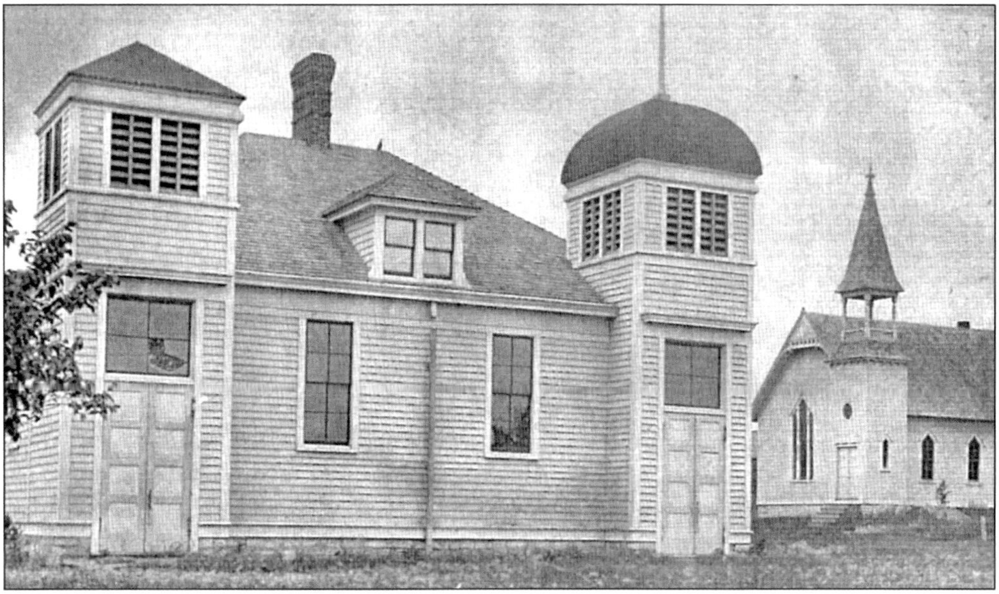

Here is a view inside Simpson School District No. 14. In 1897, a spacious two-room, ground-floor building was erected by Haney Brothers Contractors at the southeast side of the village plat of Simpson. This new well-equipped school was the second two-room building in Pleasant Grove Township. Two entry coatrooms were capped by contrasting domes. The upper-grade room to the north claimed the honor of the bell tower. Two large assembly rooms, a wide entry hall at the rear of the building, gave access to the basement and ground-level entrance. (Courtesy of Elsa Paulsen.)

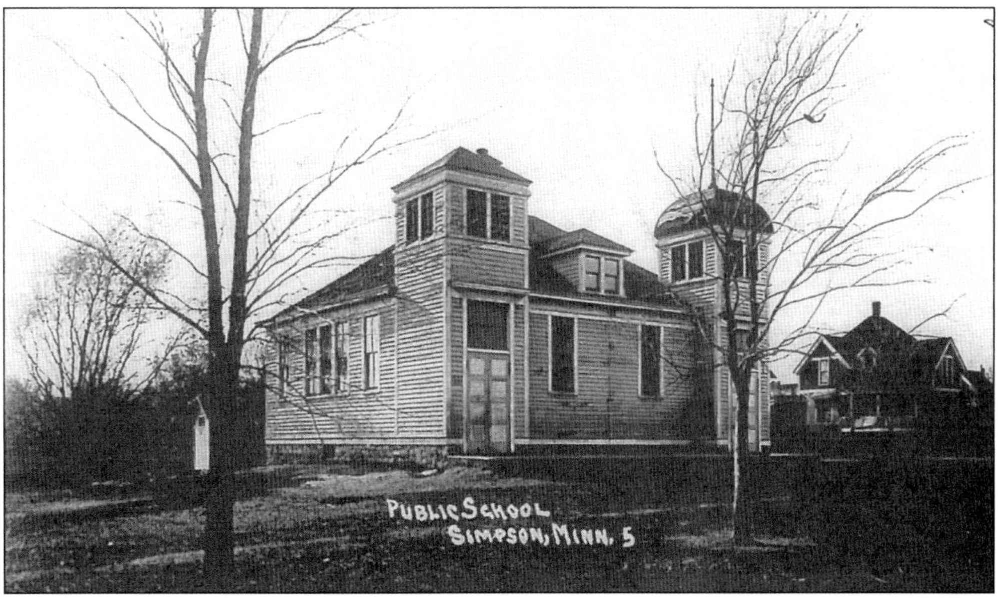

In 1898, a two-room, ground-floor frame school building was erected by Haney Brothers Contractors at the southeast one-half of block 10. There has been frequent comment regarding the difference in the towers at the entrances to the building, reportedly to identify the upper- and lower-grade rooms, to satisfy discussion of carpenters, and indecision as to which tower should contain the bell. (Courtesy of Elsa Paulsen.)

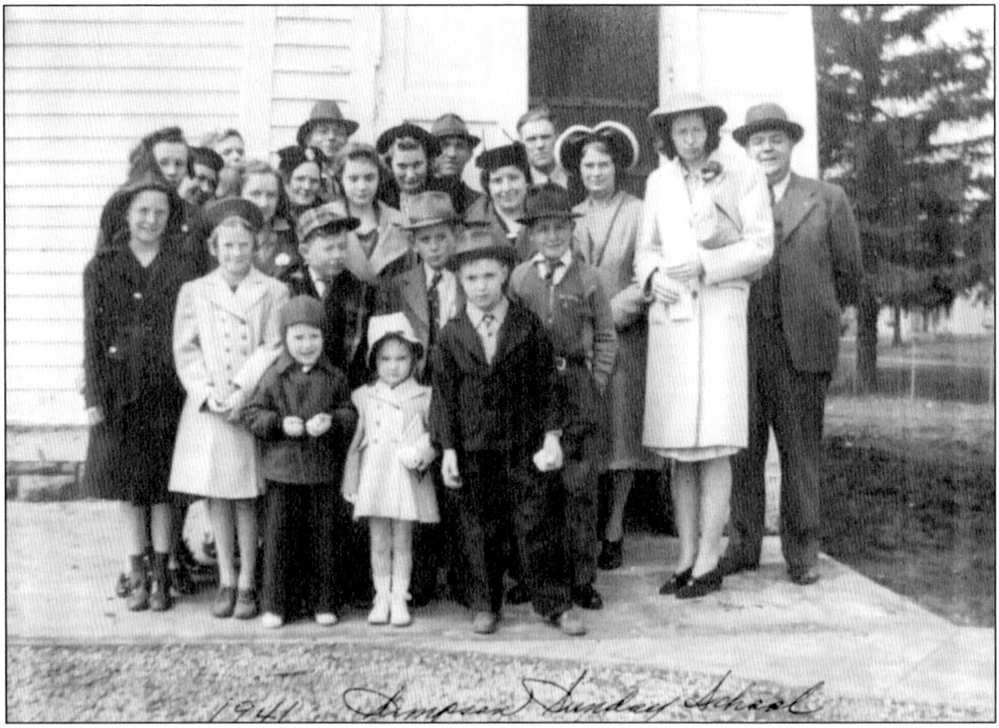

Pictured here is the Simpson Sunday school in 1941, including ? Remer, Maurice Haney, M. Lowery, Betty Row, ? Remer, Catherine Wellen, Elsie Harvey, M. Wallace Hebl, Shirley Haney Krause, ? Sparrow, Paul Colvin, Kenneth Wallace, F. Washburn, and Elsa Colvin. The teachers are Margaret and Al Crocker. (Courtesy of Elsa Paulsen.)

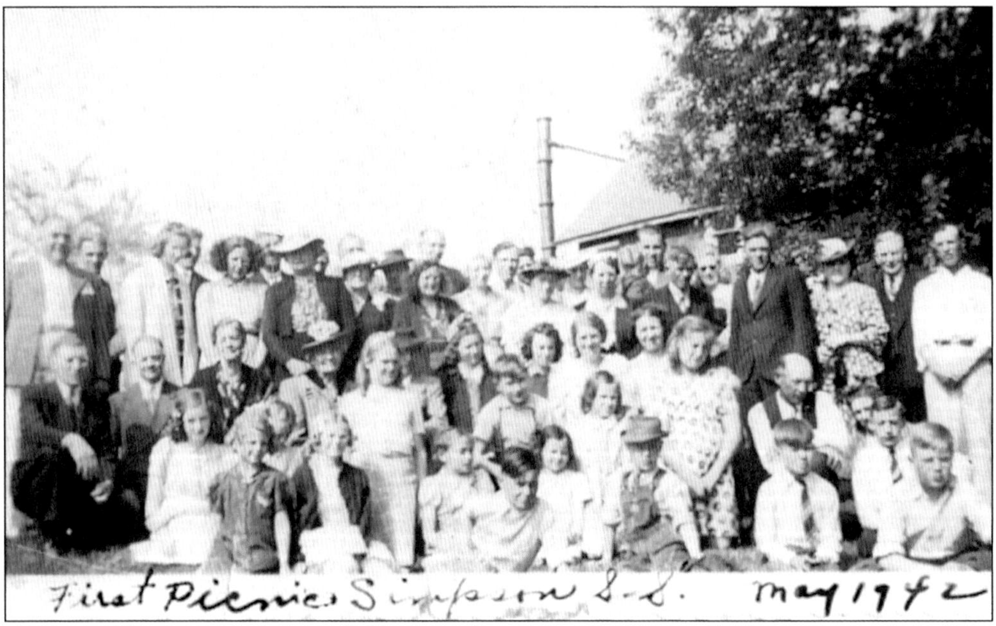

This is a Simpson Sunday school picnic. The first picnic was held in May 1942 at the Amos farm near Pleasant Grove. (Courtesy of Elsa Paulsen.)

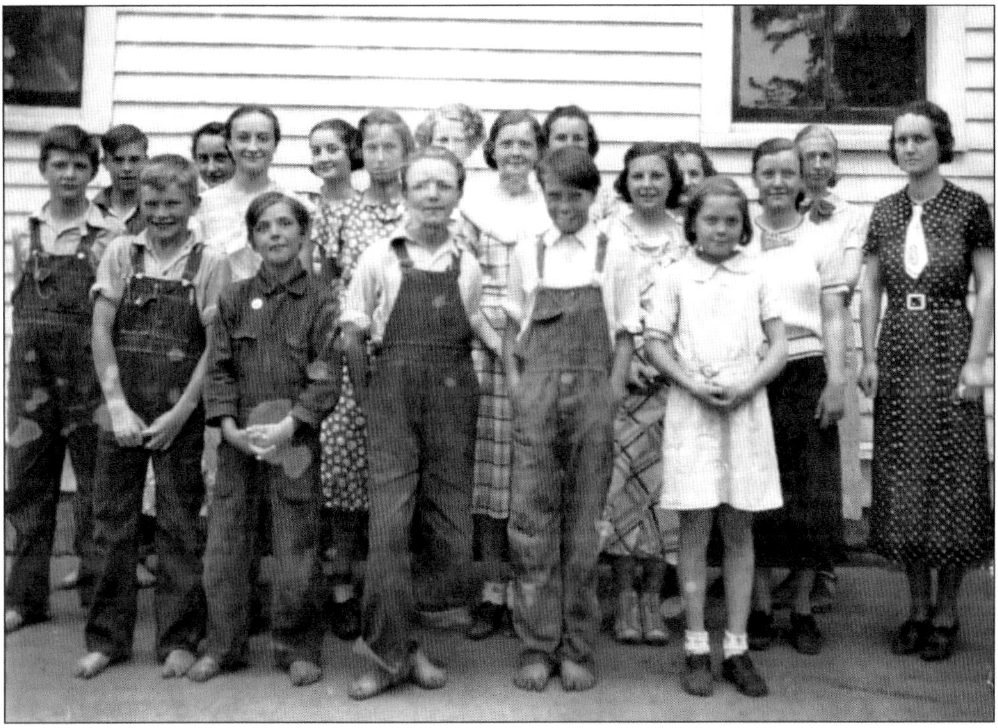

Here is a Simpson School class. (Courtesy of Elsa Paulsen.)

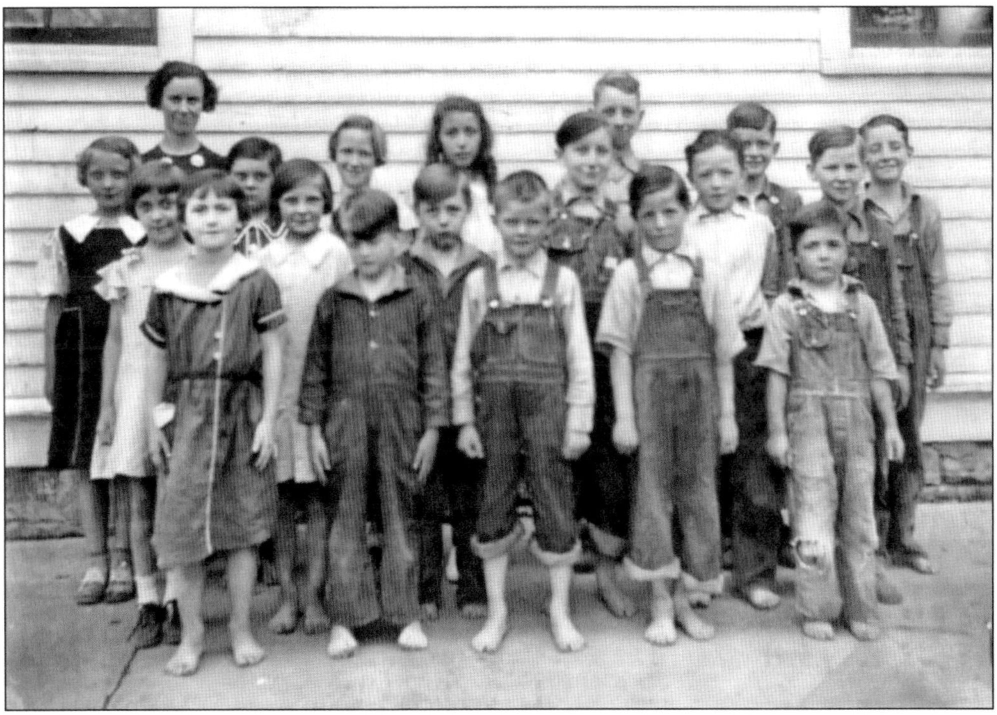

Here is the Simpson School class of Violet Close. (Courtesy of Elsa Paulsen.)

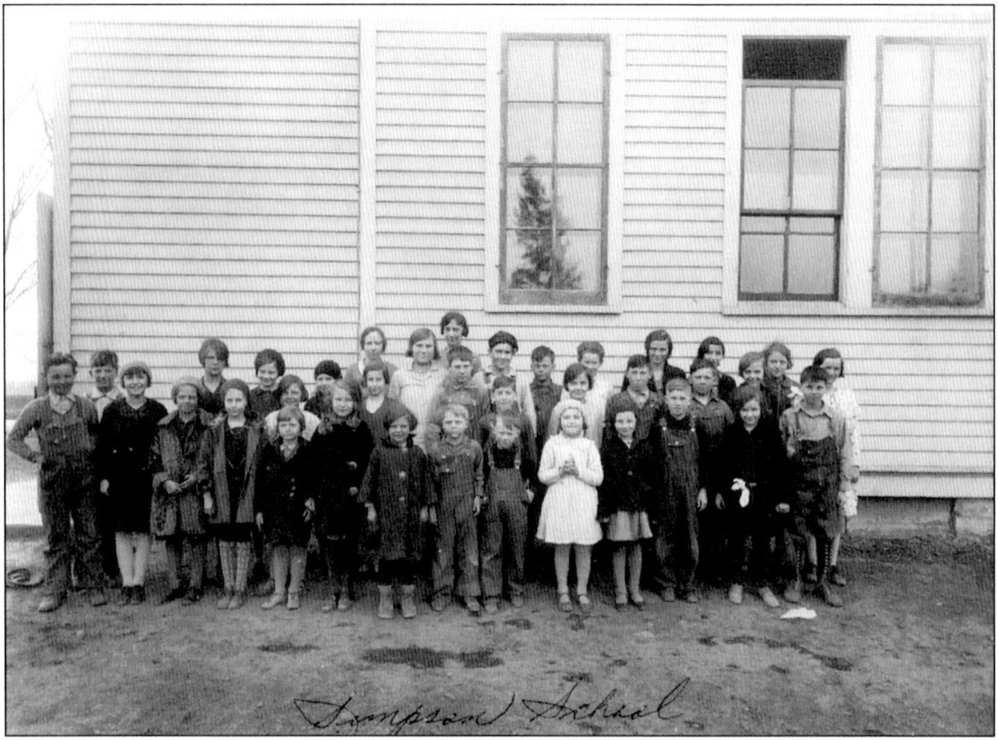

Pictured here is another Simpson School class. (Courtesy of Elsa Paulsen.)

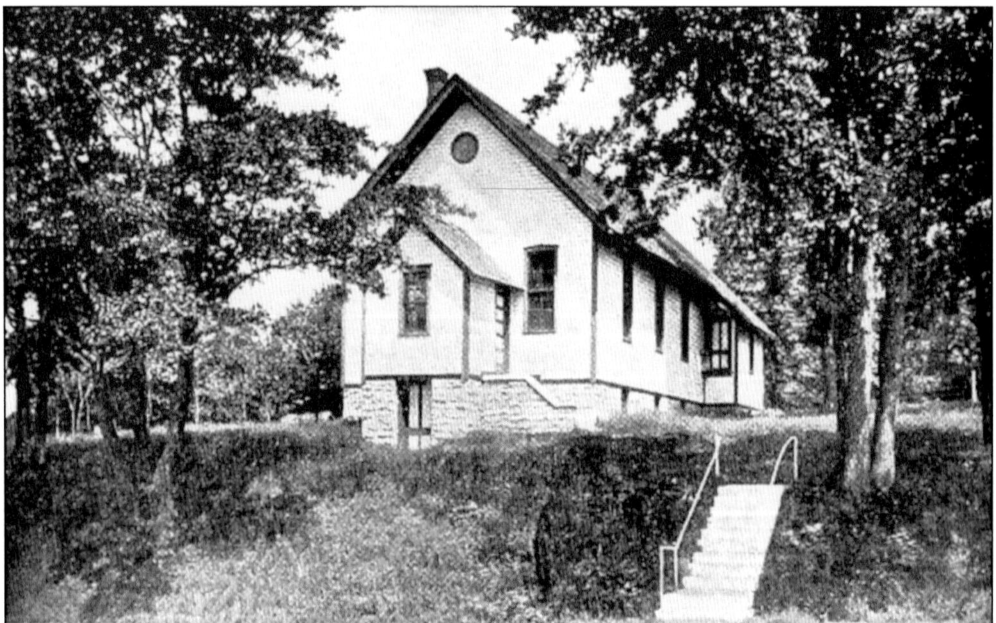

Here can be seen the St. Bridget's parish. The parish, known as St. Matthew's Temperance Hall, was built in 1872 on the hillside north of the church and highway. It was under the charge of the Winona Catholic parish until the year 1882. (Courtesy of Agnes Griffin.)

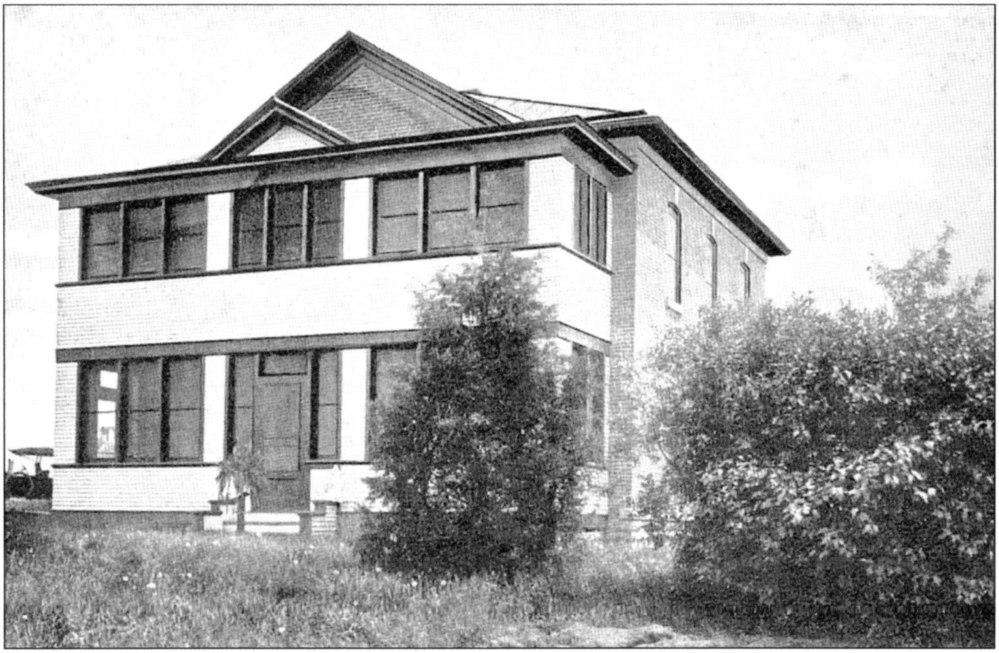

In this picture is the St. Bridget's rectory. Beginning in 1881, under the charge of St. John's Catholic Church of Rochester, a fine stone and frame parish house was begun and completed in 1882 by volunteer labor at the cost of some $23,000. (Courtesy of Agnes Griffin.)

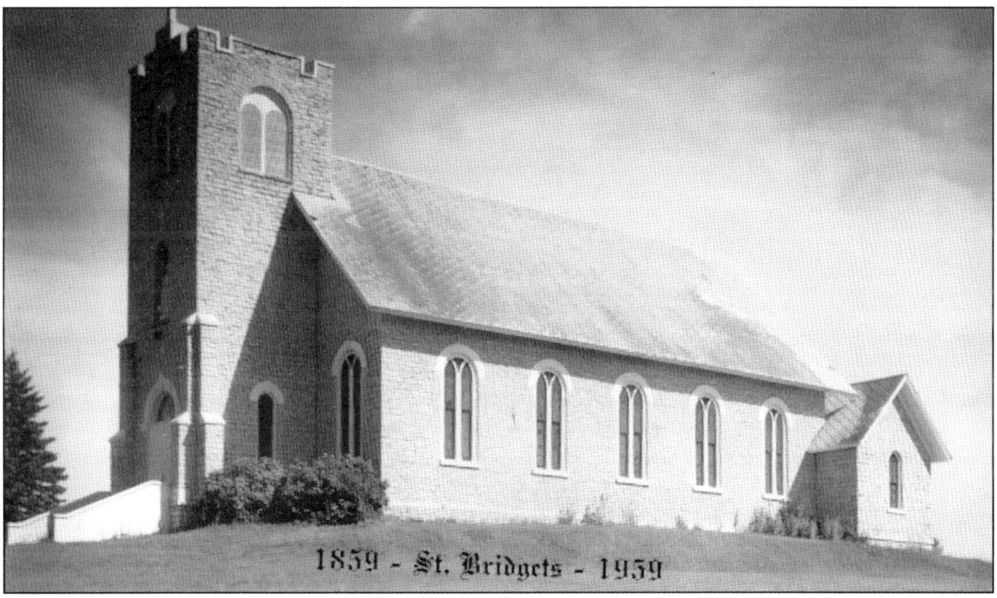

Mother church of the Catholic faith in Olmsted County, St. Bridget's Catholic Church, a large stone edifice with seating capacity for 600, was erected in 1859 west of the present village of Simpson. John C. Buckley settled along the trail from Winona to the High Forest settlement. The location was a few miles west of the present village of Simpson and was known as Buckley Settlement. Later, with the postal center at the James Carroll home, the community settlement was known as Carrollville. (Courtesy of Agnes Griffin.)

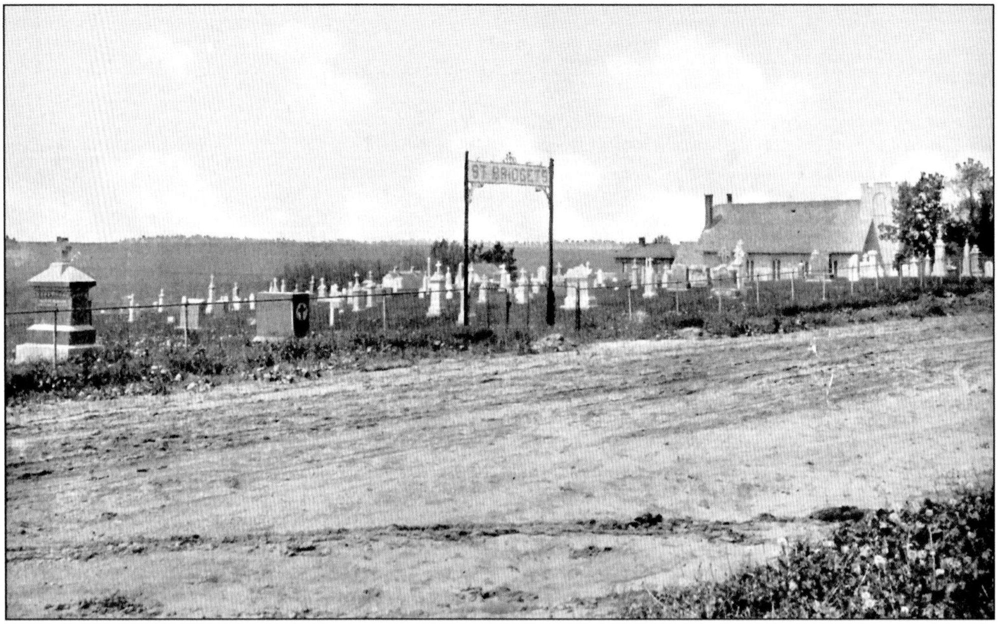

In 1854, John C. Buckley donated land in what was to become section 6 of Pleasant Grove Township as a site for a church, cemetery, and grounds for the Catholic faith. St. Bridget's Cemetery was platted to the east of the church lawns and south of the Stage Road leasing westward to Buckley Settlement and the village of High Forest. The earliest burial was that of Margaret Campion, who died on September 14, 1854. The cemetery ground has been enclosed by an ornamental fence and nameplate archway gate. (Courtesy of Agnes Griffin.)

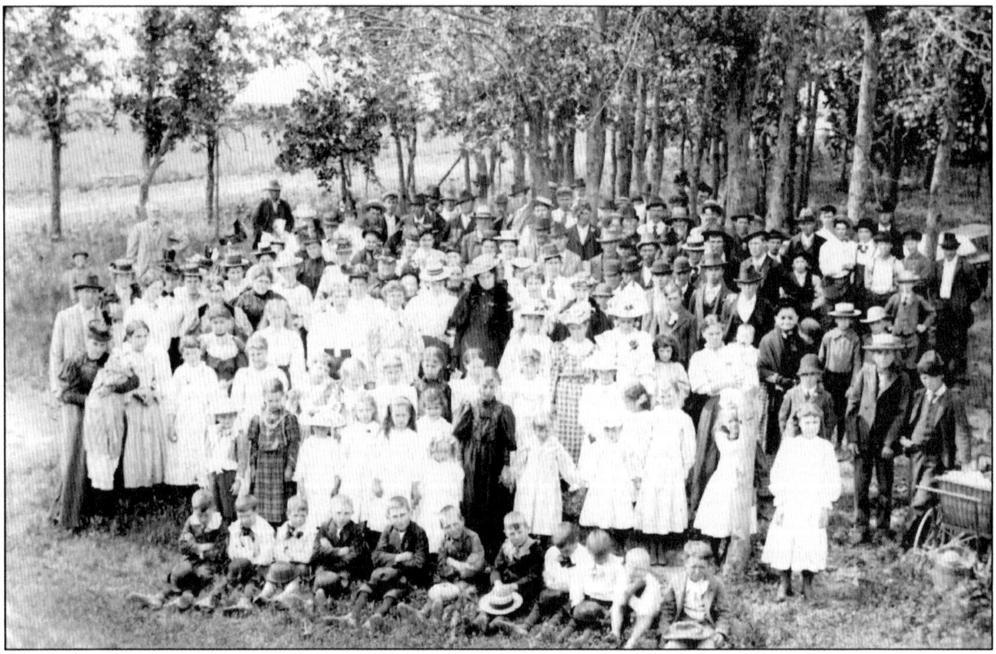

In 1895, Sumner Center and another school joined together for a picnic. (Courtesy of the SAHS.)

Three

EDUCATION

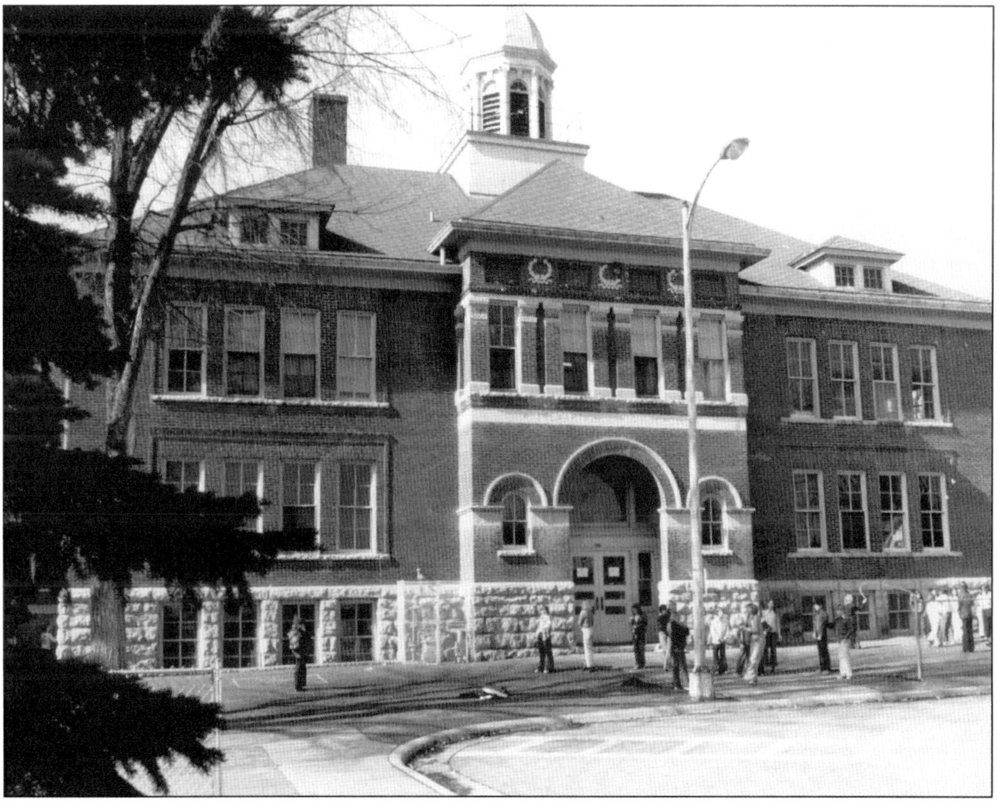

Stewartville High School (Central Elementary School) is seen here. On May 2, 1899, a meeting was called to vote on the proposition of issuing $15,000 in bonds to erect a new schoolhouse. Plans for a 10-room, modern-equipped brick building were solicited. The contract was given to Martin Hefferon of Rochester. The stone for the foundation was all quarried from the east bank of the Root River. In September 1900, the new brick building was ready to be occupied. (Courtesy of Sharon Byrne.)

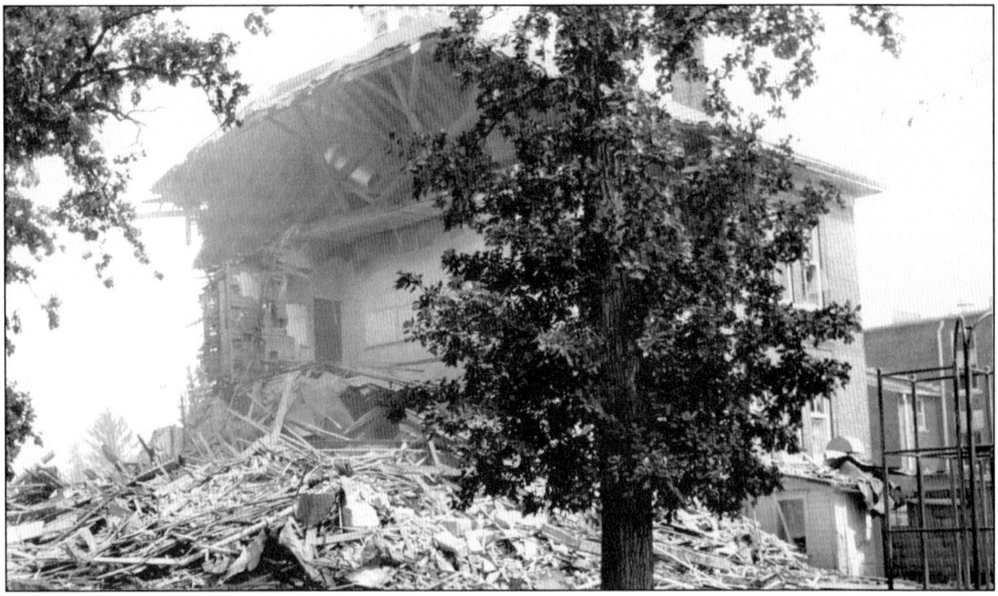

The razing of the 1900 Stewartville High School (Central Elementary School) took place on December 20, 1974. The inspection was triggered by a state board of education directive that all 75-year-old buildings be examined for safety reasons. The building was inspected by the fire marshal and architects, who found fire hazards and heating, lighting, and ventilation systems deficient in the three-story structure. They also said it had shifted on its foundation. The fire hazards were because of wooden floors, stairwells, and the roof. (Courtesy of Sharon Byrne.)

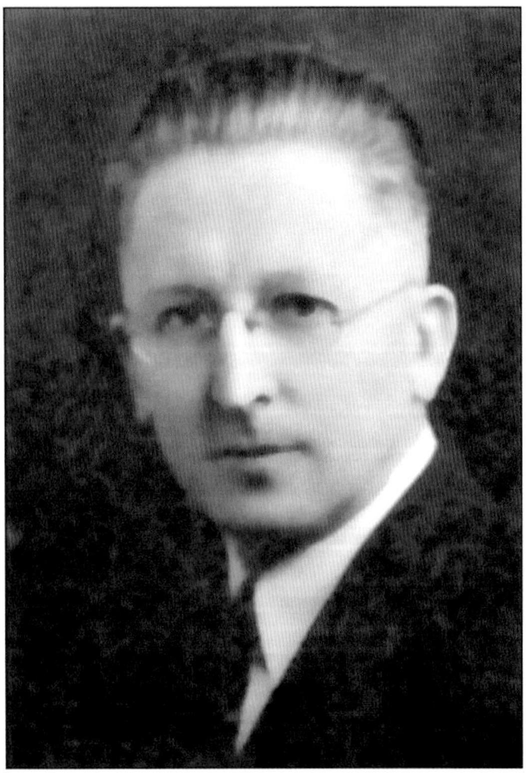

J. E. Sutherland, superintendent, was born in Chariton, Iowa, where he received his early schooling. His high school years were spent in Holtan, Kansas. He attended Campbell College and in 1921 received his bachelor's degree. In 1929, he completed his master's at the University of Minnesota. He taught at Menahga, Grasston, and Black Duck before accepting the position at Stewartville in September 1930. In 1938, he called all the pastors of all the churches for a meeting to consider weekday religious education during release time from public school for one hour per week. It was decided that one hour every Tuesday would be set aside for this program. (Courtesy of Sharon Byrne.)

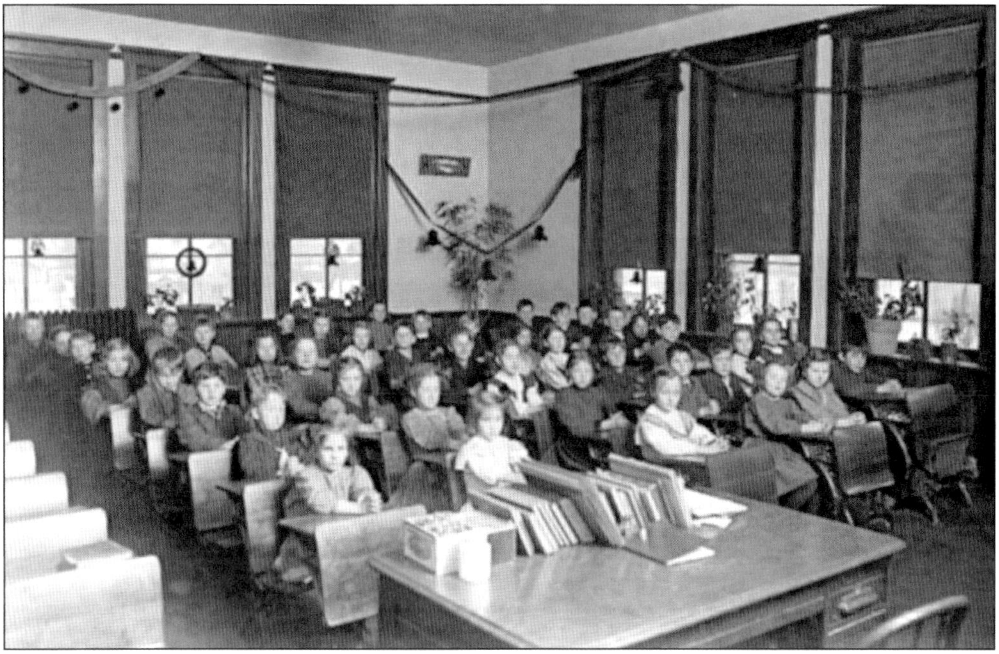

Pictured here are the second and third grades at Central Elementary School. Robinson's series of school books, desks with flop-down seats, a blackboard behind the teacher's desk, chalk that came in chunks, and a slate pencil two inches long were luxuries. Second graders learned from third graders, and third graders reviewed with their younger peers. (Courtesy of the SAHS.)

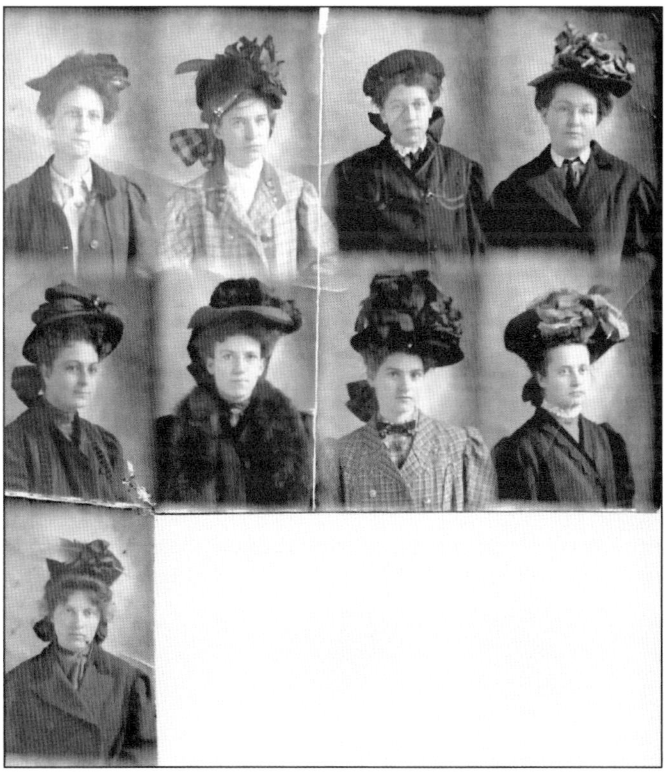

Here is the graduating class of 1908. This is a unique picture as all the young ladies have hats on. Graduates are Mabel Dodge, Esther Gahringer, Ruth Gaskill, Mable Grover, Lucy Loucks, Bertha Smith, Bessie Tews, Elsie Thayer, and Cora Wattles. (Courtesy of the SAHS.)

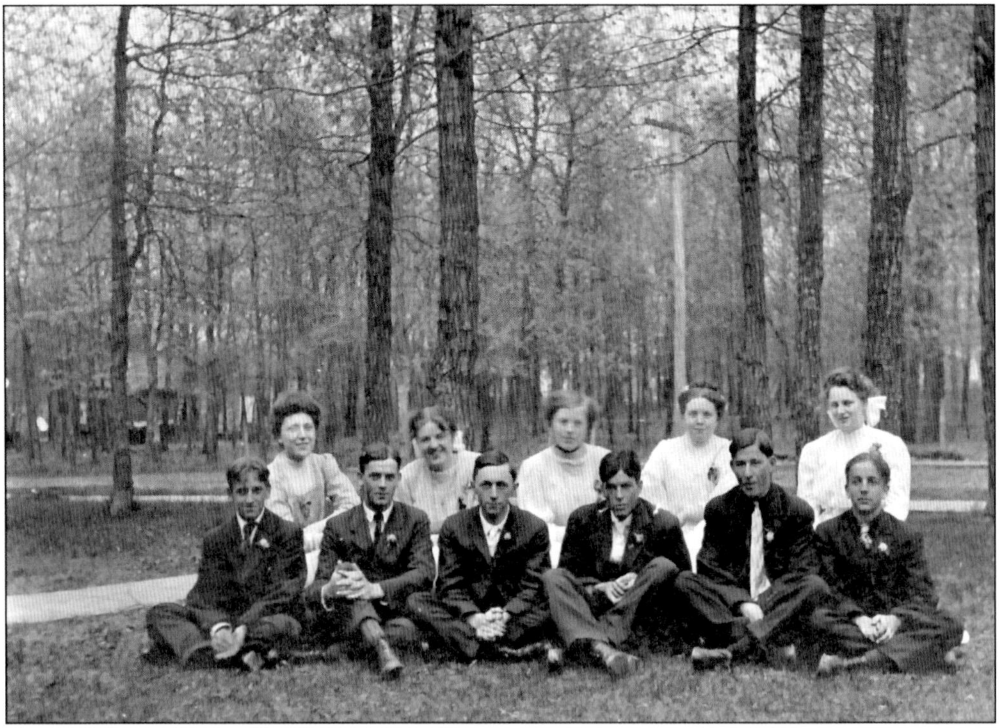

Here is the graduating class of 1909. From left to right are (first row) Clarence Christofferson, Percy Brownell, John Groggin, Joseph Brin, Harold Gahringer, and Charles Colby; (second row) Geneva Duncanson, Ora Savidge, Verna Vail, LePearl Bonner, and Casetta Lamp. (Courtesy of Sharon Byrne.)

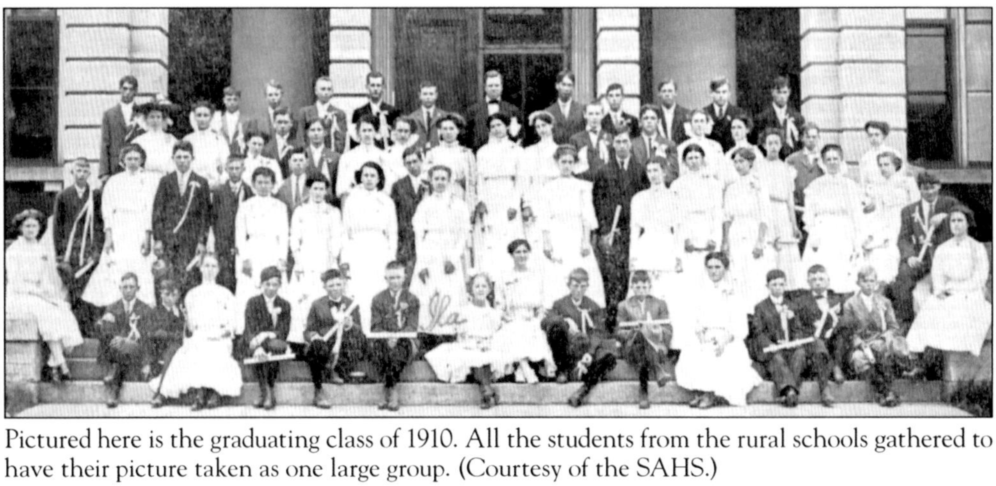

Pictured here is the graduating class of 1910. All the students from the rural schools gathered to have their picture taken as one large group. (Courtesy of the SAHS.)

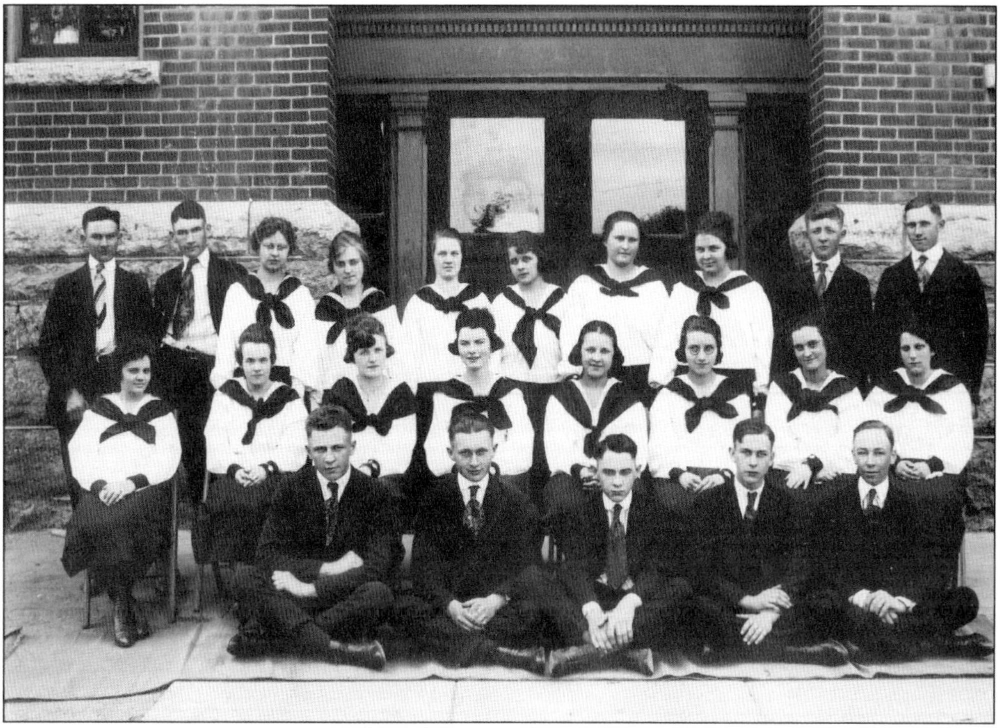

Here is the graduating class of 1920. Pictured are Russell Billings, Leslie Kingsley, Max Moore, Lester Stiles, Robert Starmer, Eilalin Thein, Henrietta Ellis, Florence Griffin, Fern Johnston, Edith Wallace, Gladys Rhoten, Lora King, John Burton, Donald Burke, Mary Sackett, Elsie Jahns, Vera Tubbs, Patricia Russell, Florence Beach, Hazel Stoyke, George Joyce, and Carl Bielke. (Courtesy of the SAHS.)

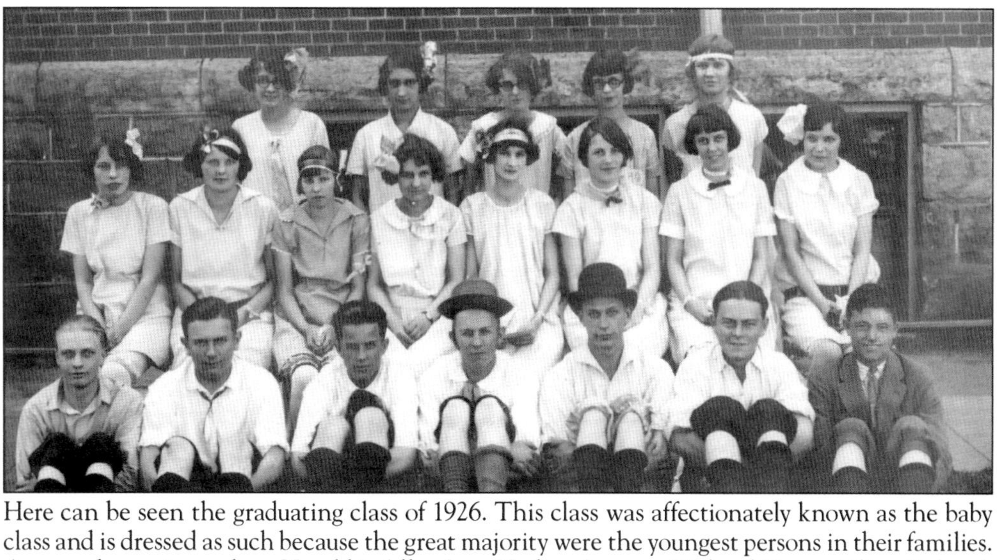

Here can be seen the graduating class of 1926. This class was affectionately known as the baby class and is dressed as such because the great majority were the youngest persons in their families. Among those pictured are Harold ?, Allen Lee, Herbert Lenton, Richard Towey, Oliver Solsrud, Lyndon Ware, Dean Hughes, Doris McClellan, Helen Ludkas, Mildred Matzke, Beth Wilson, Mattie Wood, Esther Hogenson, Lila ?, and Hilda Stensrud. (Courtesy of Sharon Byrne.)

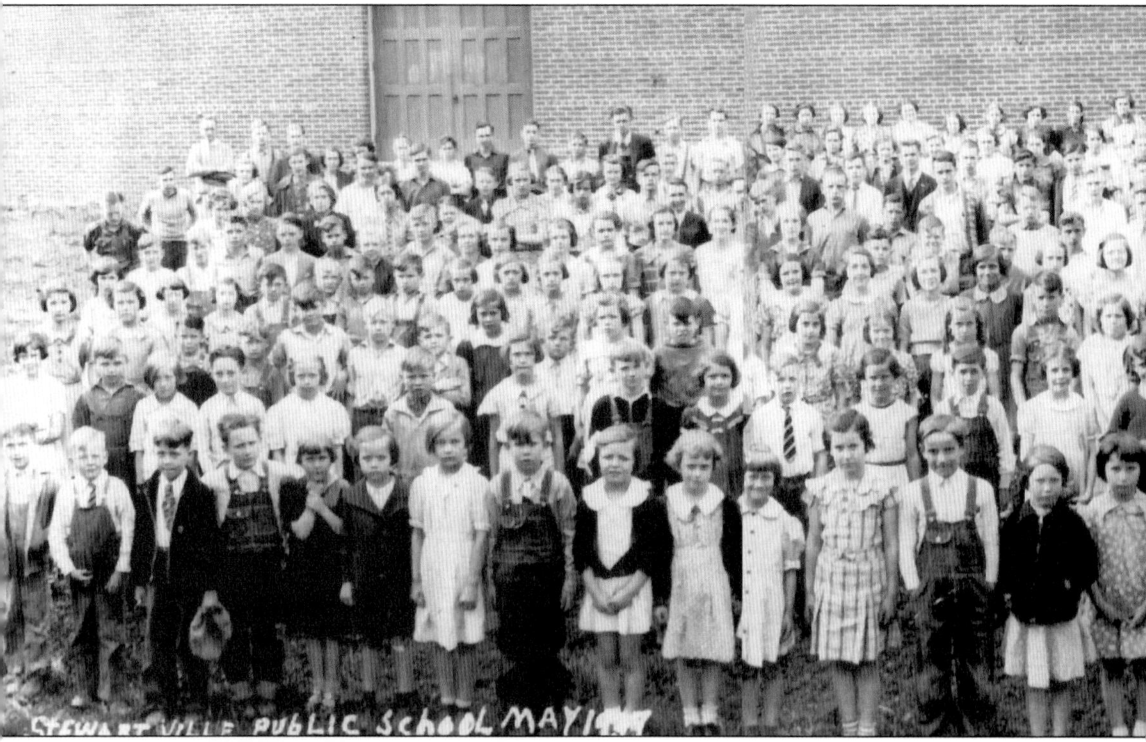

Stewartville Public School, grades kindergarten through high school, is pictured here. All the

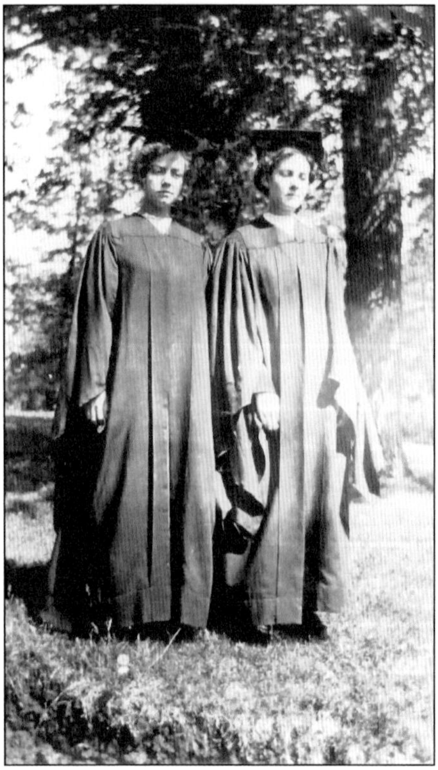

The long-awaited day, graduation, has arrived. Bess Trusty and Ila Flathers have a picture taken in their caps and gowns. They are from the Stewartville High School graduating class of 1914. (Courtesy of the SAHS.)

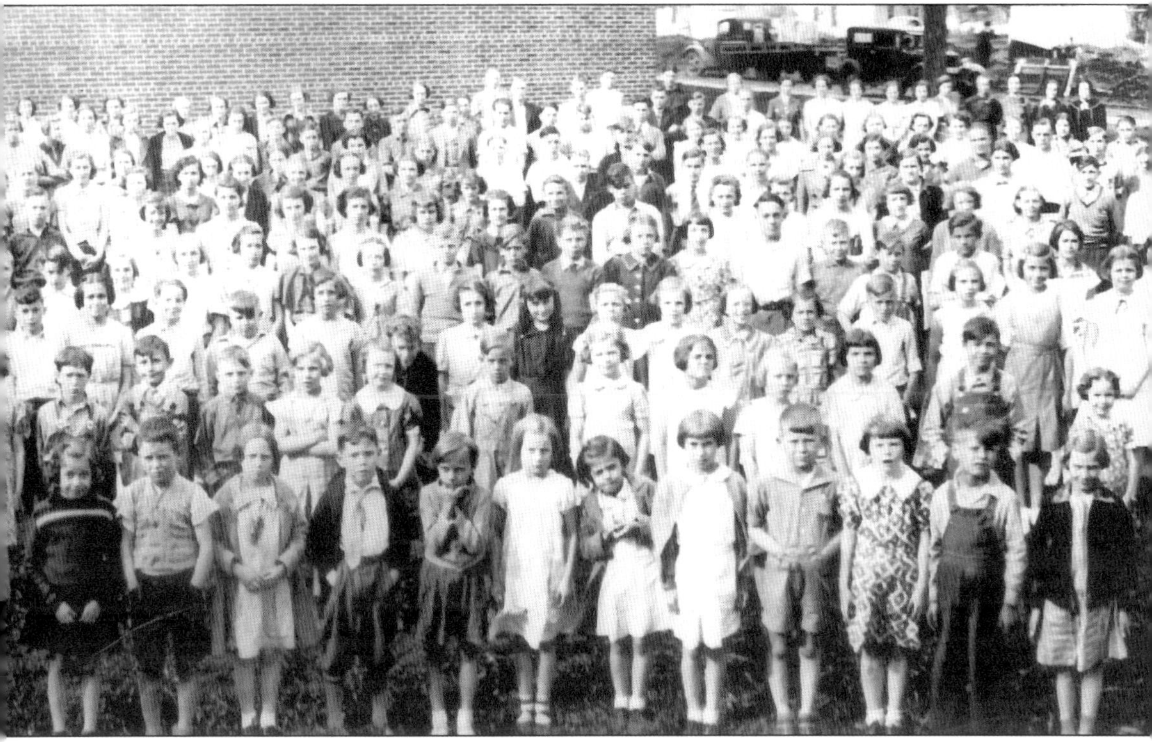

students gathered for this picture in May 1937. (Courtesy of the Gray family.)

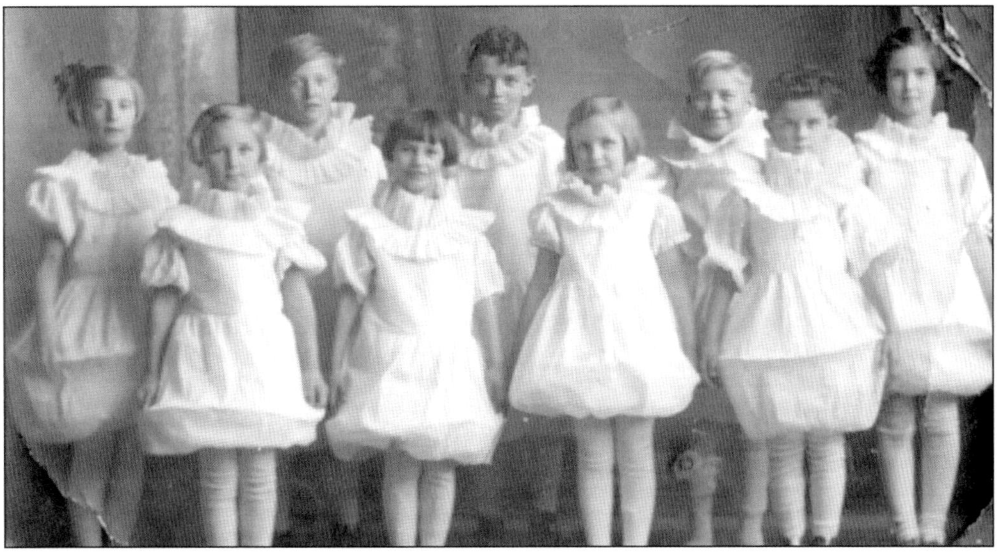

Stewartville Public School presents the operetta *Snow Queen* in November 1933. Snowflakes are, from left to right, (first row) Doris Betcher, Doris Woodworth, Gerri Gray, and Don Sullivan; (second row) Norma Janssen, Robert Peterson, Gordon Sackett, Howard Johnson, and Catherine Towey. (Courtesy of the Gray family.)

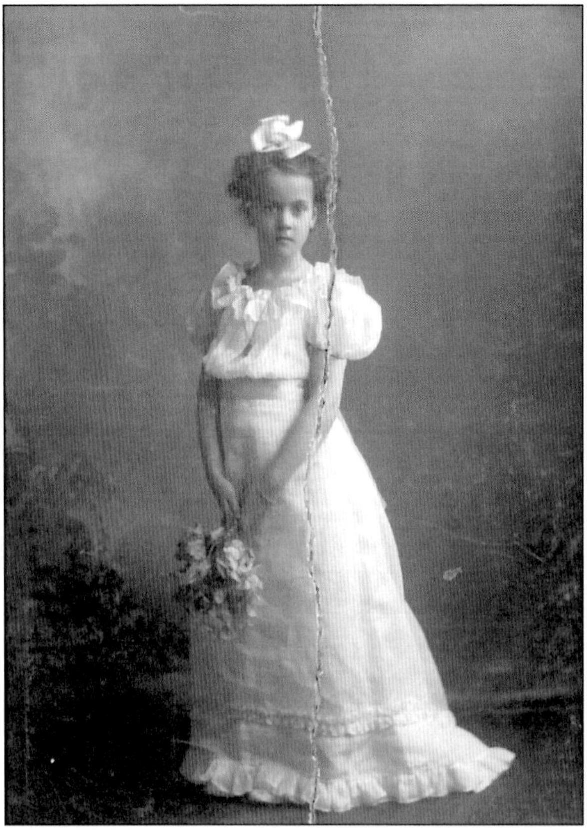

Seen here around 1902 is the Stewartville High School production of a Tom Thumb wedding. Selma Hogenson is a bridesmaid. (Courtesy of the SAHS.)

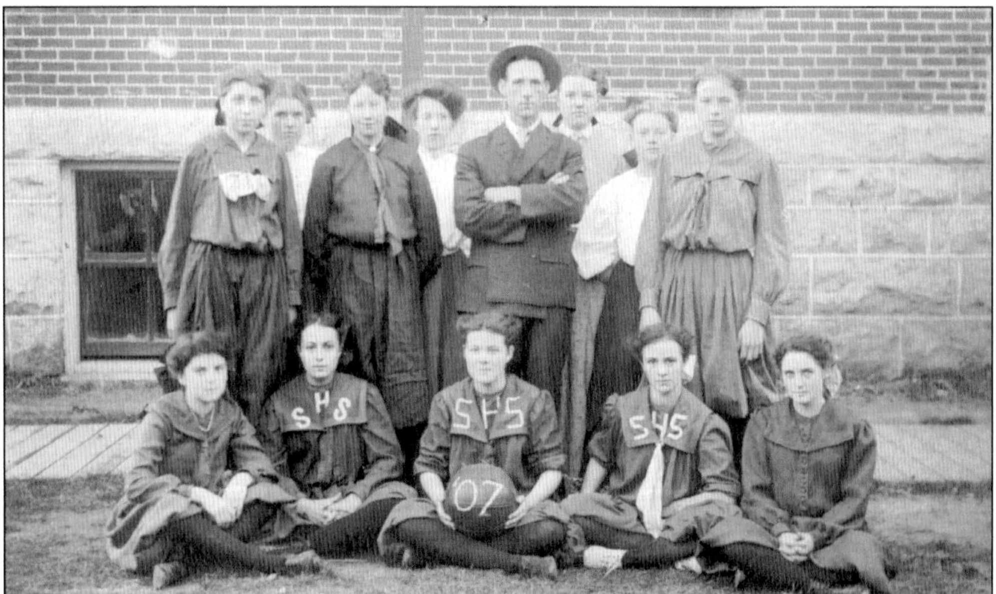

The 1907 girls' basketball team poses together here. In the early 1900s, girls participated in basketball. They wore uniforms that were befitting of young ladies and were known as the "Bloomer Girls." (Courtesy of the SAHS.)

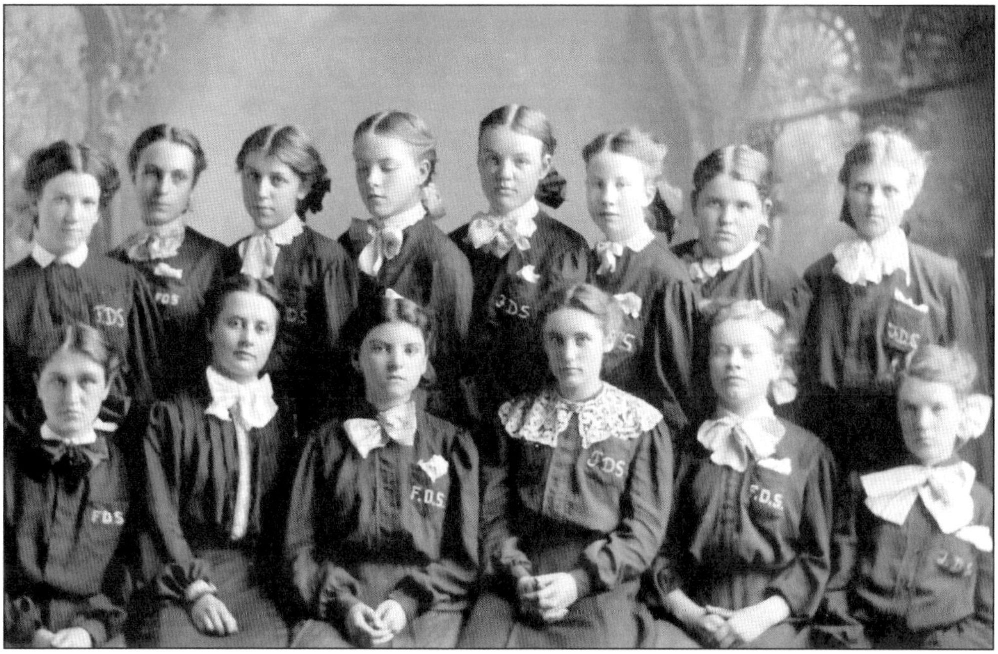

The 1908 FDS Club gathers together for a photograph. From left to right are (first row) Ellen Colby, Lucy Loucks, Stella Popple, Frances Davis, Maydalene Johnson, and Marjorie Fanning; (second row) Bertha Smith, Bess Tews, Mable Dodge, Verna Vail, Geneva Duncanson, Bessie Bibb, Mary Horton, and Mable Swenson. (Courtesy of the SAHS.)

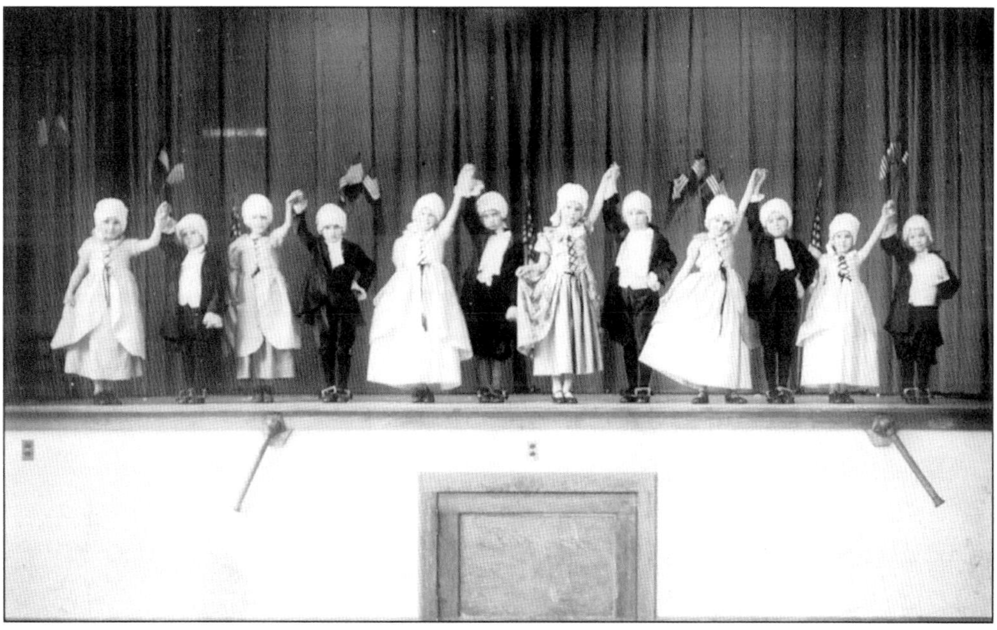

The Stewartville Public School gymnasium stage can be seen here. On February 22, 1932, students dress as George and Martha Washington. From left to right are Doris Betcher, Maurice Bentley, Norma Jensen, Jack Lenton, Marcella Kendall, Bill Tyselling, Madonna Dormady, Robert Frick, Gwendolyn Jones, Donald Sullivan, Jean Olson, and Dean Rhoten. (Courtesy of Donald Sullivan.)

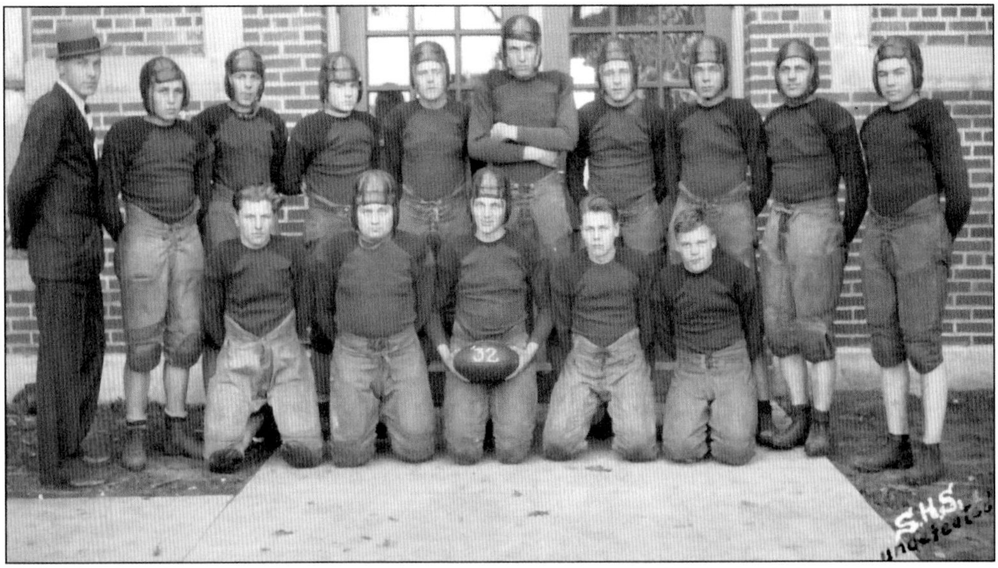

When football practice started in the fall, a large number of high school and grade school students answered the call. However, after a few weeks of practice, several players dropped out due to ineligibility. When Stewartville was ready to play the first football game, there were only 14 players left. Members of 1932 team are coach John Gruys, captain Robert Kuhle, Harold Betcher, Robert Matzke, Robert Ballard, Zephry Peterson, Herschel Hoaglan, Lloyd Russell, Robert Lane, Derwood Howe, Arthur Fields, Leonard Towey, Richard Runkle, Harry Light, George Weiland, and Homer Wooldridge Jr. (Courtesy of Sharon Byrne.)

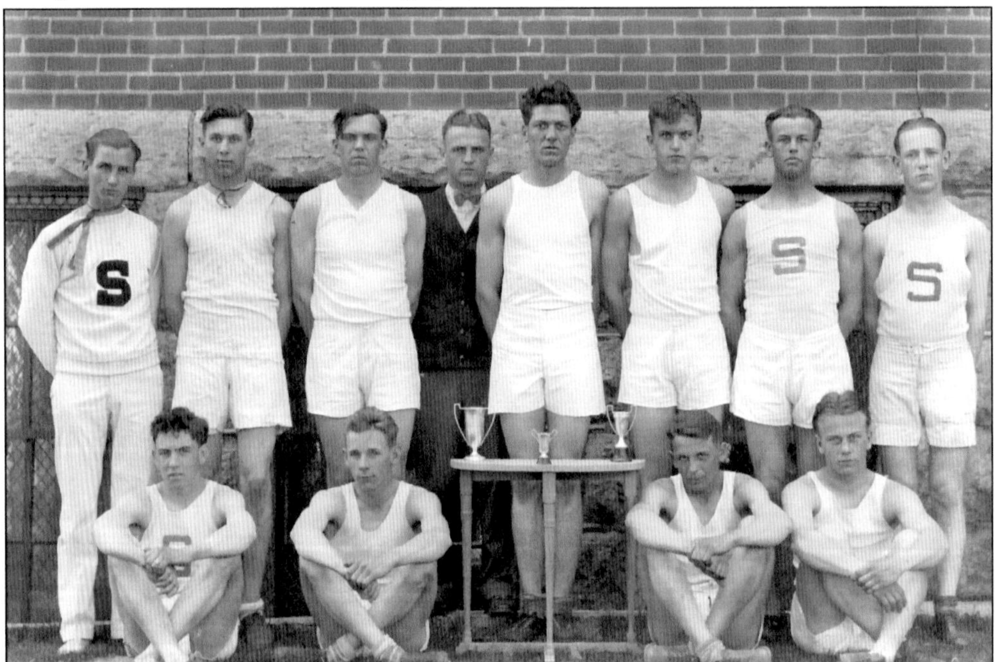

Fleet of foot to run short distances, long on endurance for the distant run, and strong enough to jump and throw, this track team added trophies to the trophy case. (Courtesy of Sharon Byrne.)

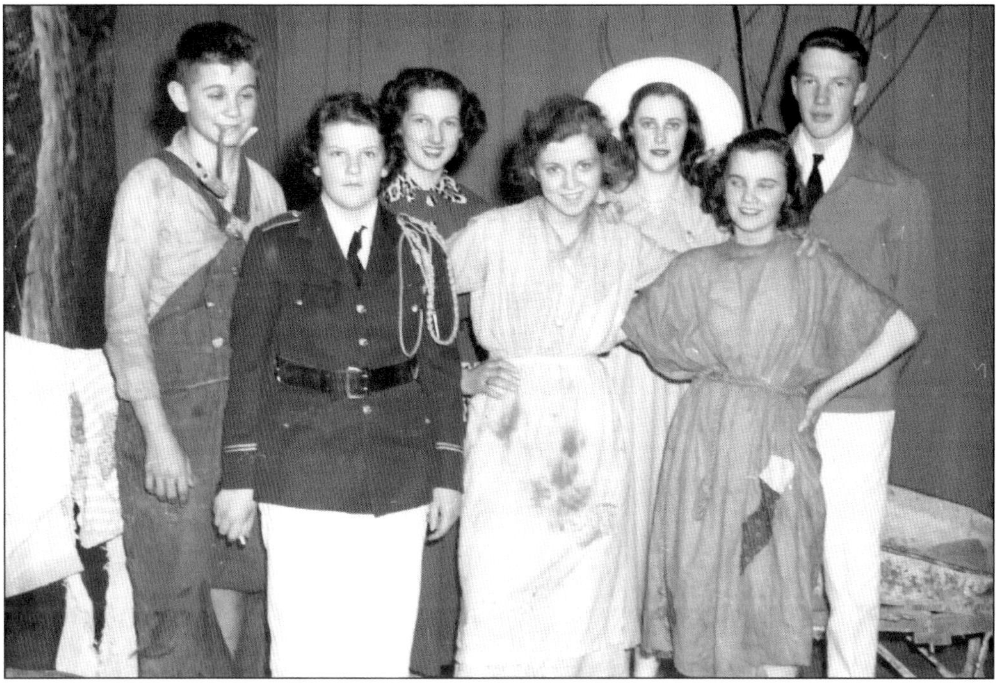

Here is a one-act play performed in the late 1940s. Pictured are Bud Walters, Audrey Buckholz, Mary Lou Conaty, Russ Wilson, Pauline Engel, and Dorothy Brownell. (Courtesy of Sharon Byrne.)

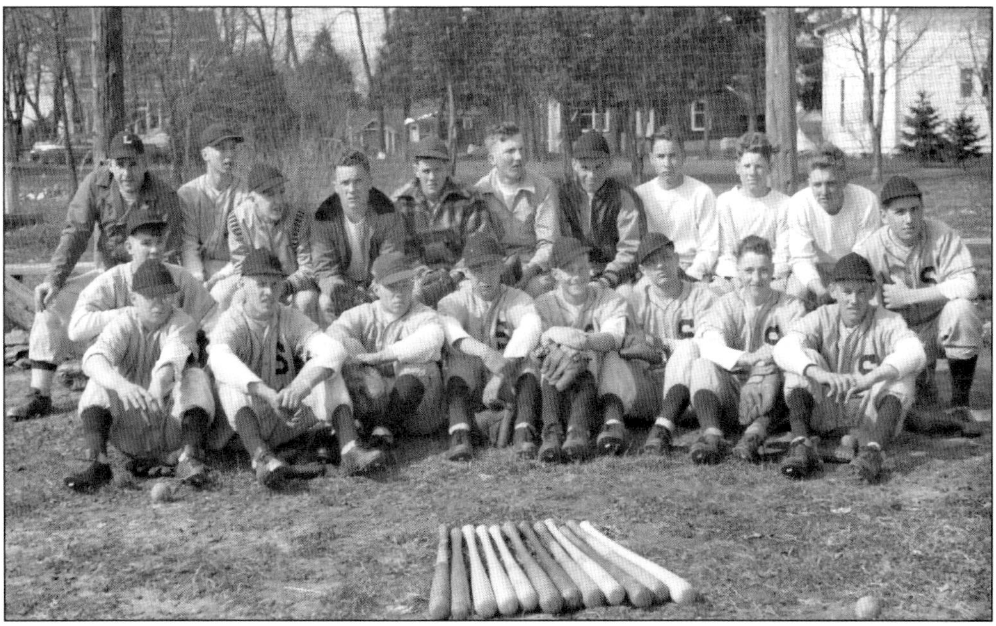

The 1949 baseball team is seen here. From left to right are (first row) Kevin Kemmer, Ron Ferson, Bob Nelson, Don Amos, Dick Travis, Jerry Moran, Orlynn Caldbeck, and Gene Ferson; (second row) coach Curt Larson, Roger Simpson, Gordon Betcher, Bill Munstock, Wayne Denny, John Strieff, Norbert Schroeder, Don Zimmerman, Charles Wendt, Dale Alcott, Don Deyoung, and Ken Mayer. (Courtesy of Sharon Byrne.)

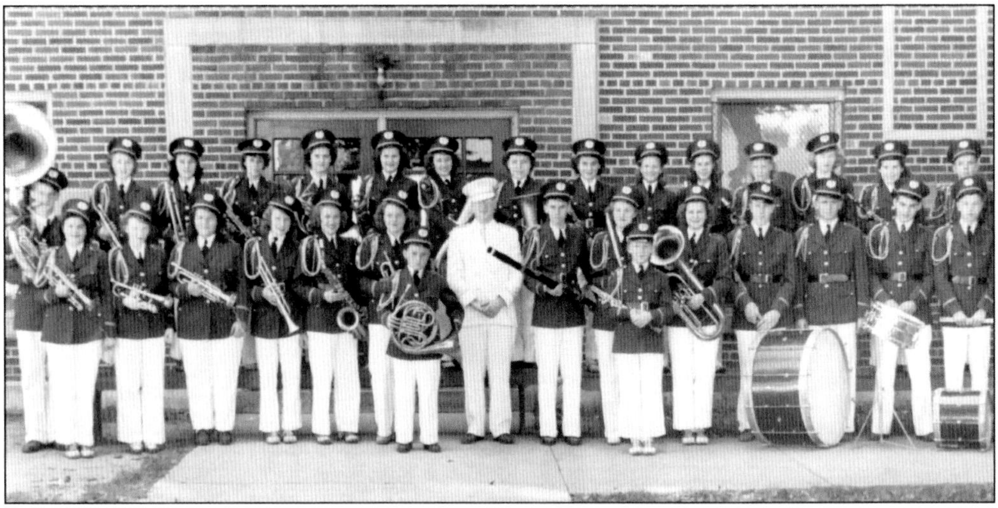

Seen here is a 1957 band photograph. Among those pictured are Ronald Kennedy, Jack Lenton, Bob Skyhawk, Lester Lyman, Betty Wooldridge, Phyllis Currier, Norma Janssen, Donald Sullivan, Vincent Kling, Robert Dixon, Carol Eppard, Gerri Griffin, Iva Mae Currier, Gwendolyn Vrieze, Shirley Barky, Delores Lenton, Melvin Brownell, Katherine McNeil, Joyce Wratz, Jean Currier, Mary Ann Kench, Patricia Griffin, Erdine Edgar, Ione Marburger, Betty Aberman, Audrey Wooldridge, Phyllis House, Carol Simpson, Francis Glover, Doris Betcher, and Roger Mappen. (Courtesy of the Gray family.)

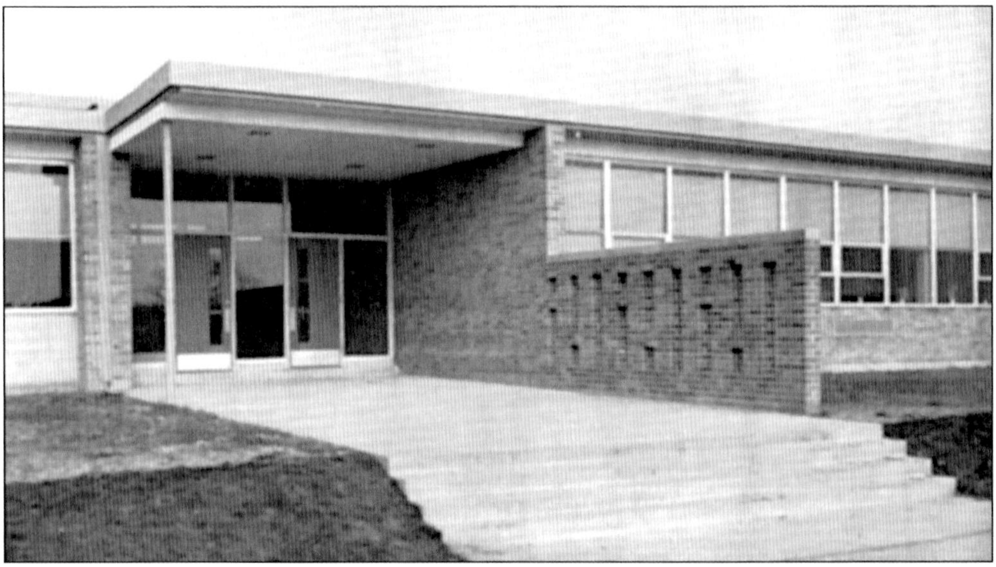

The front south entrance to Stewartville High School is seen here in 1956. About 1945, a statewide movement was started to equalize educational opportunities by enlarging school districts to educate children kindergarten through 12th grade. The board proceeded to purchase land from the village, the Tubbs estate, and Weinzettel farm. The new high school opened on September 7, 1956. (Courtesy of Sharon Byrne.)

Four

MAIN STREET

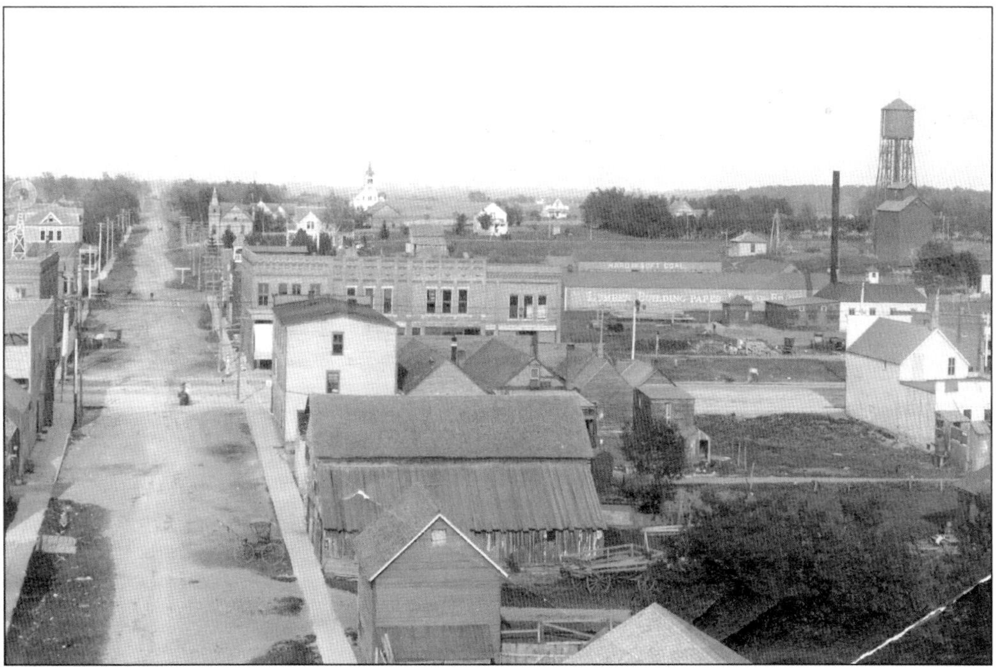

Stewartville is located at the intersection of Highways 63 and 30 East. This view, from 1910, is of Main Street looking east. In the lower right-hand side of the street, the livery barn and wooden Tews Hotel can be seen. Across the street, the row of brick buildings housed the Griffin Furniture Store, Ellis' Jewelry Store, a shoe store, a restaurant, the post office, and Stoyke's Meat Market. In the distance, St. John's Lutheran Church and St. Bernard's Catholic Church can be seen. The Stewartville water tower is in the upper right-hand corner. (Courtesy of the SAHS.)

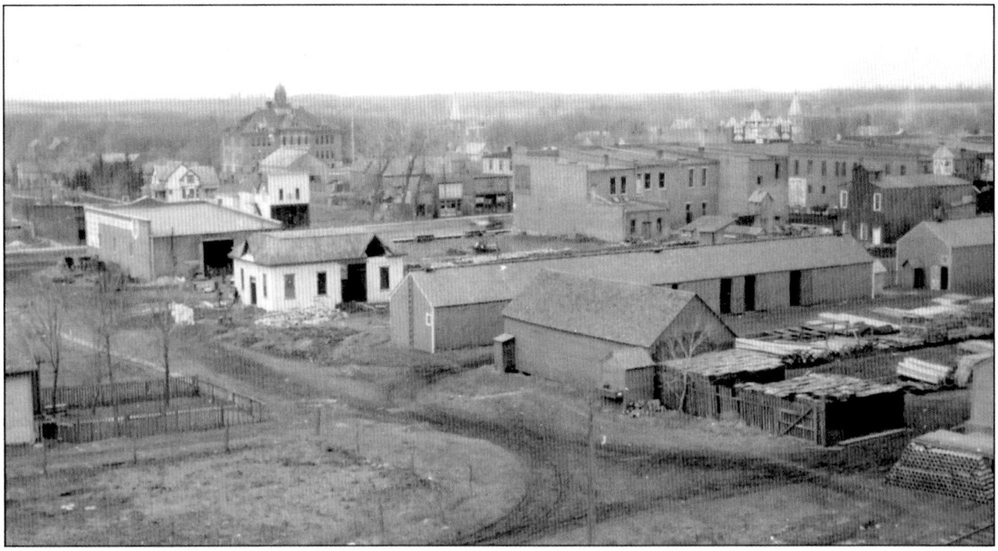

This picture of Stewartville looking west was probably taken from the water tower overlooking the Botsford Lumberyard. In the background to the upper left, the cupola of Stewartville High School comes into view. (Courtesy of the SAHS.)

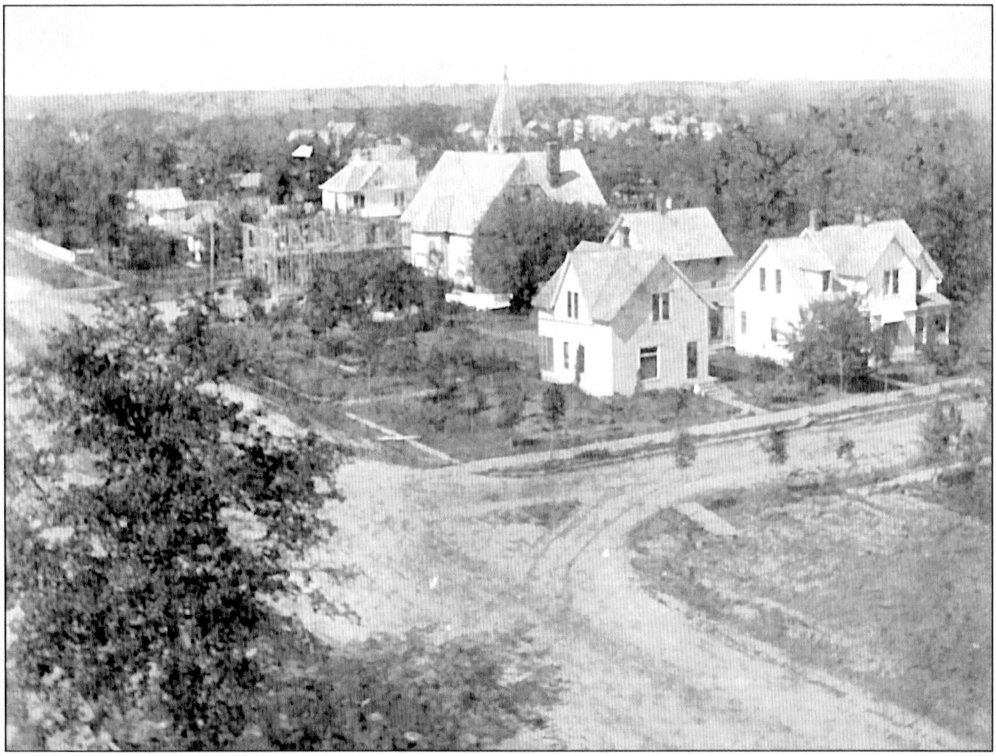

This picture was taken from the southwest looking northeast. The house on the corner belonged to Lester G. Tubbs and the Robert Starmer house is next to it on the right. The street in front of the houses is now a short, two-block one-way street running east to west. Behind both of these houses is the Congregational church. At the left of the church, the beginning structure of the parsonage being built can be seen. (Courtesy of the SAHS.)

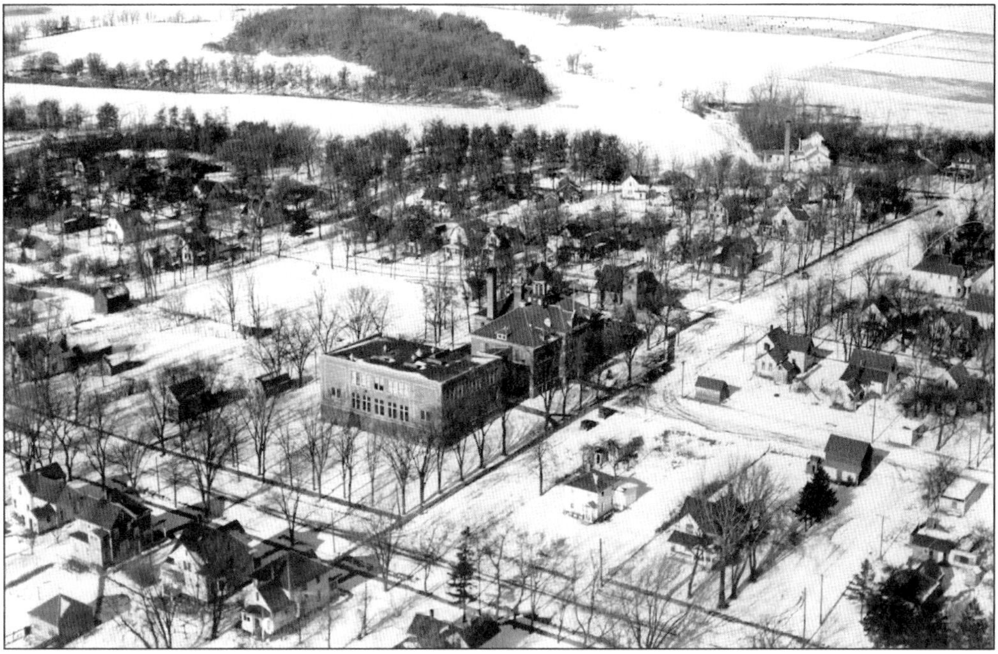

In the center of the photograph is Stewartville High School. In the background, the Root River and Lake Florence are backed up behind the dam. The waterpower was used to run the Cussons flour mill, which is visible in the upper right-hand corner. (Courtesy of the SAHS.)

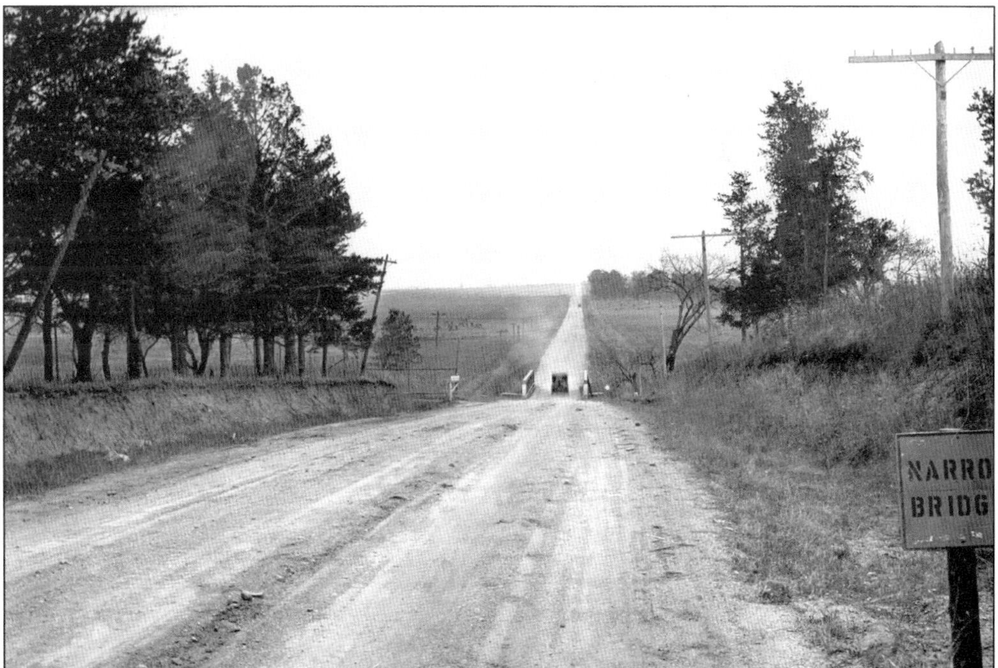

This gravel road was County Road 120 on the east side of Stewartville. It is now Fifteenth Avenue NE and marks the eastern edge of Stewartville's 5,000-plus population and home growth. Notice the narrow bridge sign on the right side of this picture. (Courtesy of the SAHS.)

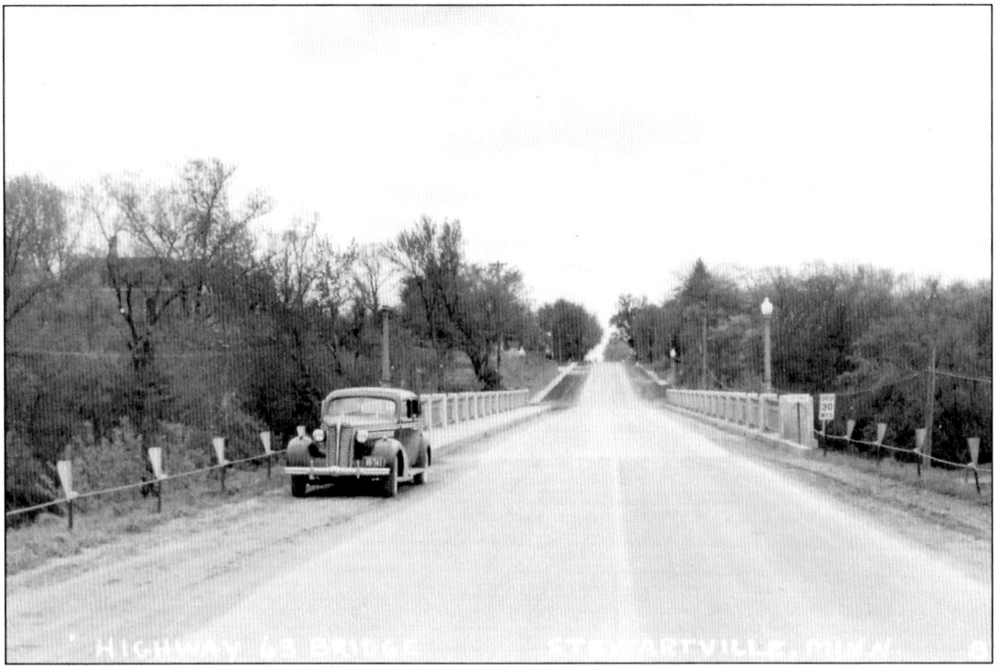

The old Highway 63 bridge crossing the Root River going south into Stewartville was approved in 1919. At the annual village election, the voters almost unanimously voted their approval of the issuing of bonds amounting to $10,000 to defray one-half of the expense of the erection of a fine 180-foot concrete bridge over the Root River on North Main Street. (Courtesy of the SAHS.)

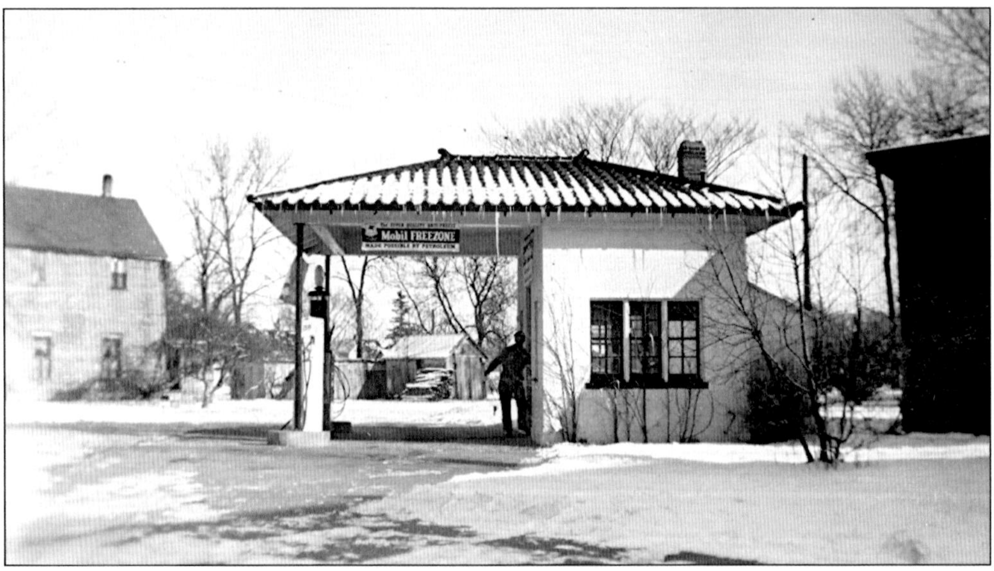

The Skelly/Mobil gas station was built by Stanley Sanborn. It was located in what is now the Family Dollar parking lot. Ray Tebay bought the station in 1944 when he returned to Stewartville from working in the Boeing plant building B-17s. Tebay opened the station in 1946 and sold Mobil gas. He tore down the house that can be seen in the background to the left and built a double-car garage from the lumber. (Courtesy of Myrtle Tebay.)

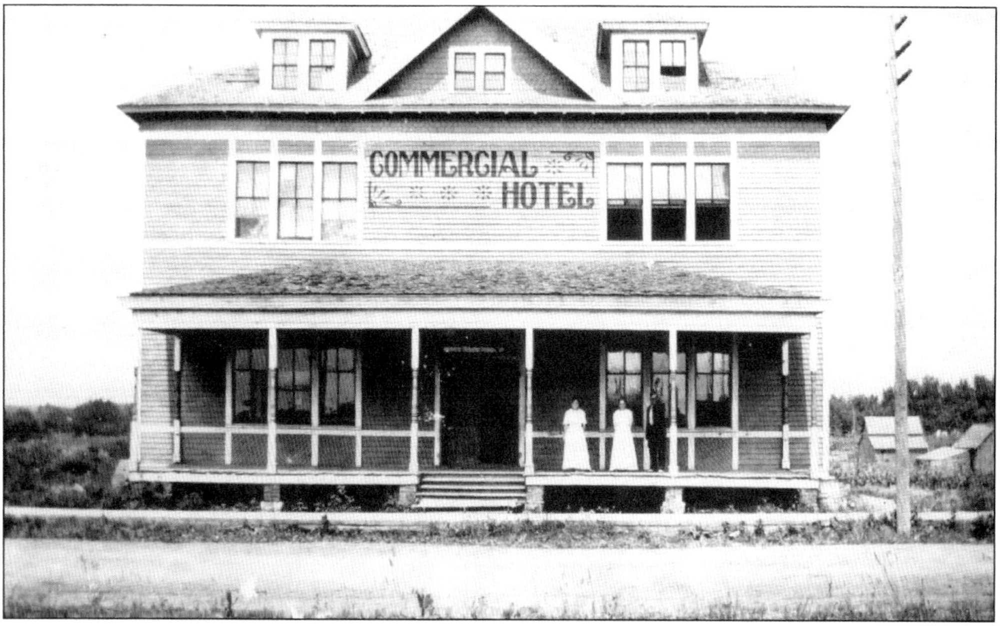

In 1899, due to the continued growth of Stewartville, a third hotel was needed. The Hotel Florence (later named the Commercial Hotel) is pictured here in 1900. Ross H. Russell Jr. bought a three-story frame school building and moved it. An addition was built, plus the large front porch. (Courtesy of the OCHS.)

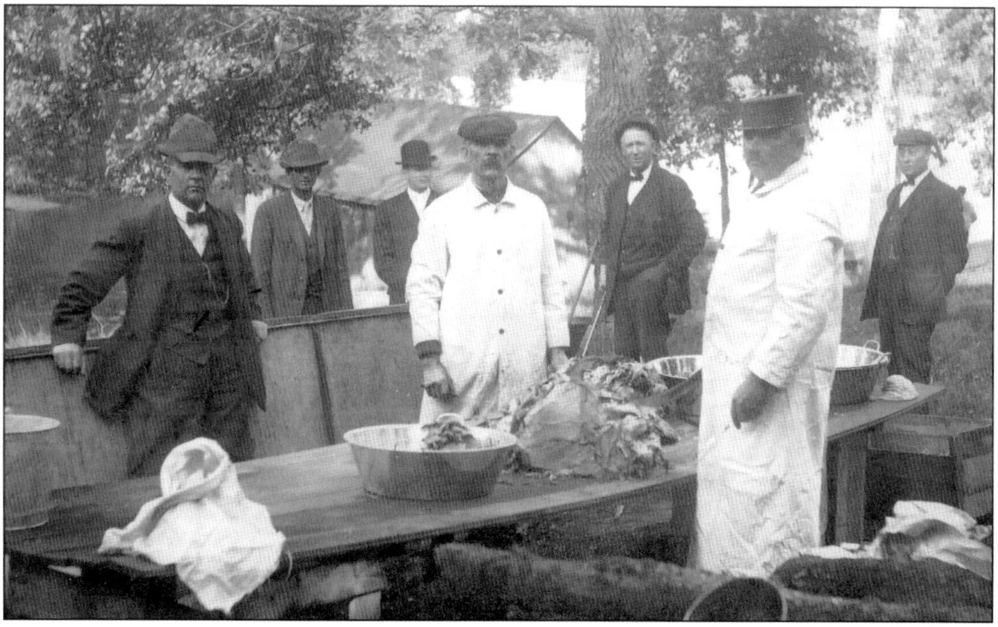

On October 1, 1913, a Mr. McGrath, Ed Hall, Homer Wooldridge, John Brooks (at center in the white coat), John Towey, Henry Ringey, and Edward Stoyke (in long white coat in the foreground) carved the ox down at the park. Barbeque Day and Stewartville's Grand Fall Holiday had the fatted ox roasted and prepared for the crowd and dished up in wooden plates for the family groups who had gathered for the day. Contests, music, and a ball game were all part of the festivities. (Courtesy of the OCHS.)

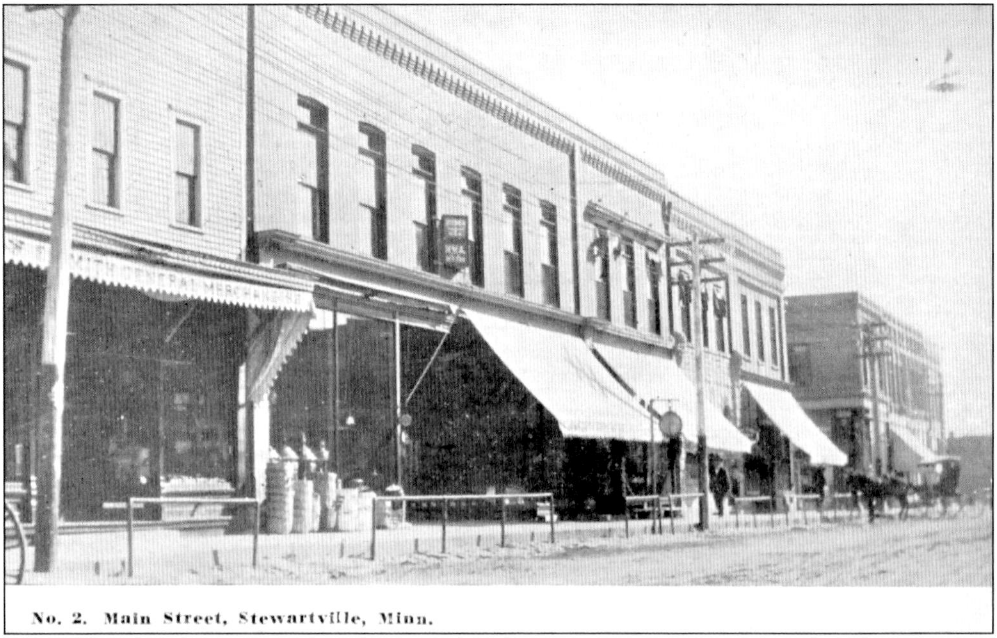

On the east side of Main Street from the lower right are the Griffin Furniture Store, State Security Bank, Illa Burke's Store, a hardware store, and Haack's Store. (Courtesy of the Gray family.)

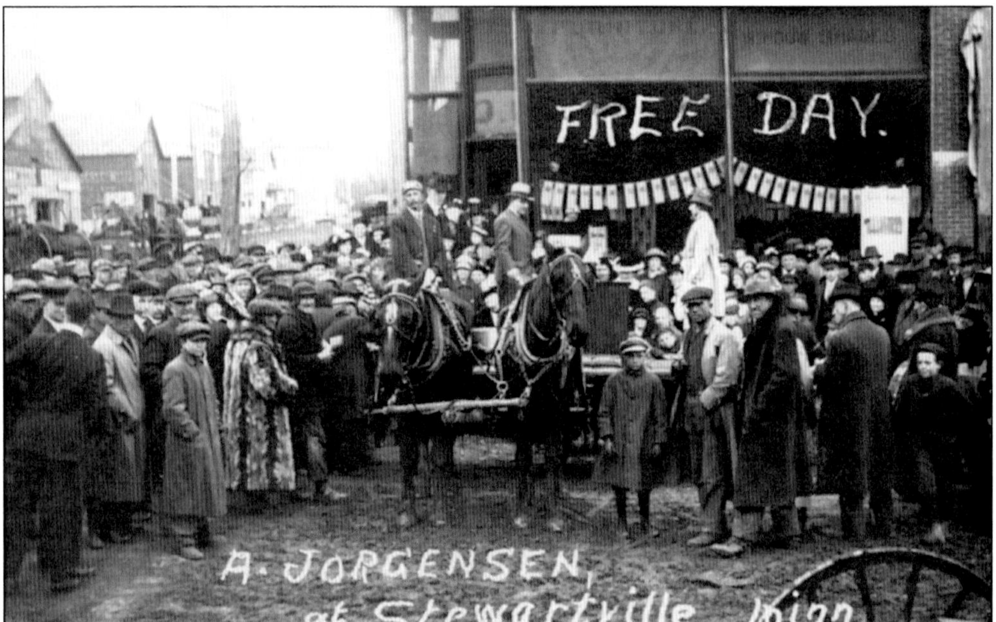

Here can be seen a sewing machine demonstration. A large crowd gathers on the corner by the Griffin Furniture Store as A. Jorgenson demonstrates the Free brand sewing machine on the back of a horse-drawn wagon. P. H. Griffin is the man with the dark hat standing on the wagon. (Courtesy of the Gray family.)

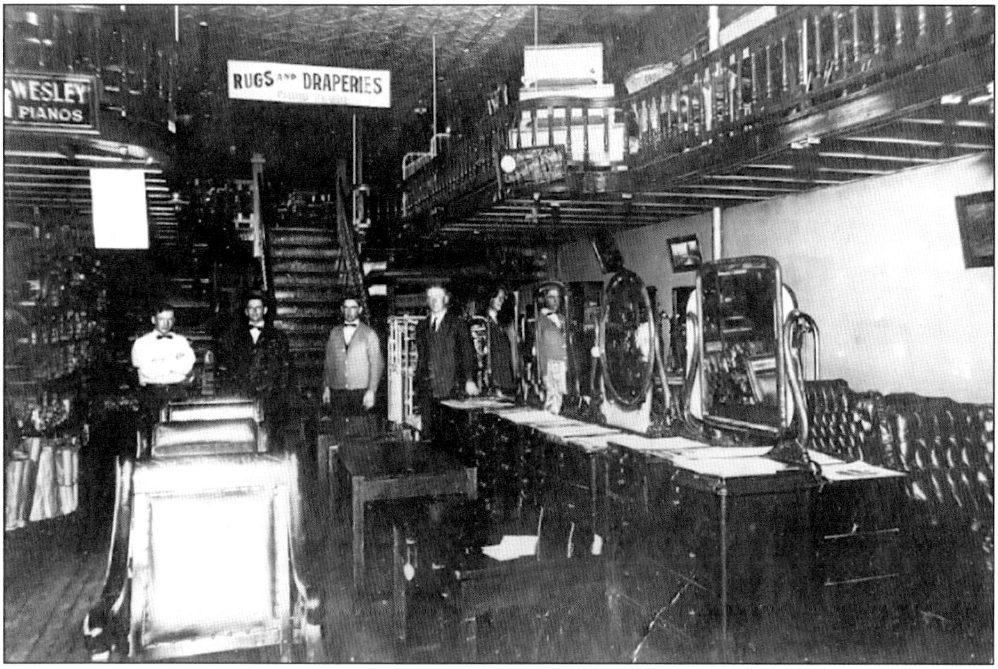

J. H. Towey built the store in 1898. In February 1914, Towey was appointed postmaster of Stewartville and sold his business to P. H. Griffin and George Vroman of Rochester. The business was a partnership until 1917, when Griffin bought the Vroman interest. In 1940, Griffin separated the funeral and furniture store businesses. (Courtesy of the Gray family.)

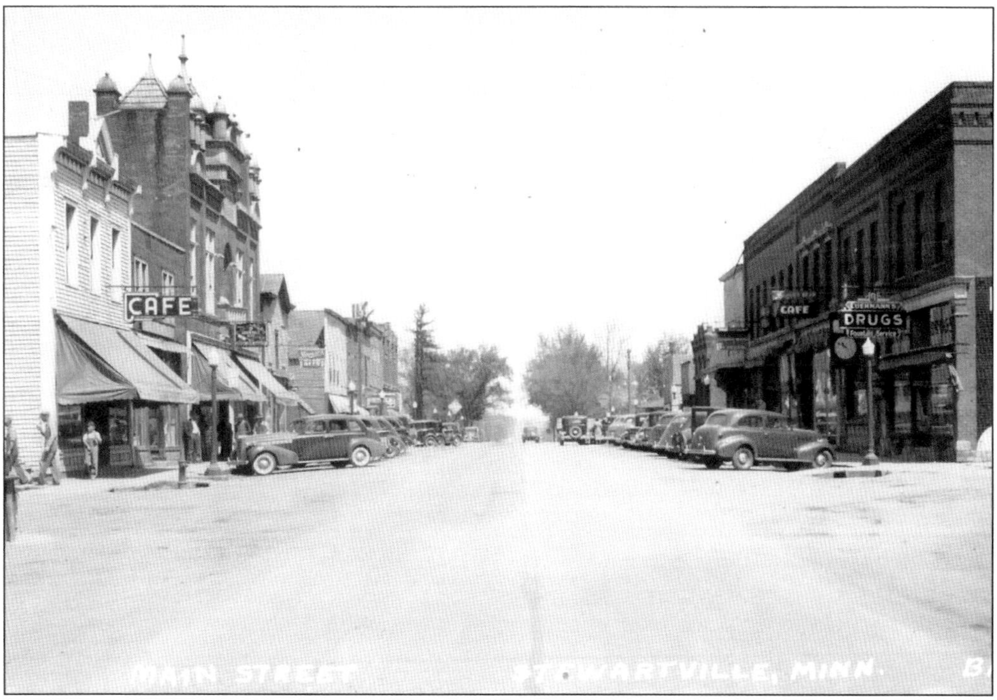

In the 1940s, here on Main Street, a hardware store can be found on the left as well as the opera house and a restaurant. On the right is Luehmann's Drugs. (Courtesy of the SAHS.)

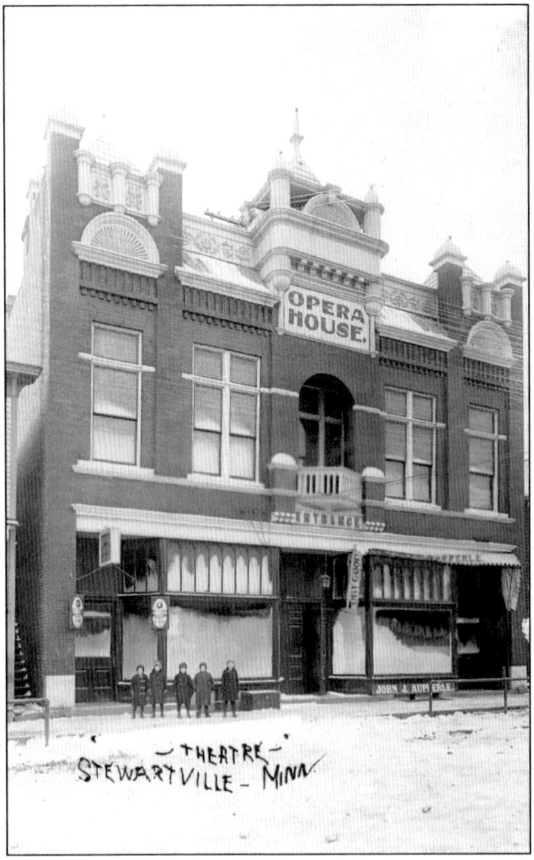

The opera house was built by William Keenan in 1896. The annual firemen's ball, the first social event held in the building, was on December 31, 1896. The building was used for a movie theater, high school plays, baccalaureate, graduation, medicine shows, revival services, wrestling matches, dancing, and a gymnasium. It also housed John Aupperle's General Store, Conaty's Men's Clothing Store, and McFarland Land Company. The upper portion was removed in 1972 and the lower portion annexed into the Coast to Coast/Hanson's Country Store. (Courtesy of the SAHS.)

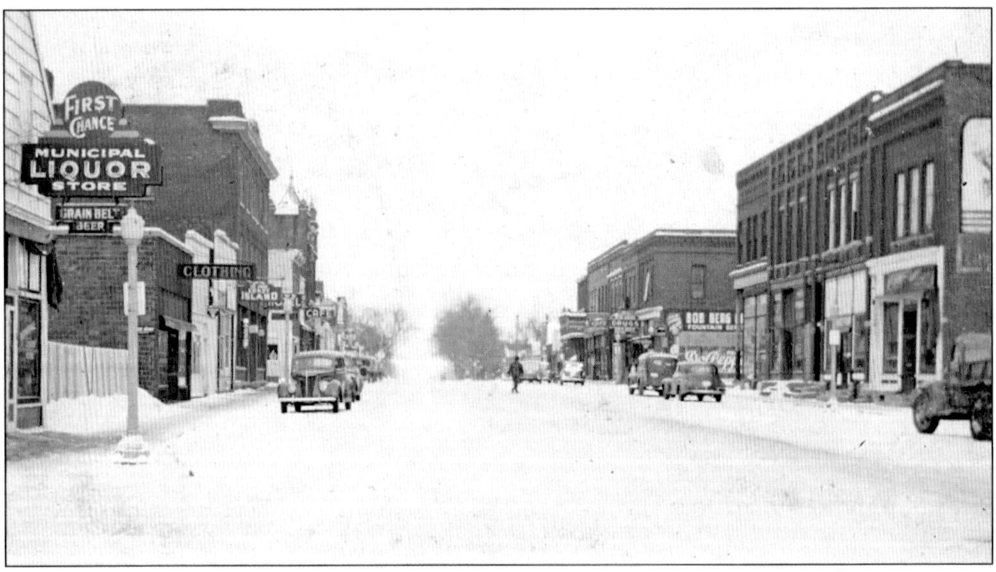

Main Street is seen here in 1945. On the left is the Municipal Liquor Store with a sign stating that it was one's "first chance" for liquor if they were coming from the south and the "last chance" if the were going back south to Fillmore County or Iowa, which were dry at the time. (Courtesy of the Gray family.)

The Lake Theatre was located where the present Dahl's Copiers now resides. In 1919, the movie theater was closed due to a shortage of fuel. In March 1943, former mayor Lynn Mulhern gave a free movie for the school pupils of the Racine, High Forest, Pleasant Grove, and Stewartville districts. Price of admission was a donation of scrap copper or brass, which was brought to the teacher of their class or school. (Courtesy of the SAHS.)

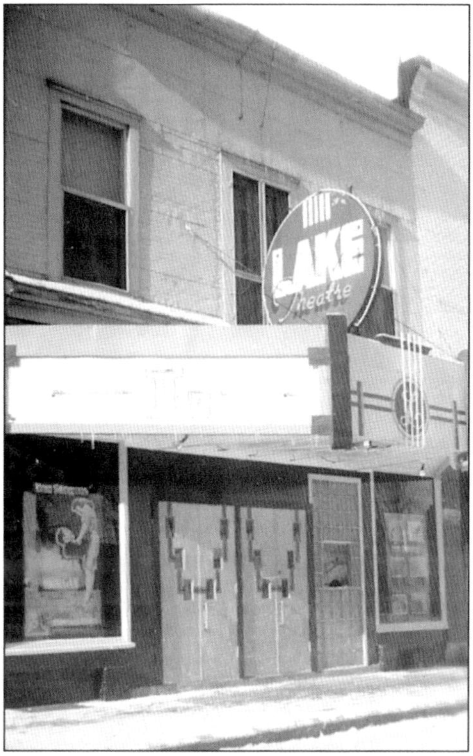

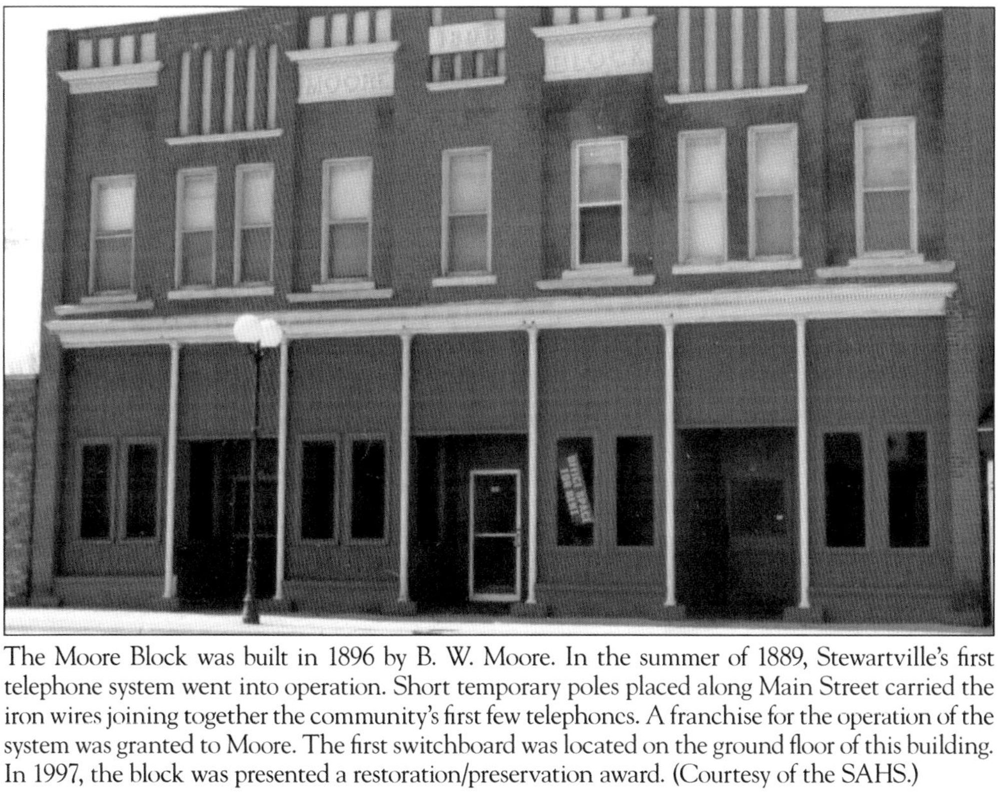

The Moore Block was built in 1896 by B. W. Moore. In the summer of 1889, Stewartville's first telephone system went into operation. Short temporary poles placed along Main Street carried the iron wires joining together the community's first few telephones. A franchise for the operation of the system was granted to Moore. The first switchboard was located on the ground floor of this building. In 1997, the block was presented a restoration/preservation award. (Courtesy of the SAHS.)

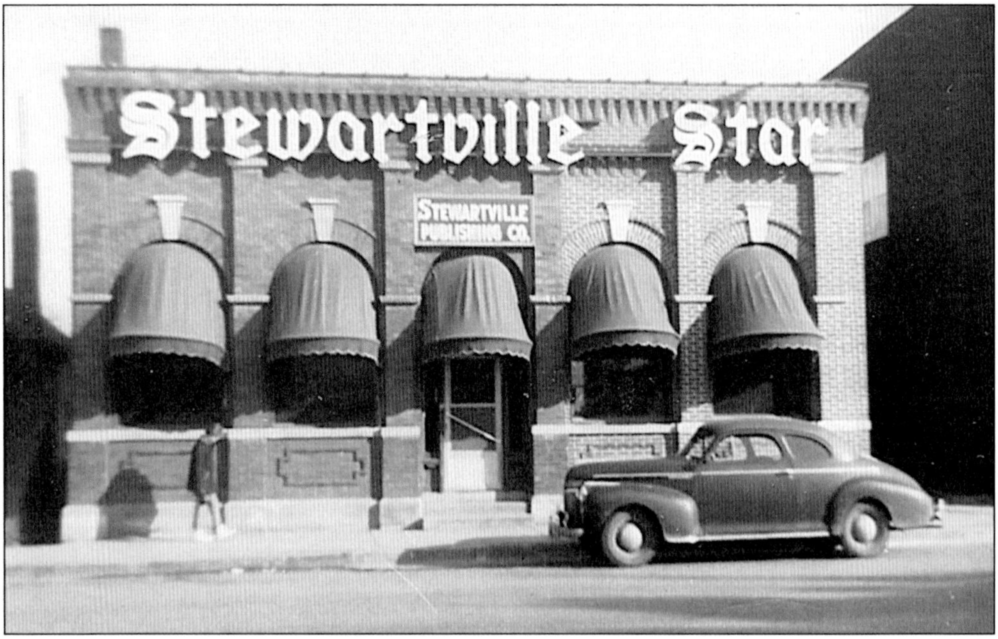

The oldest active business establishment on Main Street was the Stewartville Star. It was first issued on May 1, 1891, with L. K. Allen as publisher and Linus Blank as editor. The weekly edition incorporated lively advertisements of area merchants and accurate accounts of news happenings and sports. (Courtesy of the SAHS.)

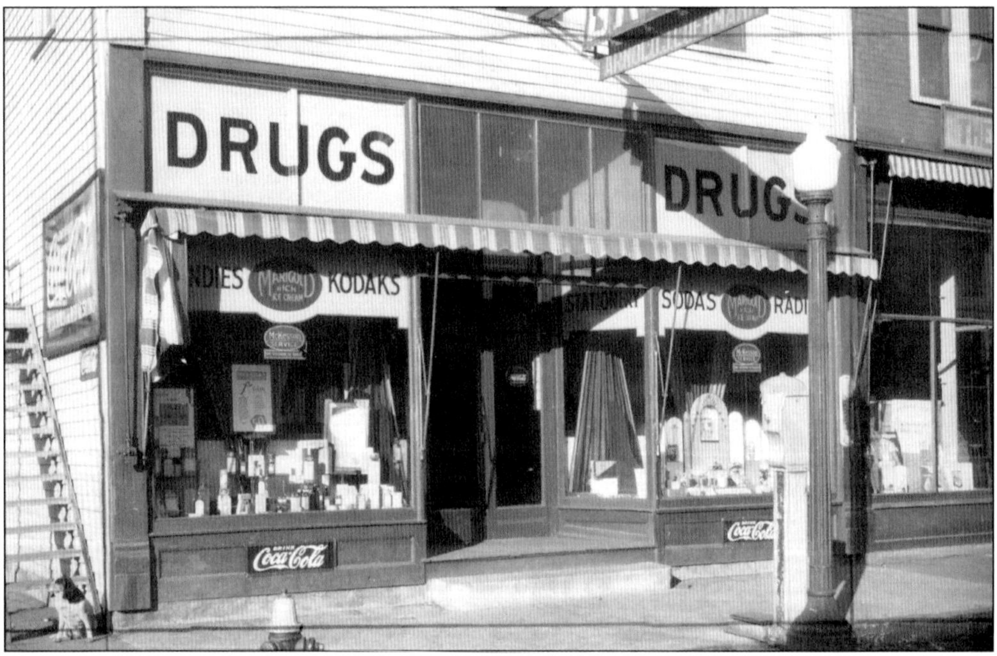

Arnold J. Luehmann purchased the Wagner Restaurant in June 1923 and converted it into a drugstore. A year and a half later, he purchased the Stoddard Drugstore and combined the two businesses at the Stoddard location. He continued the business until 1940, when he sold it to Robert F. Berg. (Courtesy of the SAHS.)

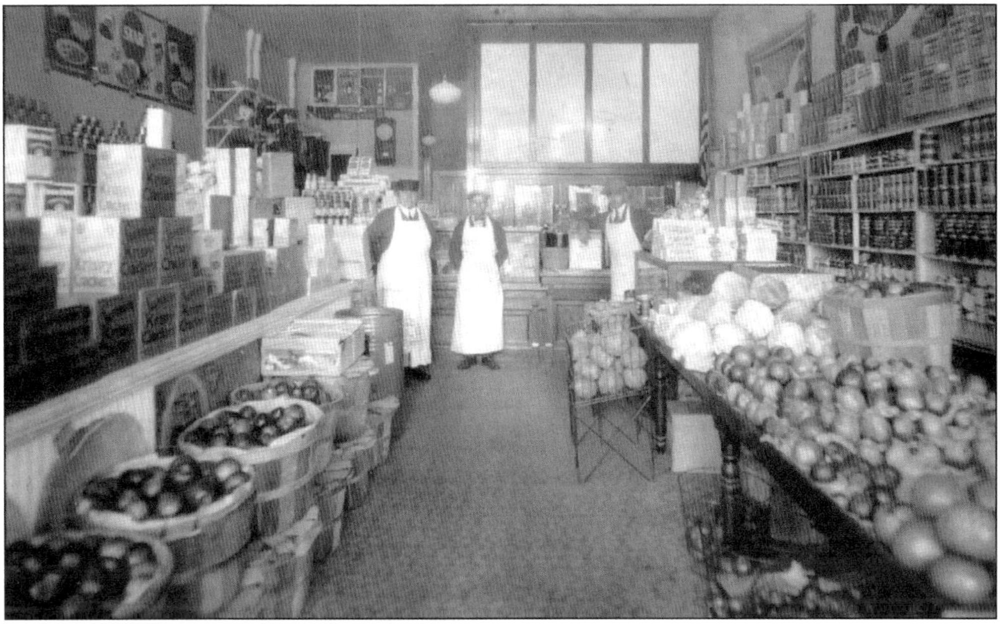

The oldest continuous business (excluding the newspaper) was Stoyke's Meat Market. Edward Stoyke was born in Germany in 1870 and immigrated to the United States at age 13. His first occupation was in a grocery store, and he also learned the butcher's trade. In 1896, he and Ed Hall bought out the meat market of H. H. Rice. Stoyke died in 1933, and the store was then operated by Ronald E. Stoyke, the youngest member of the family. (Courtesy of Kathleen Stoyke.)

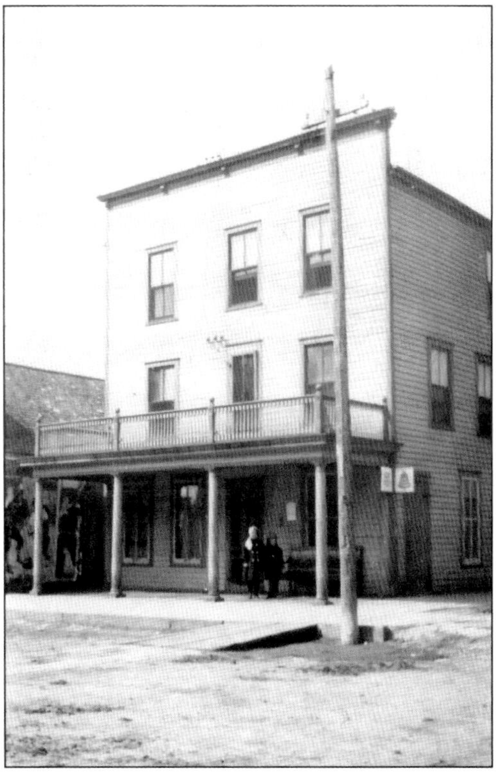

The original hotel was built by John F. and Ida May Owen in 1890. It was a three-story framed building occupying the corner lot of Main and Owen Streets. The hotel consisted of 23 guest rooms. Three large cottonwood trees were removed so the porch could be added. (Courtesy of the SAHS.)

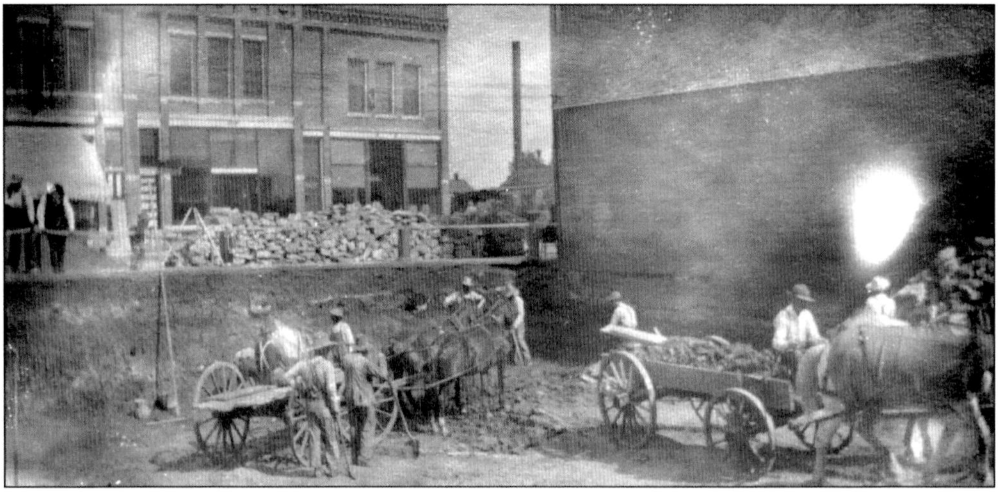

In this picture, the men are digging the basement of the new brick Tews Hotel using horse-drawn wagons to haul the dirt away. Notice the people watching the operation from along the edge to the east. (Courtesy of the SAHS.)

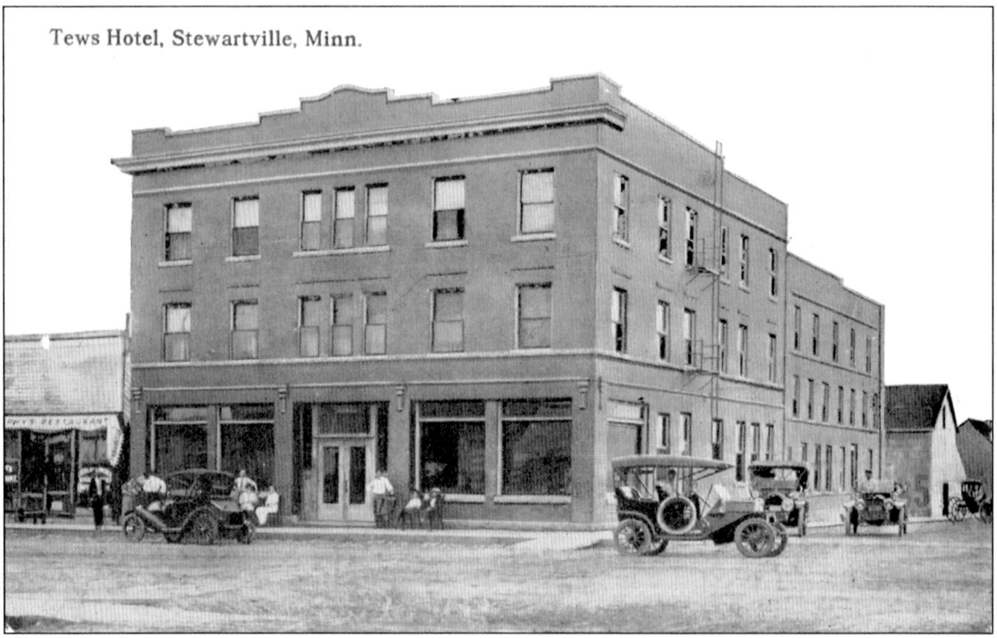

On March 1, 1900, Fred and Alice Tews purchased the hotel from O. G. Mack. Business increased and the wooden framed hotel was moved to the west. A new three-story brick building was erected and connected with the frame building. Traveling salesmen stayed at the hotel. Prices were $1 per day, including meals and lodging. Feather beds and layers of quilts kept the guests warm, and when a knock came at the door, a response was welcomed so the hotel keeper knew that the guest had not frozen to death overnight. (Courtesy of the SAHS.)

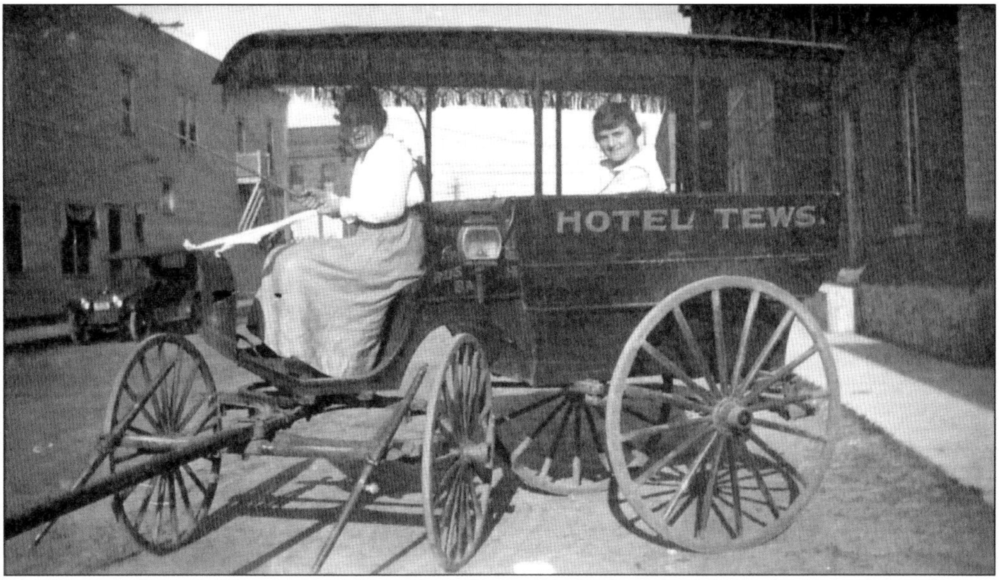

William Siman operated a hack service, which in reality was a horse-drawn taxi service to and from the railroad depot. In keeping with all first-class hotels, a feed barn was maintained. Farmers and guests could put up their teams for 10¢ for hay and 15¢ for hay and oats. The barn was originally built for use as an icehouse and cold storage for beverages. (Courtesy of the SAHS.)

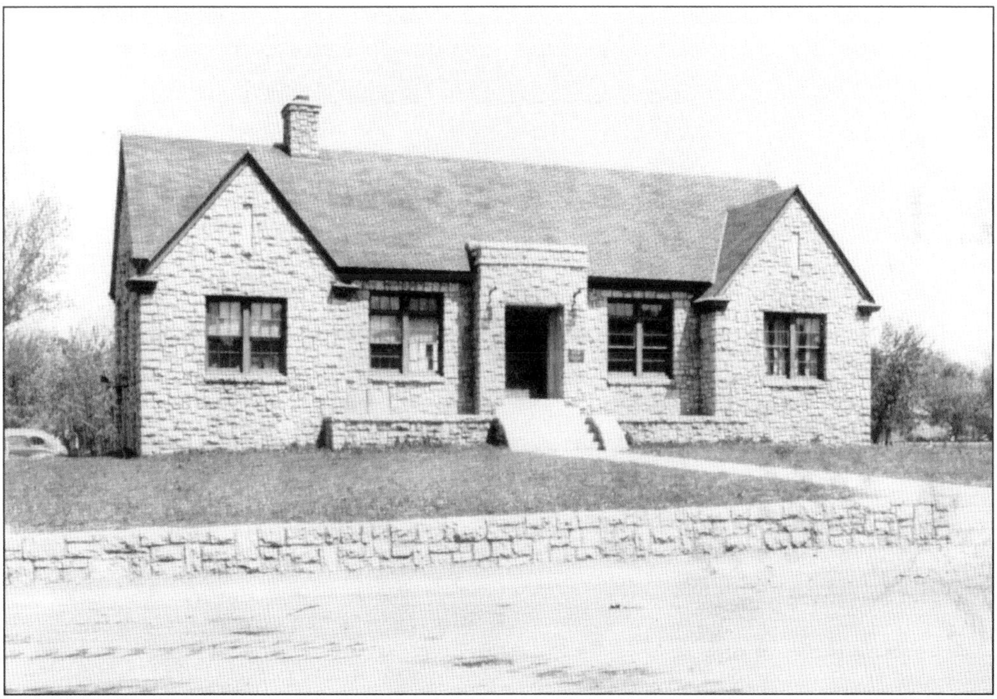

The Stewartville Community Center building was erected in 1938 as a Works Progress Administration project. This building was used to house city government, the town's first library, 1948 kindergarten classes, and community gatherings over the years. (Courtesy of the Gray family.)

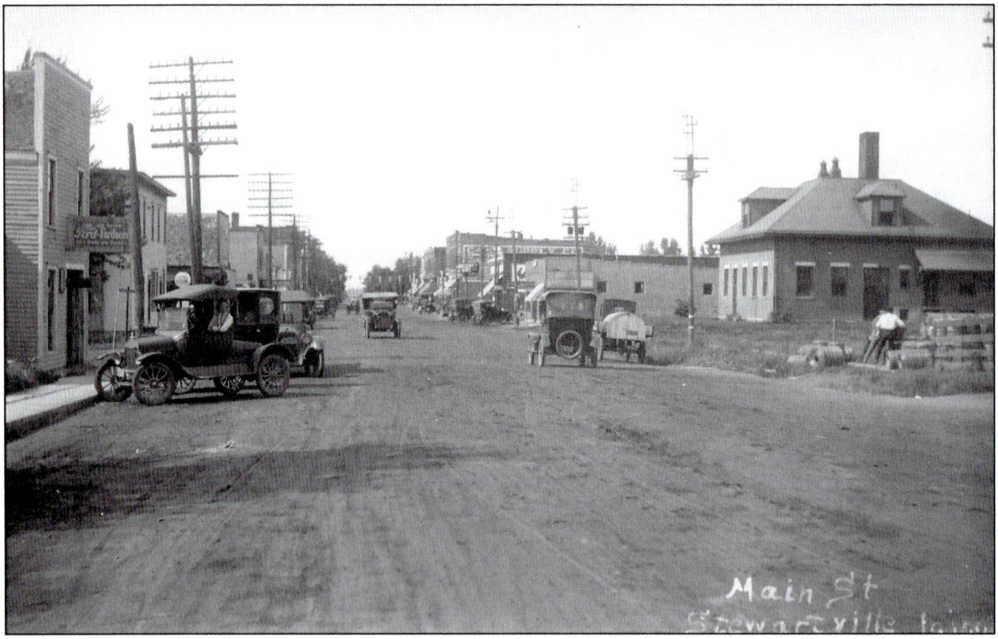

Main Street is seen here with cars. Looking north, on the right side of the street is the Farmer's Cooperative Creamery, and on the left are O. E. Hagen's Shoe Store, Brown's Chick Hatchery, Tuttle's, and Barthleme's Dry Cleaners. (Courtesy of the SAHS.)

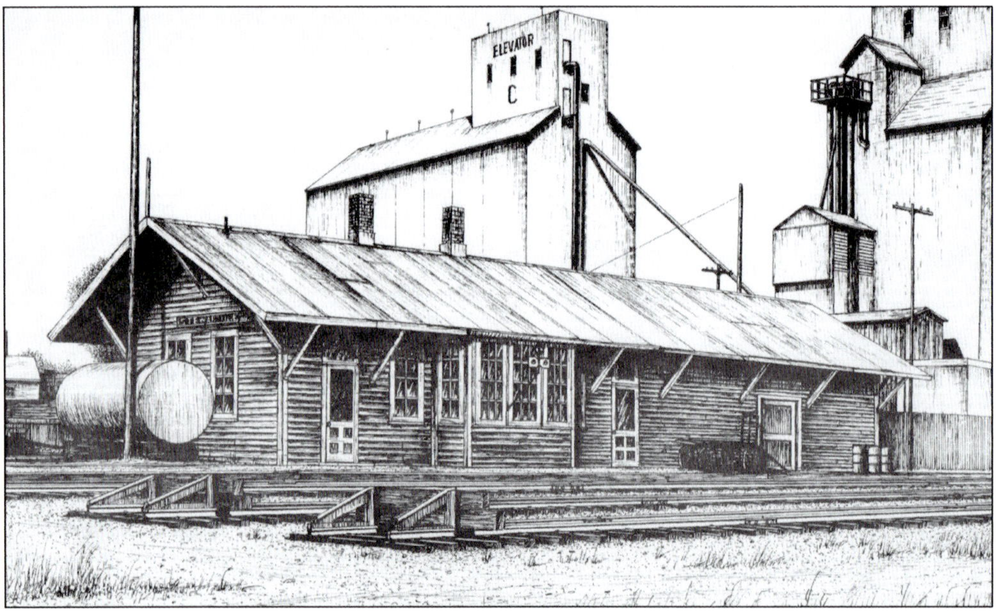

The railroad came to Stewartville in 1890 with the Winona and Southwestern Railway of a line from Osage, Iowa, to Winona. One of the most important factors of the building of the railroad was the rapid development of Stewartville. It was a village centered in a rich farming community and had a flourishing flour mill as its main enterprise. In 1899, the line was built from Simpson to Rochester, and the name changed to the Winona and Western Railroad. On September 19, 1901, it was purchased by the Chicago Great Western Railroad. (Courtesy of All American Co-op.)

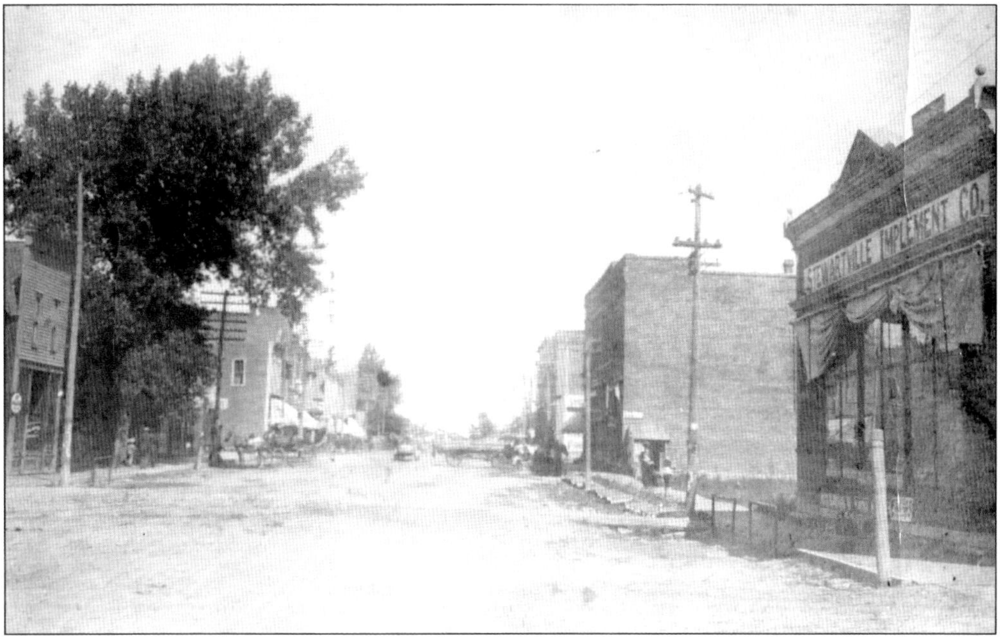

The Stewartville Implement Company was located where Weinhold's Professional Building now stands on Main Street. The brick building to the north is Stoyke's Meat Market. (Courtesy of Elman Hanken.)

Haack's Store in the late 1930s shows, from left to right, Alice Haack-Smidt, Edgar Haack, owner Frank Haack, Verna Schroeder-Reich, and customers Milton Haack and Donald Haack-Smidt. (Courtesy of the Smidt family.)

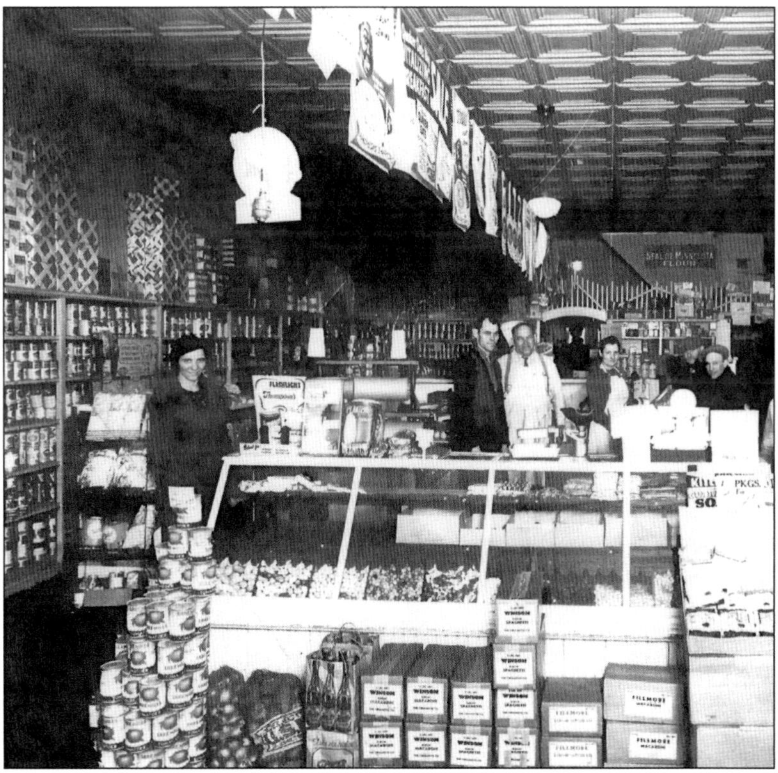

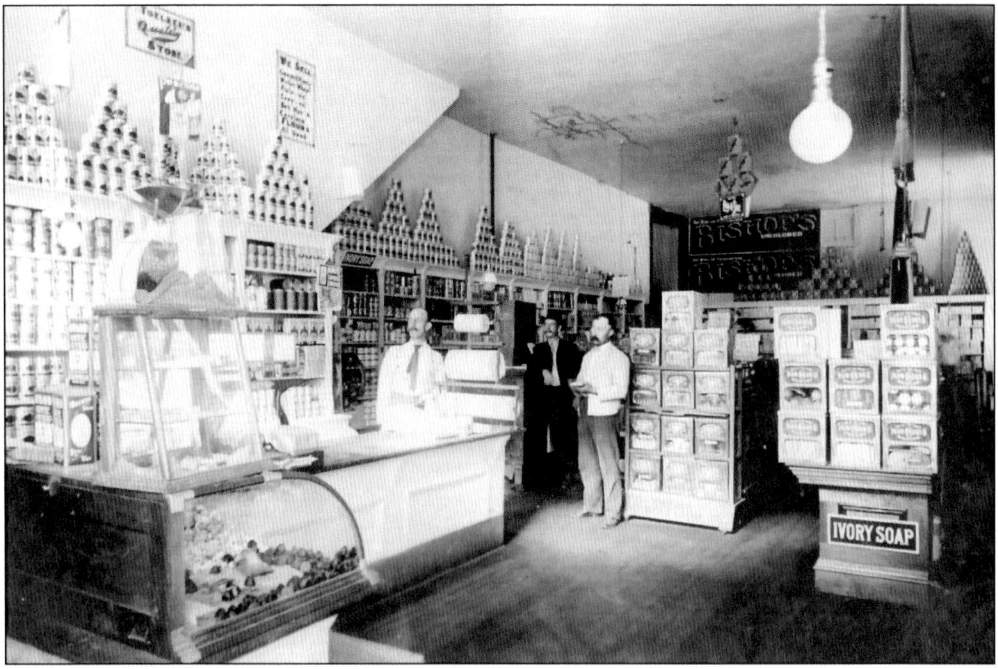

The earliest Shelley Horton Store was located on Depot Street. Pictured from left to right are Shelley Horton, unidentified, and Henry Ringey. (Courtesy of the SAHS.)

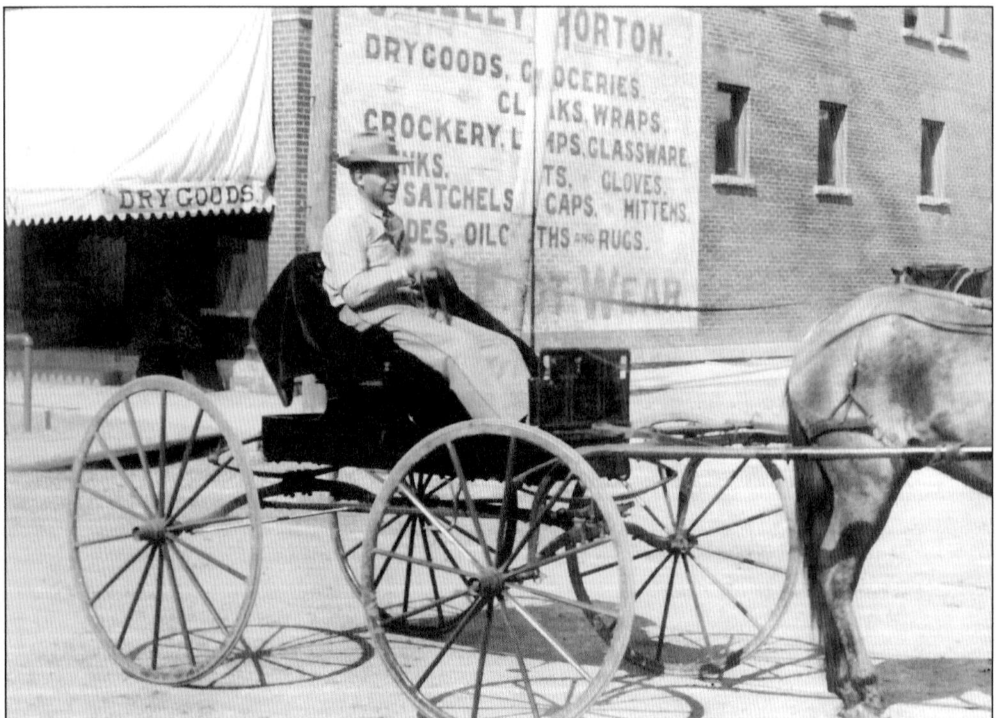

Shelley Horton is pictured in a horse-drawn buggy with the advertising for his store in the background at right. (Courtesy of the SAHS.)

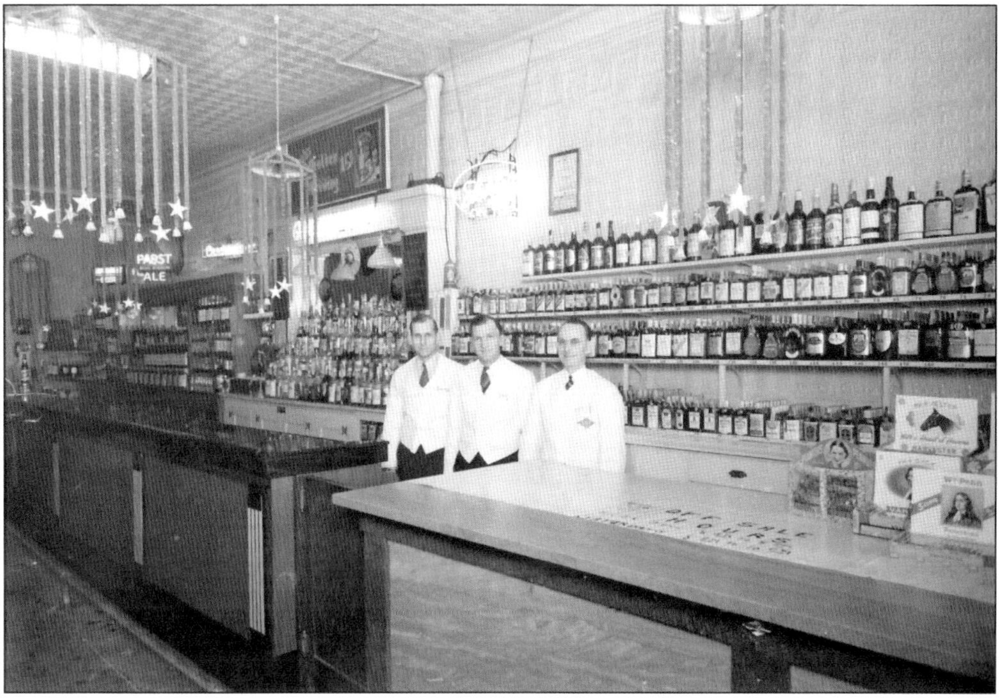

Inside the Municipal Liquor Store are, from left to right, Larry Gathje, Gus Bleifus, and manager Guy Gillis. (Courtesy of the SAHS.)

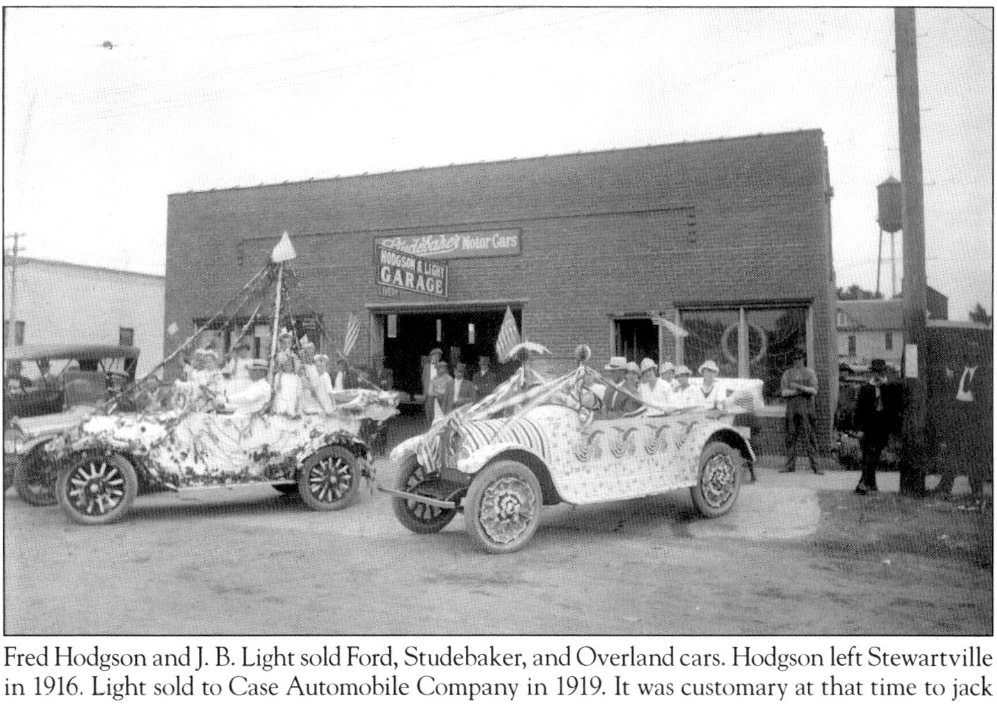

Fred Hodgson and J. B. Light sold Ford, Studebaker, and Overland cars. Hodgson left Stewartville in 1916. Light sold to Case Automobile Company in 1919. It was customary at that time to jack up the cars and remove the batteries in November and then replace them in May. The use of snowplows brought this custom gradually to a close. (Courtesy of Joel Packer.)

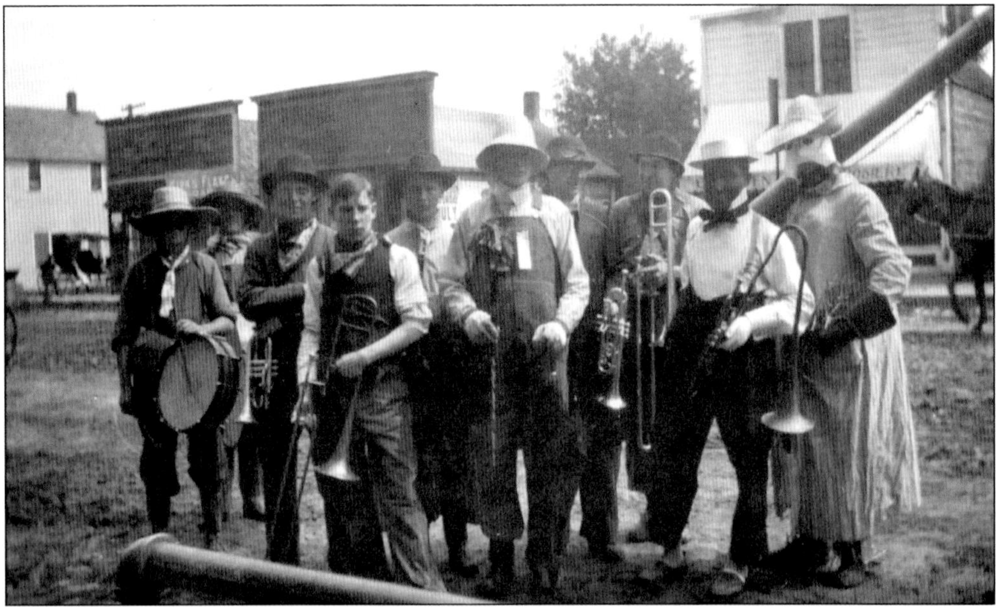

A rube band met its neighbors from LeRoy to celebrate the clerk's picnic day on August 5, 1915. It was an enjoyable event for these important and very necessary persons to the business and social activities of any city. After an excellent dinner in the park, many contests were participated in with the last contest being a tug-of-war. The winner was treated to a box of cigars. (Courtesy of the SAHS.)

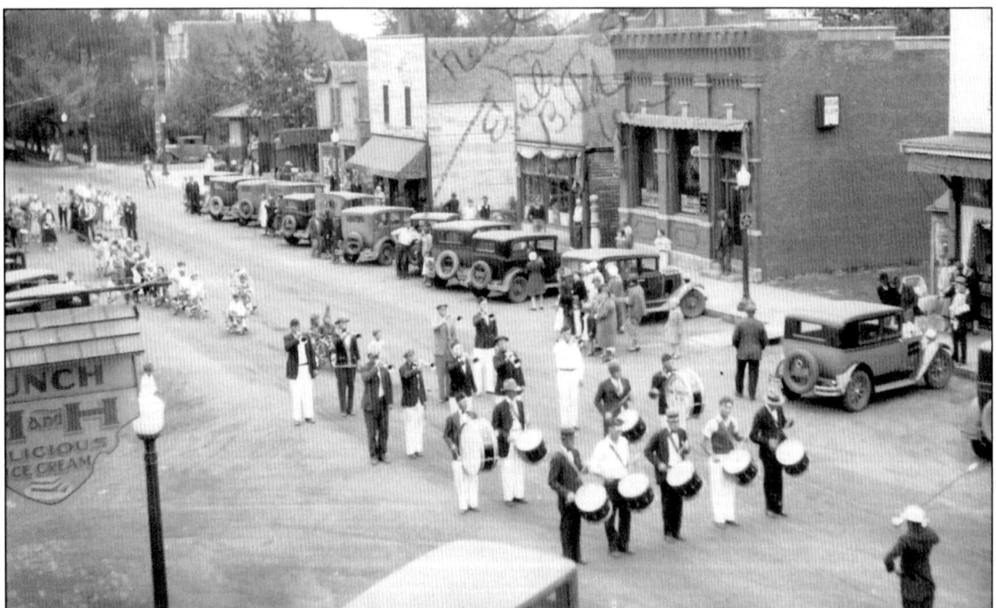

A Fourth of July parade on Main Street is seen here. On the far right are the Haack's Store, the bank, and a barbershop. (Courtesy of the Smidt family.)

In 1901, Albert L. Brush of Osage, Iowa, organized the First National Bank of Stewartville and built the bank building across the street from the opera house. In 1932, at one of the first meetings held with 118 stockholders at the opera house, officers and directors elected president Dr. C. E. Fawcett, vice president Edward J. Schatz, and cashier Homer Wooldridge. In later years, Schatz served as president until his death in 1956. (Courtesy of Joan Hill.)

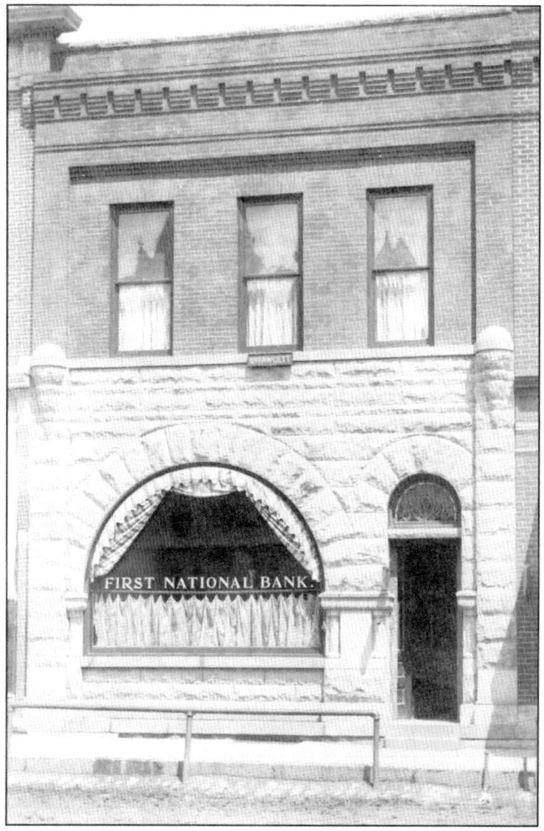

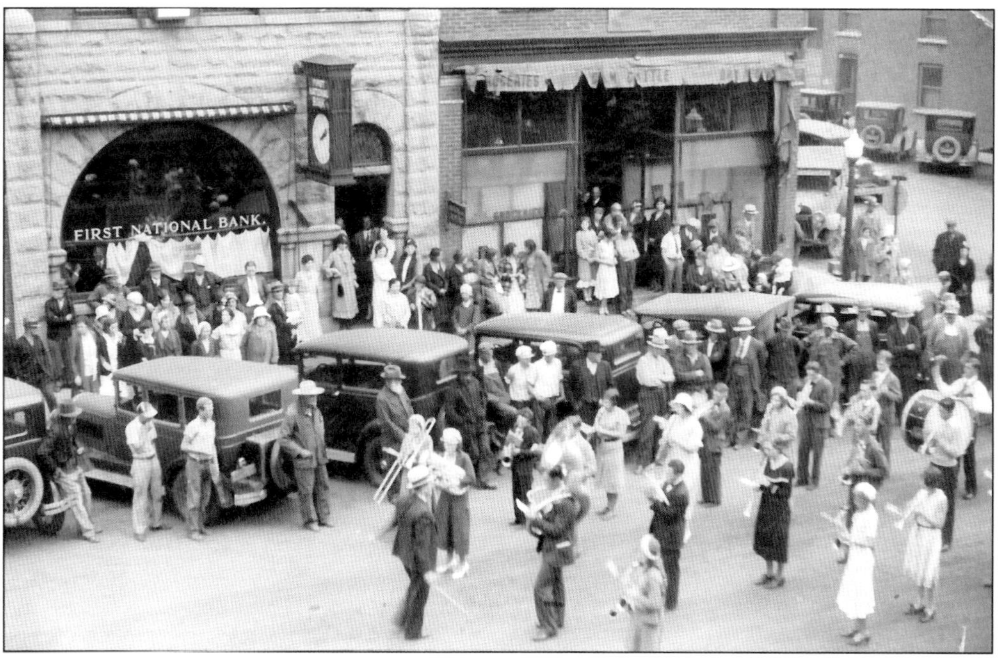

The new First National Bank was opened on May 21, 1932. The high school band gave a concert on Main Street in the afternoon in honor of the event. (Courtesy of Joan Hill.)

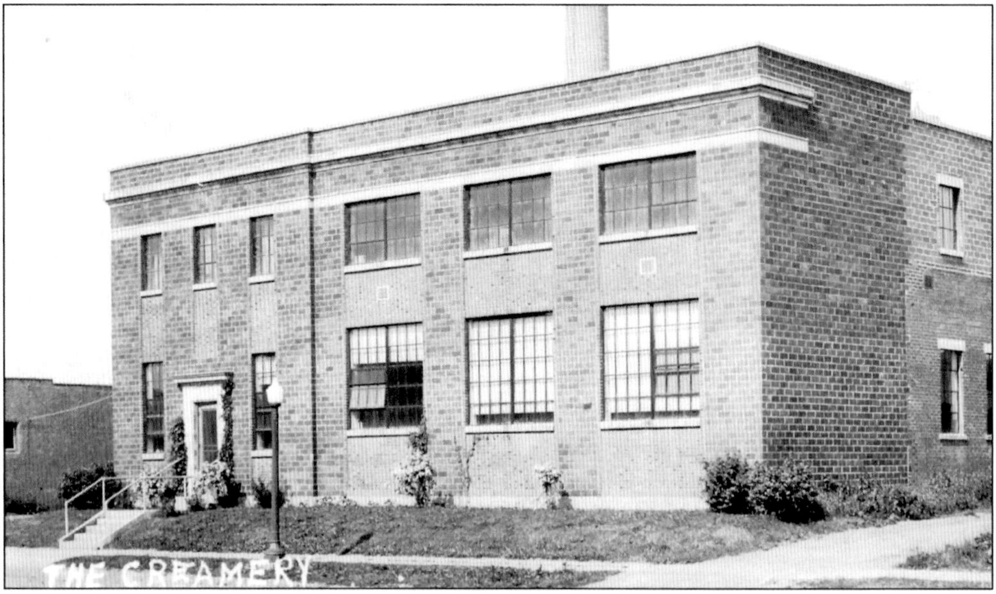

On April 4, 1914, a meeting of farmers from the vicinity was held in the town hall for the purpose of organizing a farmers' cooperative creamery. It was decided that the farmers must have at least 80 cows and that each farm member must purchase one share of stock for each cow he owned at $1 per share or he might purchase stock as a patron deducting 10¢ per month, per cow, from his cream check. On October 1, 1914, a contract was let to Henry Schellin to construct the building, and it was used until 1927. (Courtesy of the Smidt family.)

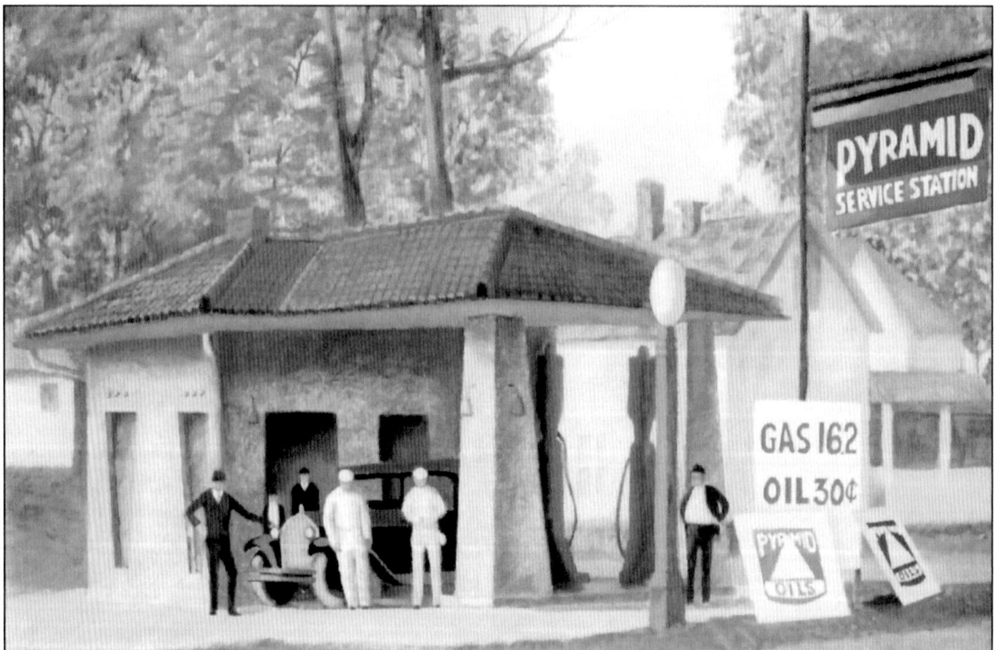

This is a painting by Jim Elton in 2004 of John Lins's Pyramid service station on North Main Street. To the right is the Richard W. Sears birthplace home, which now serves as a museum run by the Stewartville Area Historical Society. (Courtesy of Jim Elton.)

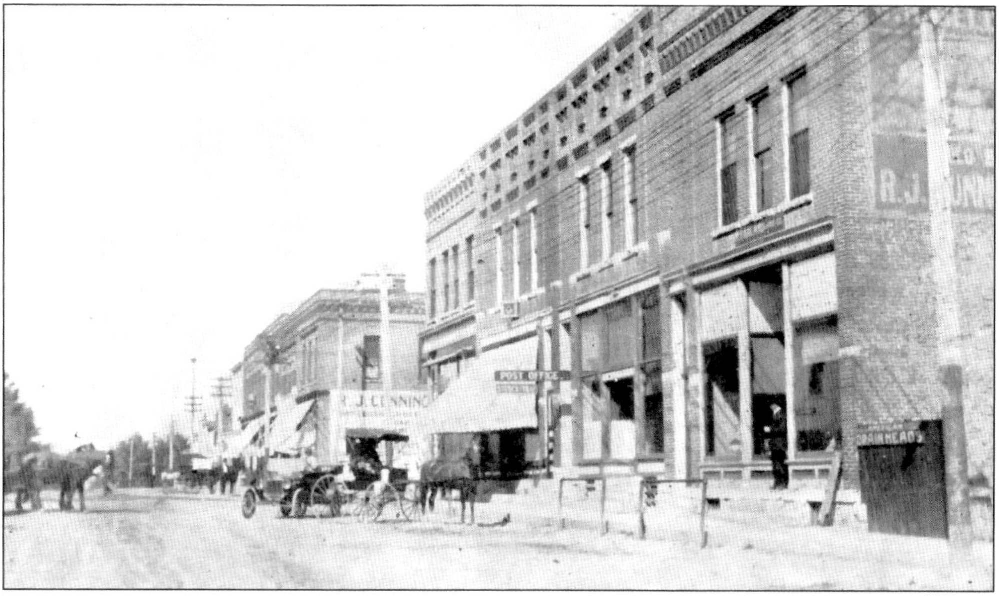

In the middle of this picture by the awning, the post office sign is visible. The post office at Stewartville was established on November 26, 1858, with Charles Stewart as postmaster. He held the office for 10 years. W. E. Smith was appointed postmaster on August 20, 1878. He installed a suite of patron mailboxes, the rental of which helped to compensate the service. The first rural route started in 1897 served by Ben Yates and Will Sparkes. (Courtesy of the SAHS.)

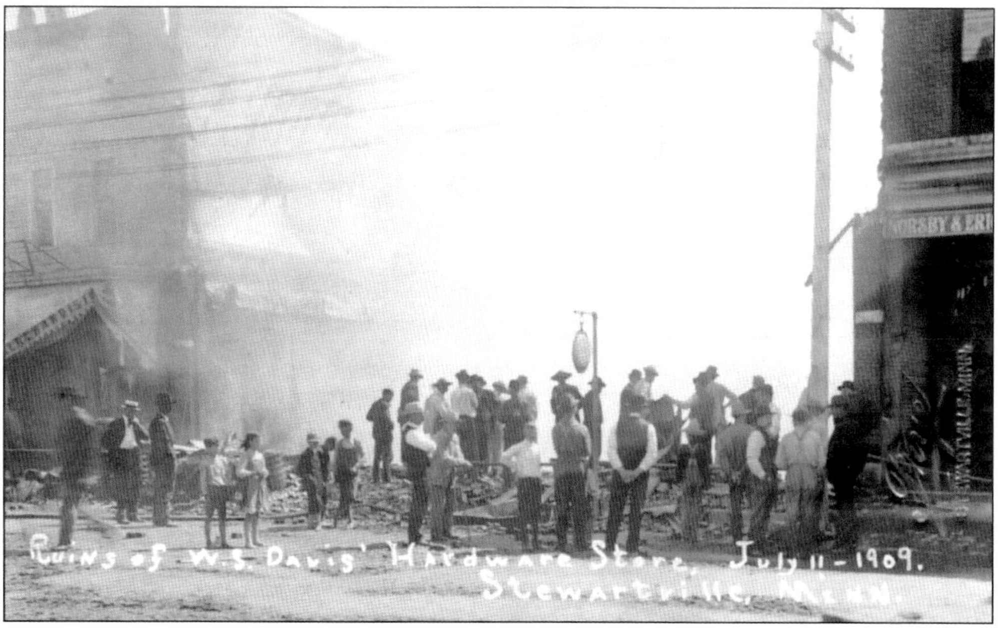

A disastrous fire destroyed the Davis Block. The large hardware and seed store owned by W. S. Davis was totally destroyed by fire on Sunday afternoon, July 11, 1909. The origin of the fire was unknown. Books, paper, and stock were carried across the street and stored with merchants on the west side. Cartridges in the store began to explode and represented a battlefield. Sparks set fire to neighboring roofs, but the fire was allowed to burn out. The stock and building were valued at $30,000. (Courtesy of the SAHS.)

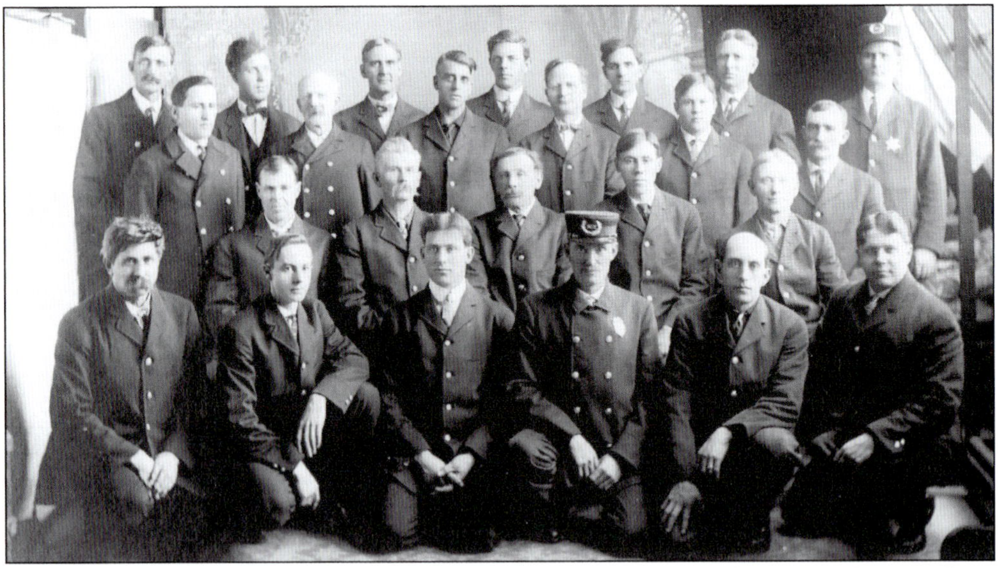

The Stewartville Fire Department was organized on July 31, 1895, with a roster of 25 members. James Larkin was the first chief and N. C. Carey was assistant chief. From left to right are (first row) James Bonner, Avery Tews, Eli Dreblow, George McMoran, Roy Horton, and John Aupperle; (second row) Fred Tews, Walter Grover, David Johnston, Charles Strifert, and Charles Zierath; (third row) Ed Strifert, James Dickey, Fred Hoaglan, Jul Bergeson, Charles Grover, and James McMoran; (fourth row) Ed Hall, Ed Anderson, Lester Tubbs, Frank Hodgson, Jackson Cussons, John Towey, and Patrick Courtney. (Courtesy of the Stewartville Fire Department.)

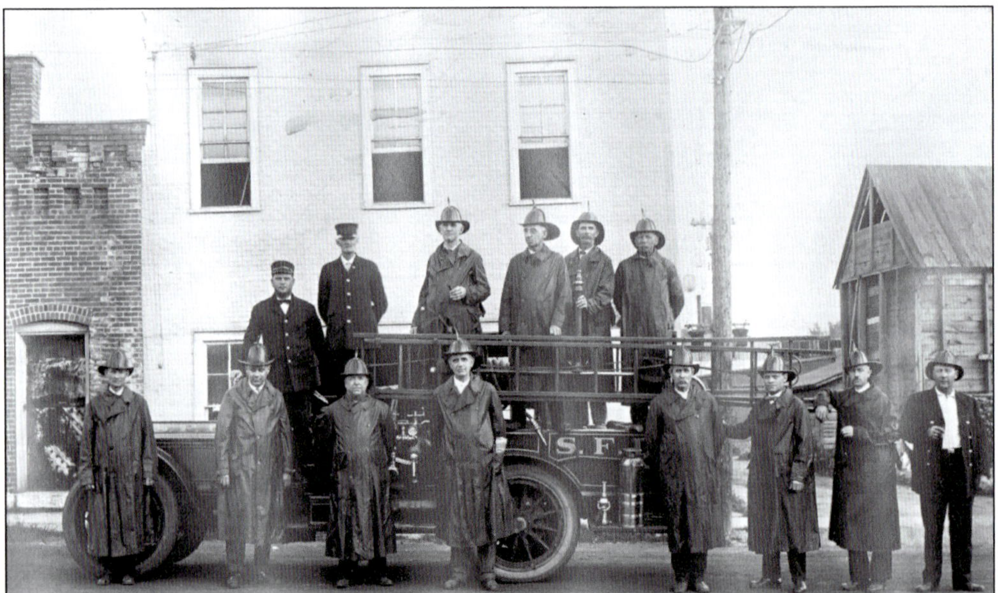

In 1920, the department was motorized when the village council purchased a Packard chassis onto which a modern chemical outfit was placed. This truck served until 1930. Since the department was organized, it has been called to battle for several big fires, the three largest being the Davis Block fire in 1909, the Chicago Great Western Railroad station fire in 1915, and the Farmer's Elevator fire on July 28, 1938. (Courtesy of the Stewartville Fire Department.)

Five

LAKE FLORENCE

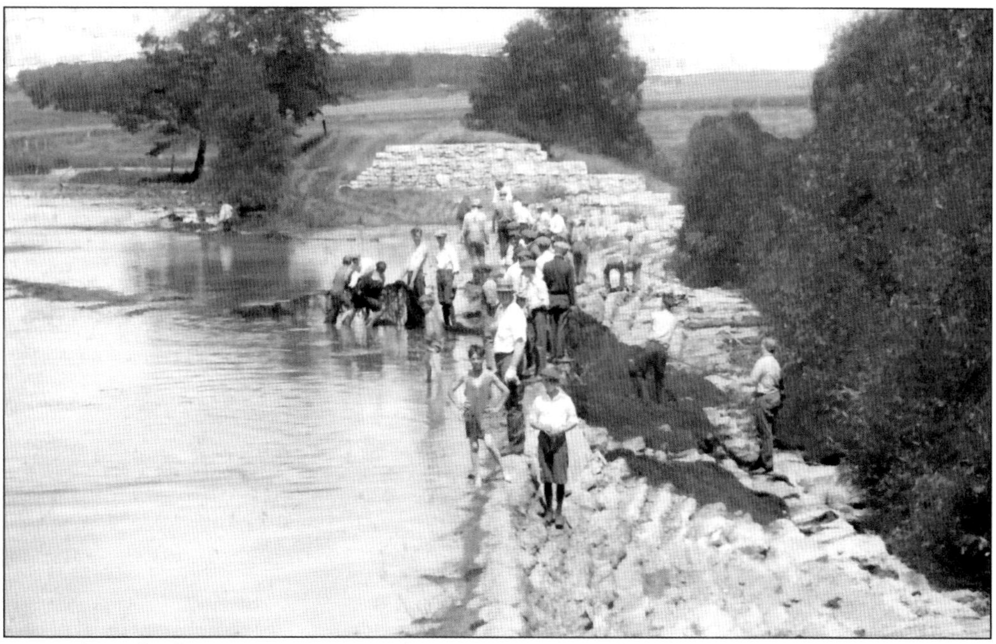

Soon after Charles Stewart came to this vicinity in 1857, he obtained a permit from Truman Wooldridge to dam the river. The first dam was small, made by a few of the first settlers using logs, boards, rocks, and stones—the materials they had at hand. (Courtesy of the Gray family.)

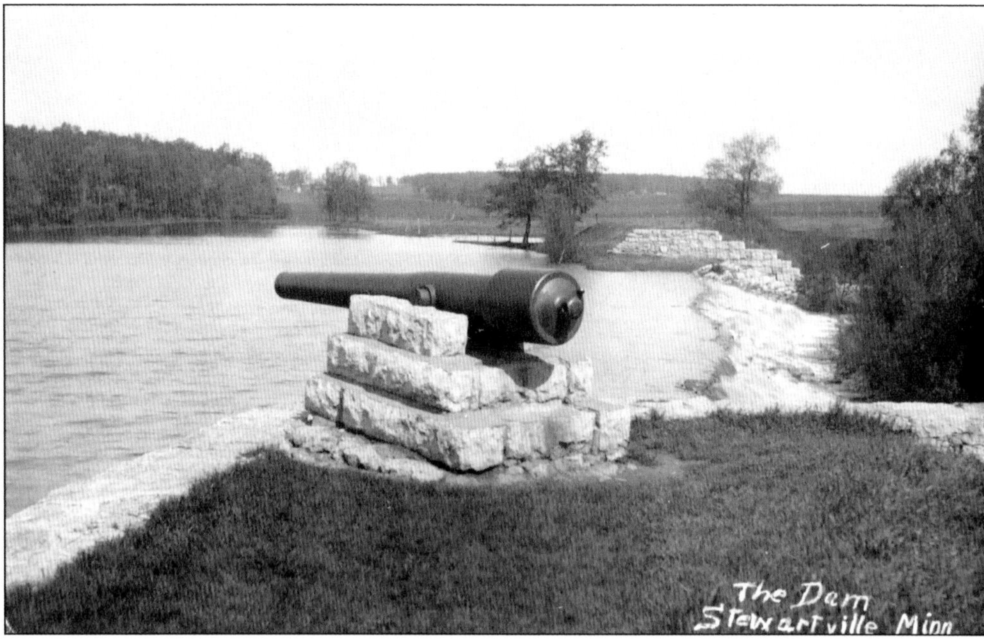

The dam caused the river to widen, and picturesque Mill Pond (as it was always called by the Stewart family) was formed. Much later, the lake became know as Lake Florence, named for Florence Stewart, wife of Charles Neil Stewart. One evening when the Stewarts were enjoying a boat ride, Florence, letting her hand glide through the water, lost her diamond ring. It was never found. (Courtesy of the SAHS.)

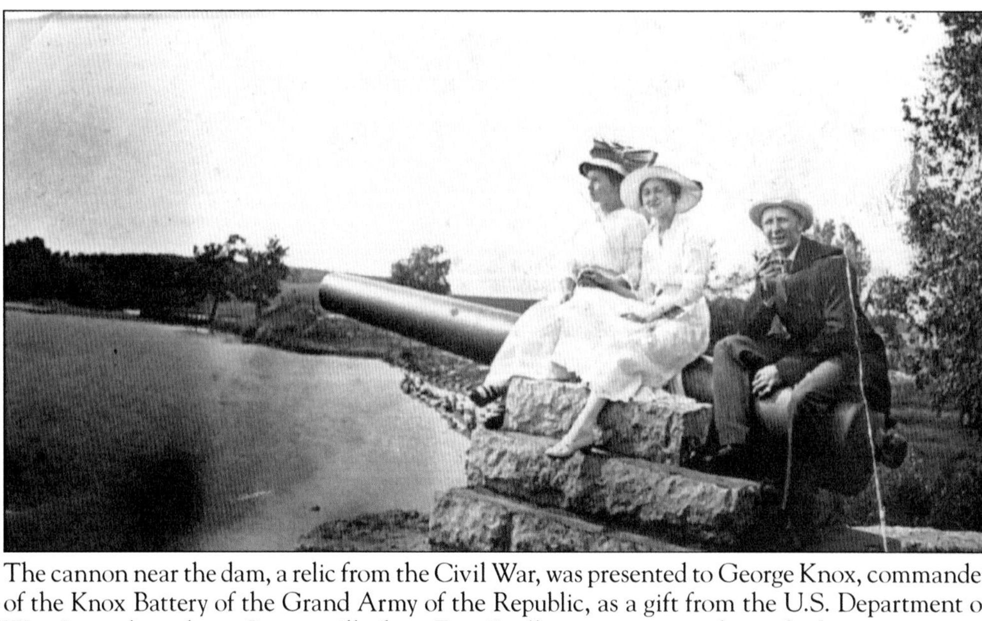

The cannon near the dam, a relic from the Civil War, was presented to George Knox, commander of the Knox Battery of the Grand Army of the Republic, as a gift from the U.S. Department of War. It was brought to Stewartville from Fort Snelling on a wagon drawn by horses sometime in the 1890s. Knox would fire off the cannon at 4:00 a.m. every Fourth of July for many years. (Courtesy of the SAHS.)

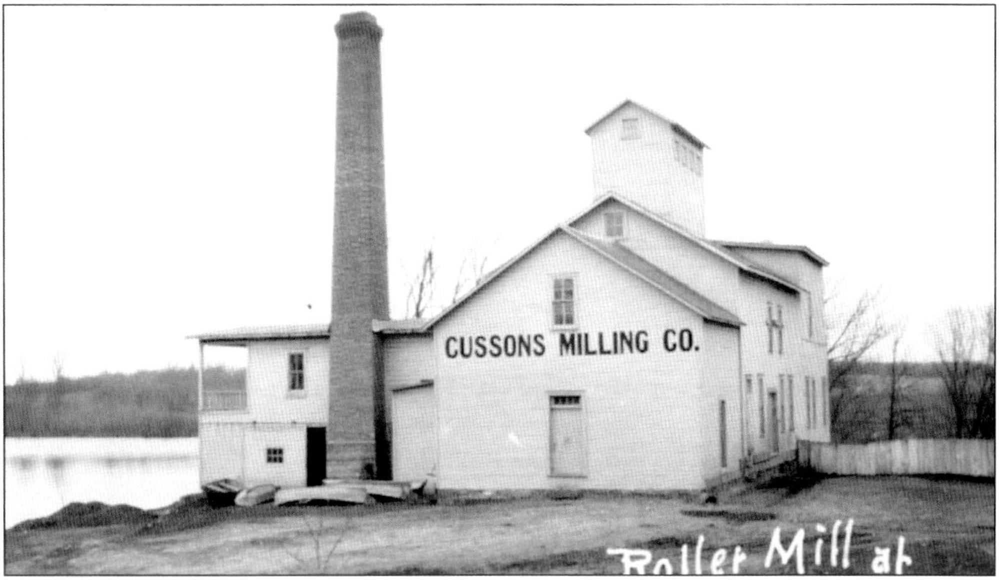

In April 1898, John M. Cussons and his four sons, who operated a mill at Chatfield, purchased the Stewartville mill from Charles Neil Stewart. The mill was remodeled and new machinery added, which brought it up to the modern methods of milling. The Cussons Milling Company was then organized with Wauzee and John elected to operate the mill. John operated the mill until his death in 1938. The mill was leased to A. R. Roberts then closed and was later razed. (Courtesy of the SAHS.)

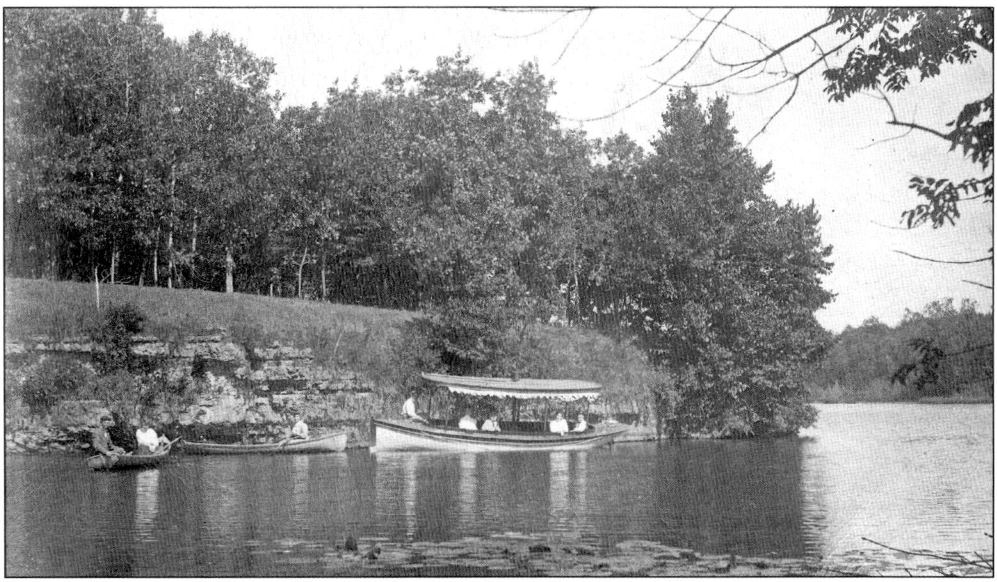

In 1890, the Cussons brothers purchased the *Idle Hour*, a 24-foot gasoline launch that carried 25 passengers. It had a canopy top and side curtains that could be pulled down if a party were caught out on the lake in a shower. This launch was used Sundays, evenings, and holidays until 1917 when it was sold. (Courtesy of the SAHS.)

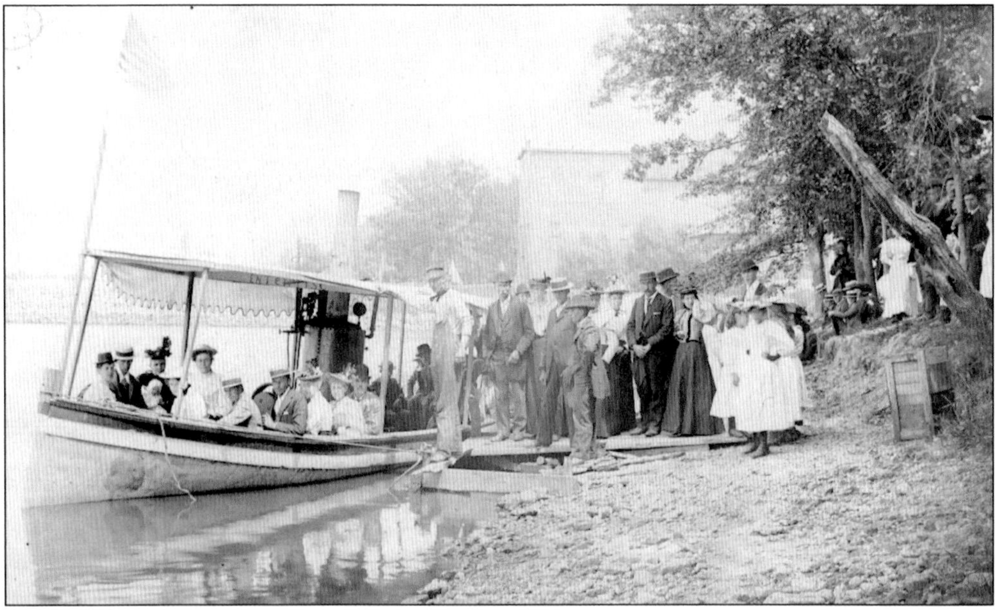

About 1906, large picnic parties would come from Osage, Iowa, and other stations south on an excursion train. They would walk from the depot to the park with their well-laden picnic baskets, go upriver in the *Idle Hour* for the day, and return via the railroad in the evening. (Courtesy of Madelyn Betcher.)

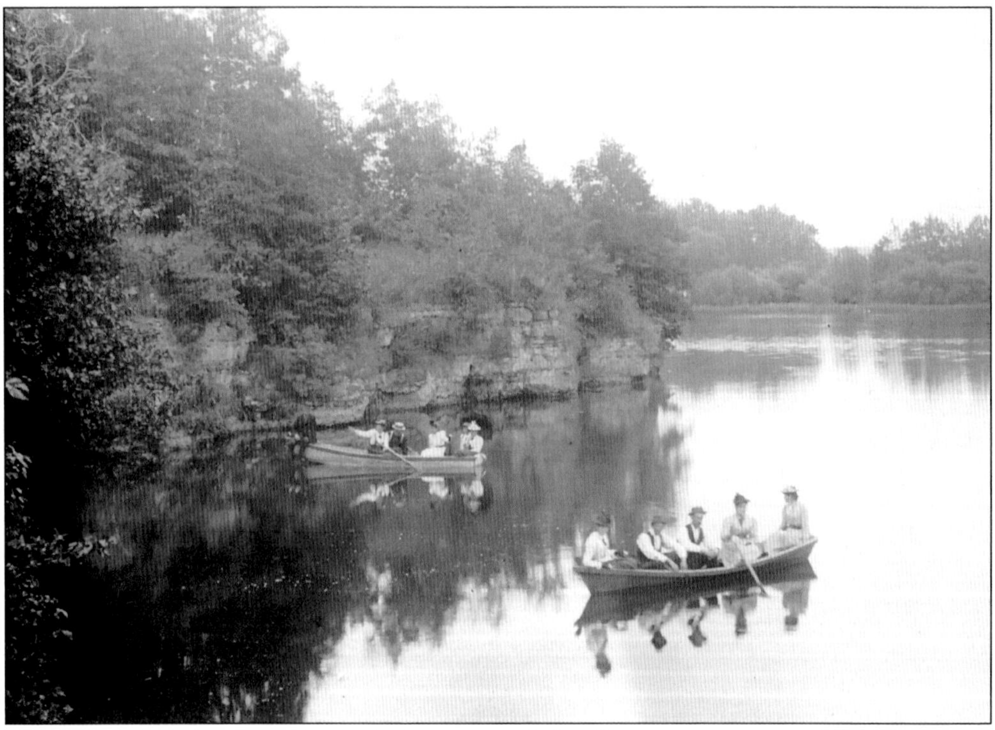

A Sunday afternoon boat ride on the Root River/Lake Florence was a treat. The Root River/ Lake Florence acts as a mirror for these two boats full of well-dressed ladies and gentlemen enjoying a day on the water. (Courtesy of the OCHS.)

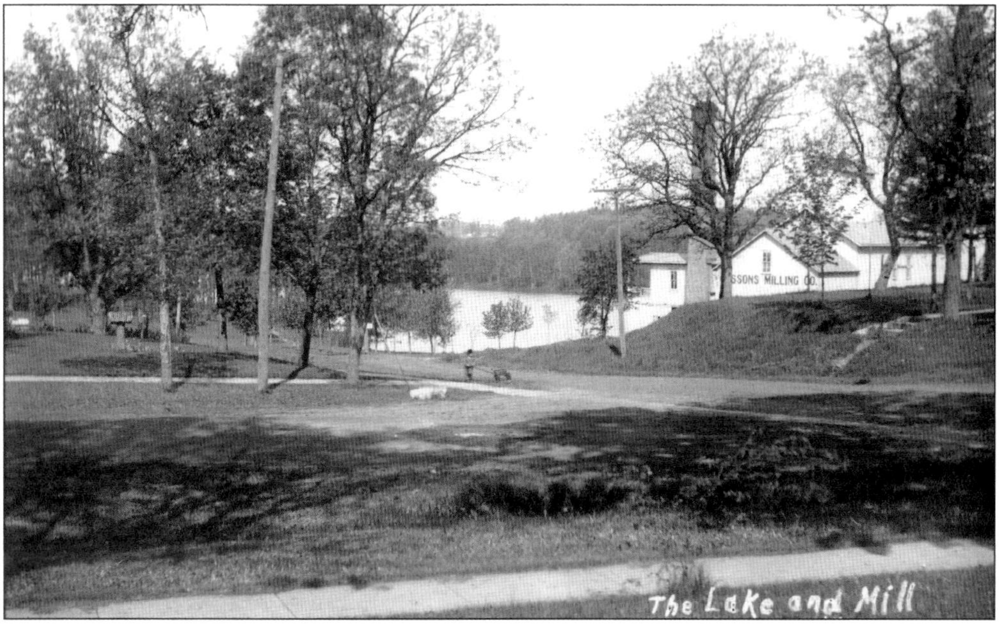

In this early picture, the Cussons mill can be seen off to the right, and the lake and park are on the left. People who enjoyed the great outdoors would return to Lake Florence Park to enjoy all the pleasures afforded there. Children loved to cross the dam to pick pails of wildflowers. Bird-watchers found the natural wooded shores of the area an ideal place to enjoy their feathered friends. Swimming and fishing were always a fun summer activity by the shores of the lake. (Courtesy of the Gray family.)

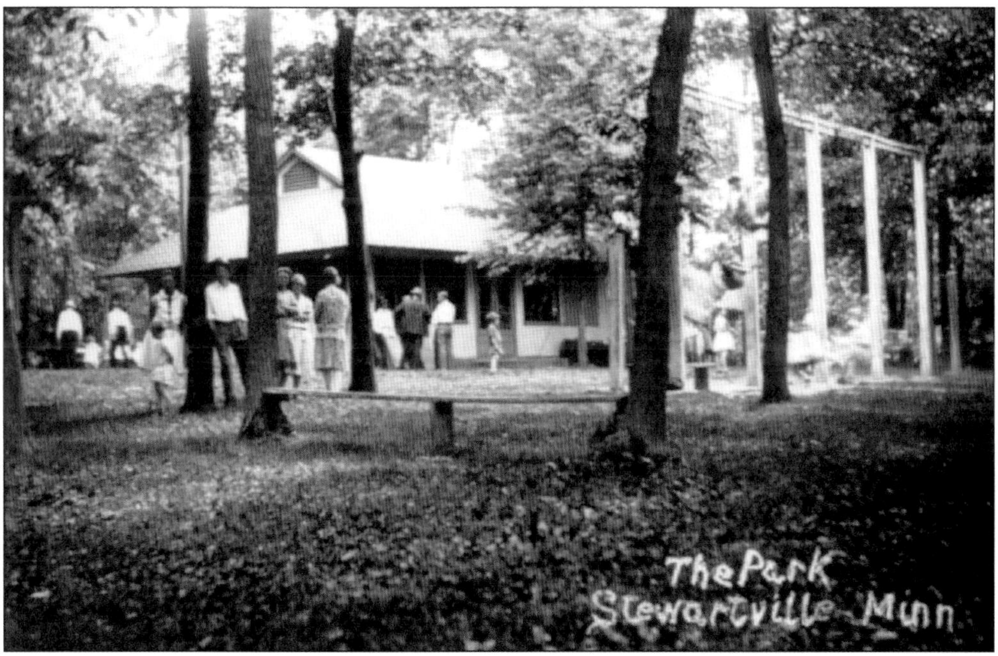

The picnickers can enjoy the comforts of eating in a screened kitchen that is provided with two gas stoves, a sink with running water, tables, and benches. Three outdoor fireplaces are also very popular, along with the swings for young children. (Courtesy of the Gray family.)

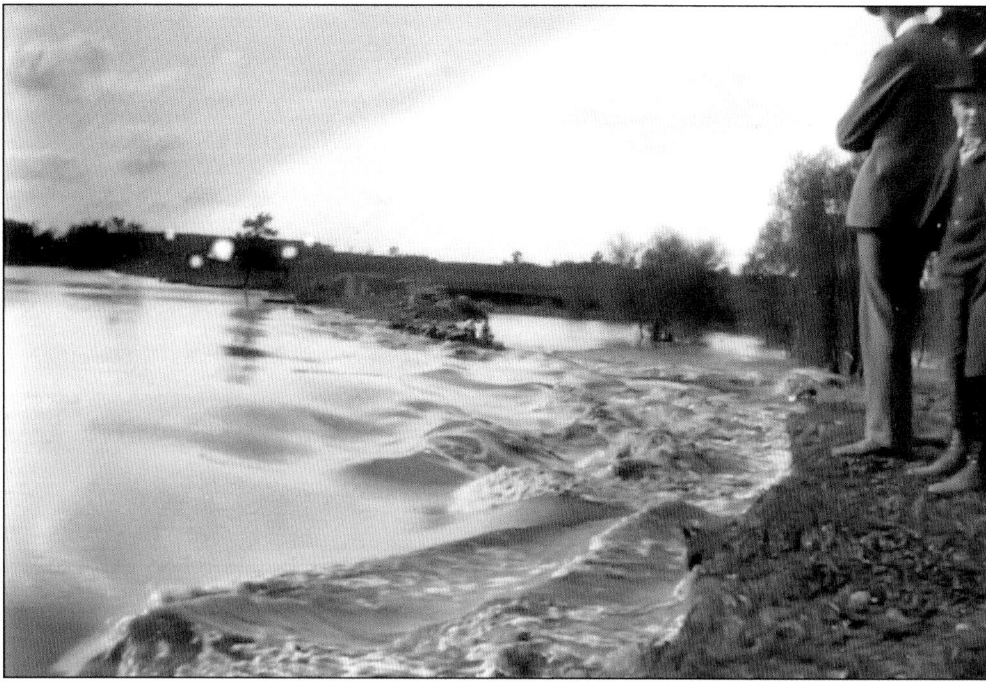

Everyone came down to the lake when the ice went out and the spring runoff brought the level of the lake up. Here men are standing by the edge by the cannon to observe the waves lapping at their feet. (Courtesy of the Gray family.)

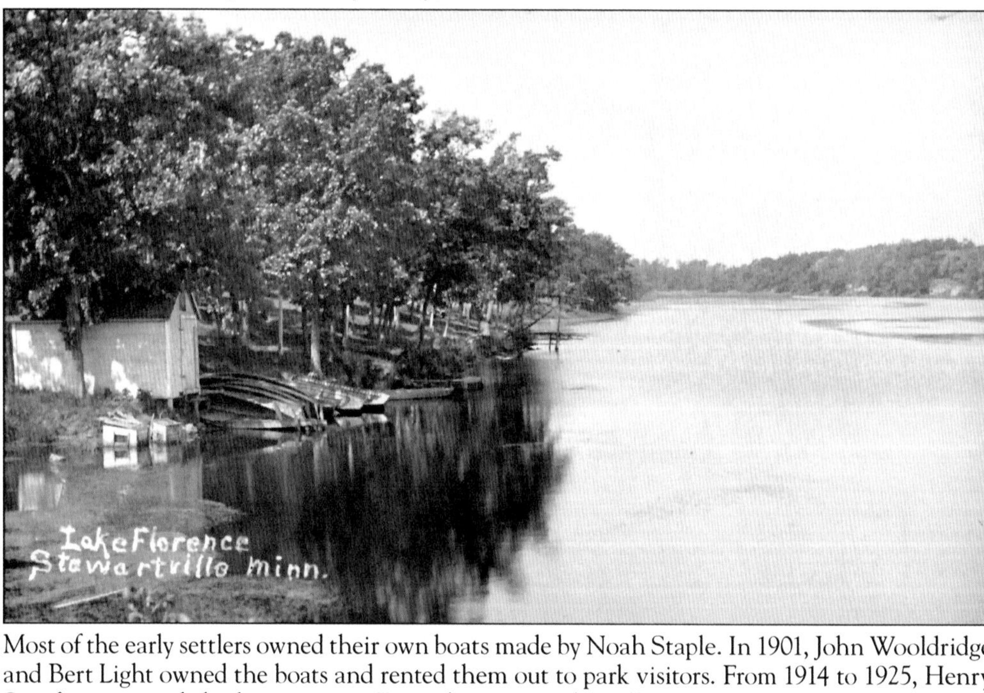

Most of the early settlers owned their own boats made by Noah Staple. In 1901, John Wooldridge and Bert Light owned the boats and rented them out to park visitors. From 1914 to 1925, Henry Streifert operated the boat service. For a short time, the village owned the boats, and people would use their own motors. Eugene Kuehntopp was in charge of renting and repairing them. (Courtesy of the SAHS.)

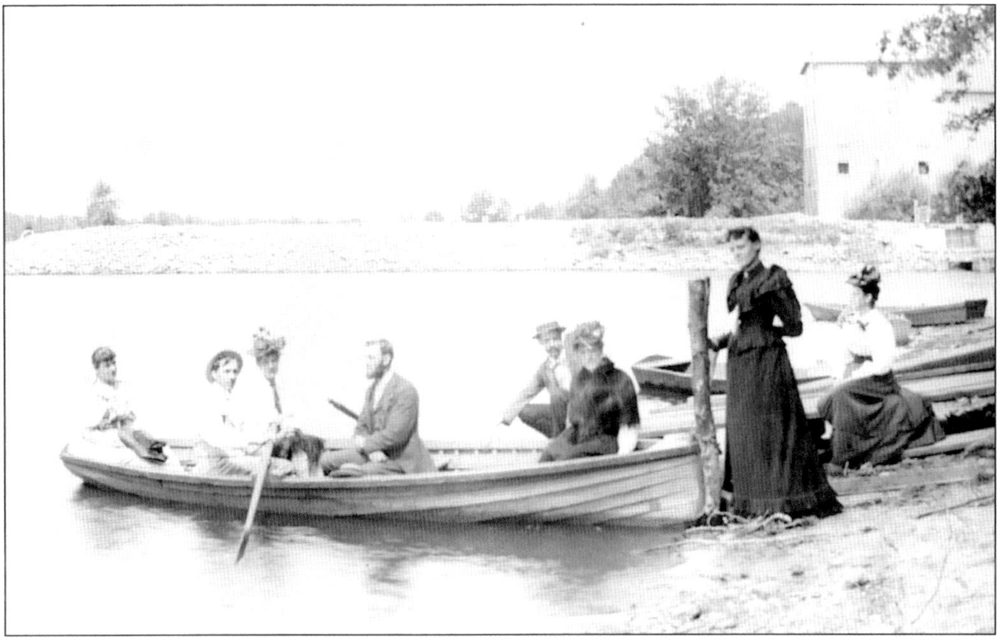

People in the boat are, from left to right, Burr Tuttle, Dr. C. E. Fawcett, May Stillwell, Leslie Stillwell, and Mabel Fawcett. (Courtesy of the SAHS.)

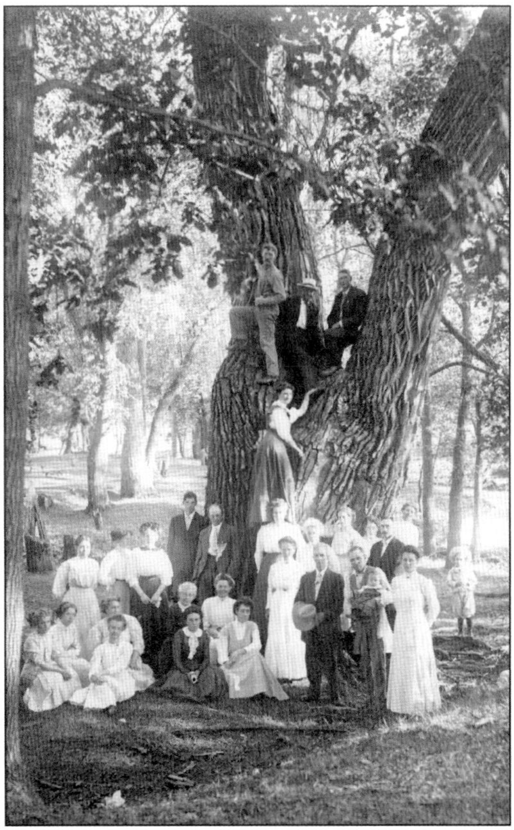

The "Big Elm" was a favorite gathering place for pictures and picnics. Pictured are Ed Rutledge, John Beach, Joseph Anderson, Mrs. John Beach, Fred Bonner, William Prinz, Lillian Duncanson, Myrtle Savidge, Mabel Dodge, Rev. C. E. Mead, Mrs. Frost Parkinson, William Parkinson, LePearl Bonner, Bessie Bobb, Bertha Smith, Mrs. Ed Rutledge, Martha Anderson, William McGrath, Vern Smith, Helen Smith, Mrs. Vern Smith, Bessie Bentley, Ora Savidge, Mrs. C. E. Mead, Mrs. E. J. Dodge, Mrs. John M. Cussons, and Stella House. (Courtesy of the SAHS.)

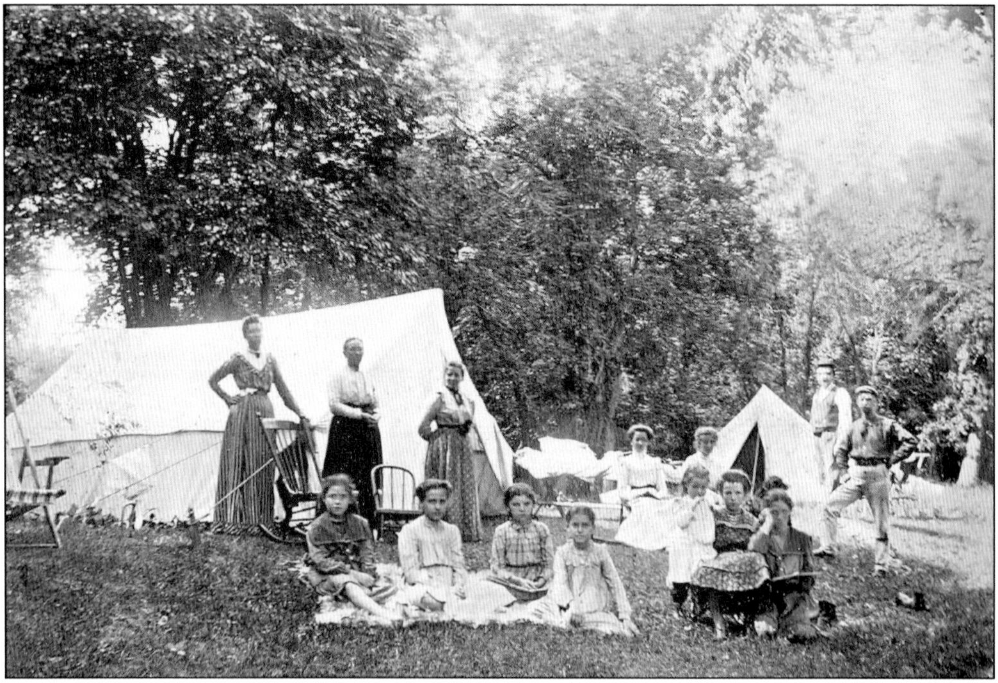

The Big Elm was located one and a half miles upriver. The stone quarry and the park have long been favorite picnic and camping spots for people of this whole area. (Courtesy of Madelyn Betcher.)

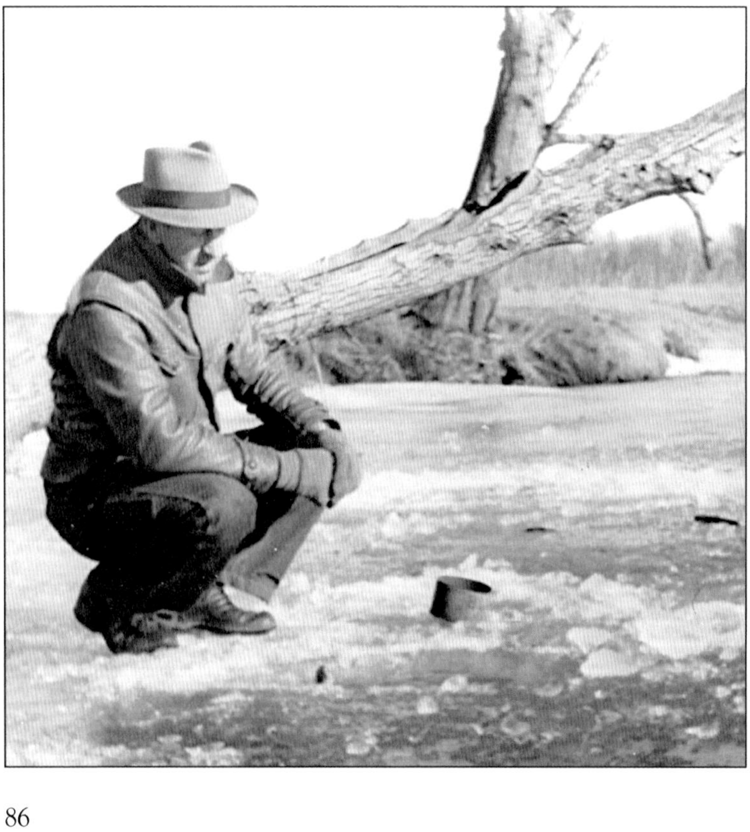

Ice fishing was a favorite winter pastime. Here a gentleman hunches down beside his hole in the ice, bait can to the left on the ice, and intently watches his bobber in the hole in the ice for a strike. (Courtesy of the SAHS.)

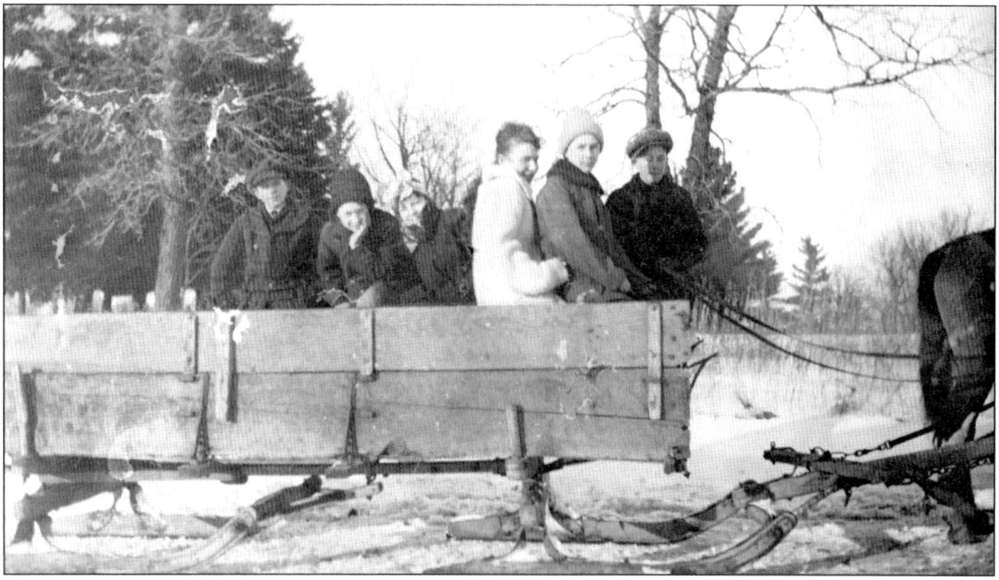

Cutter riding on the ice was a popular pastime on Sunday afternoons and moonlit nights. The clanking of horses' hooves on the ice, the merry jingle of bells, and the happy singing voices were sounds never to be forgotten. A carload of cutters was often unloaded at the Farmer's Supply Company back in 1907. (Courtesy of the SAHS.)

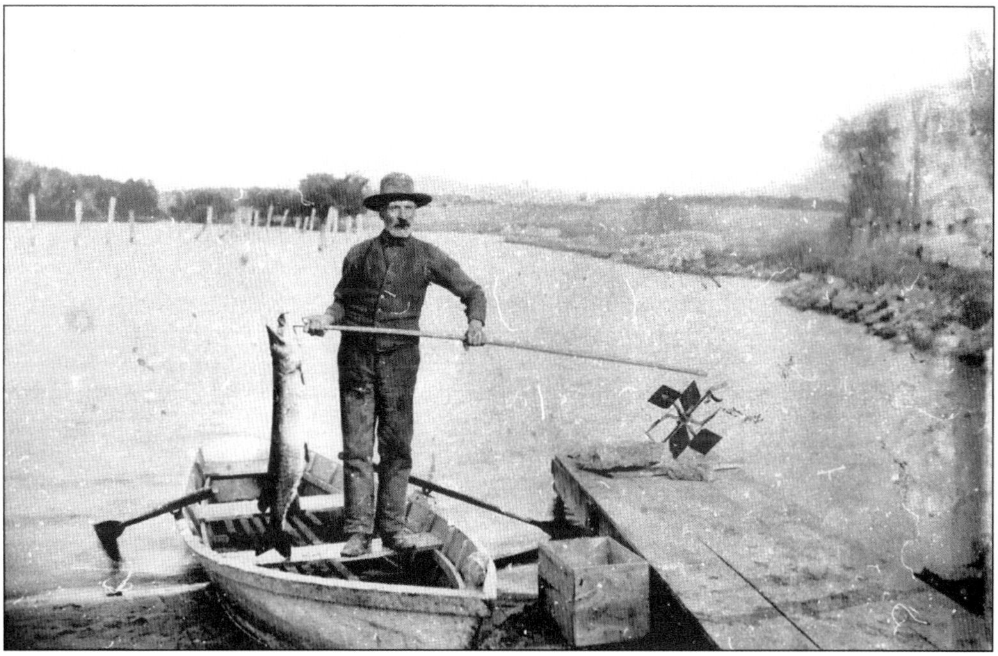

On October 10, 1888, "Scotch Tommy" Fairberne, the village blacksmith, caught the first muskellunge ever taken from Lake Florence. It was caught in front of the mill. In 1906, Henry Ringey won the distinction of landing the biggest fish ever caught here. It was a 29.5-pound muskellunge, which he landed below the dam. The fish was on exhibition at the Stoyke and Hall Meat Market for two days, after which it was cut up and distributed among Ringey's friends and furnished fish for over 50 people. (Courtesy of the Gray family.)

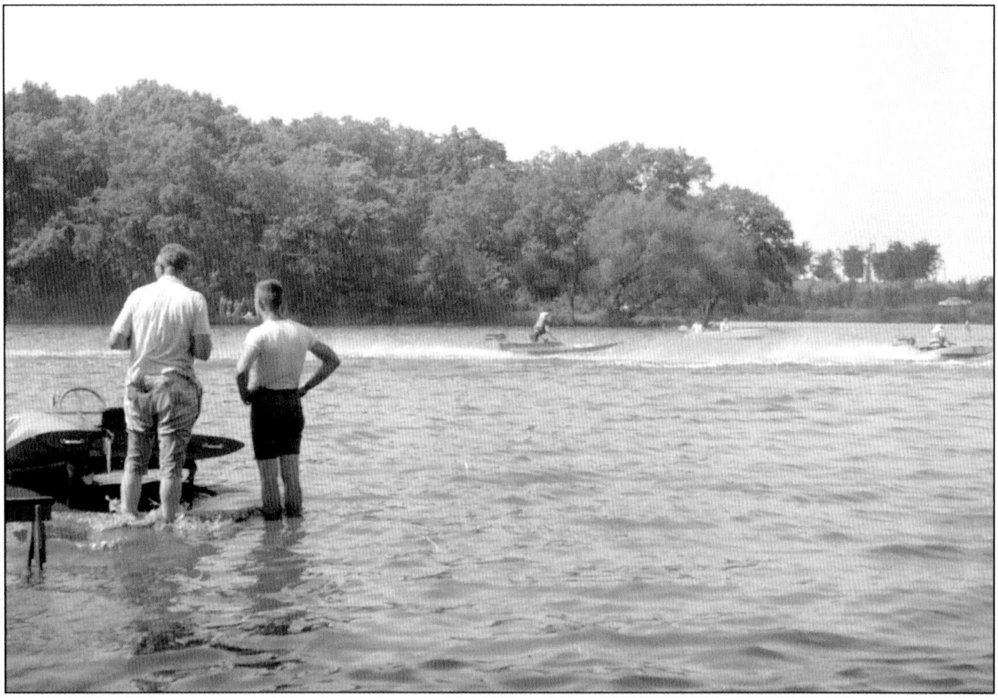

Speedboat races were held on the lake during the summer festival, and in later years, snowmobile races were a favorite winter festival activity. (Courtesy of Elman Hanken.)

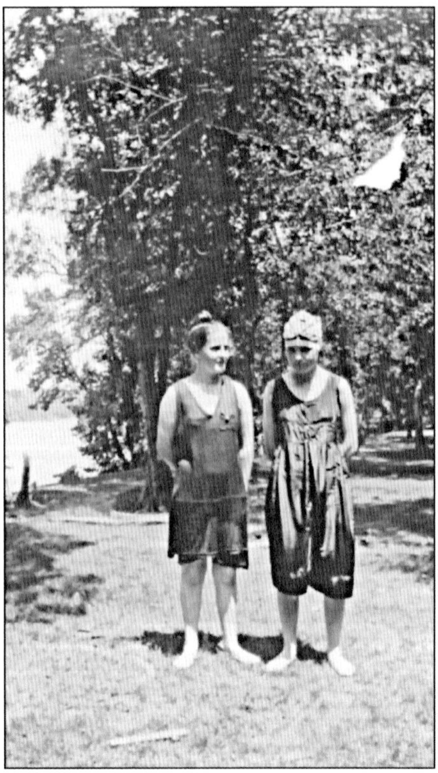

Swimming has always been a popular sport here. A rocky bed of the lake in the early days and the muddy bottom of later years has never discouraged the enthusiastic swimmers. Although the fashions in swimming suits have greatly changed from the full woolen dress bloomer type to the scanty suits of today, the fun of swimming is still the same. (Courtesy of the SAHS.)

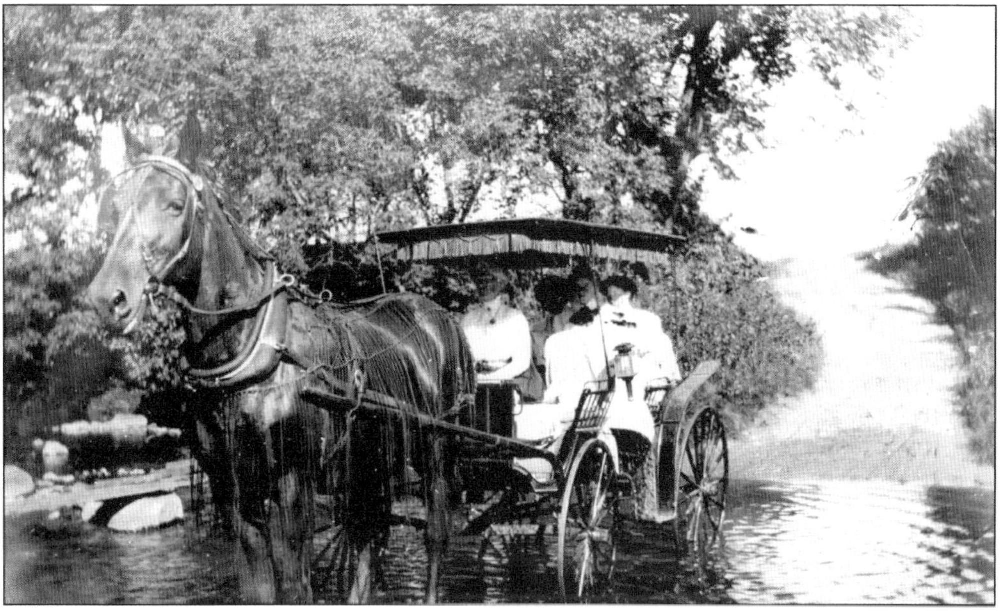

In 1910, a Mrs. Davis and Harriet Herrman cross the low-water bridge by High Forest, taking County Road 6/Panhandle Road past the Sportsman Club and stone quarry. (Courtesy of the SAHS.)

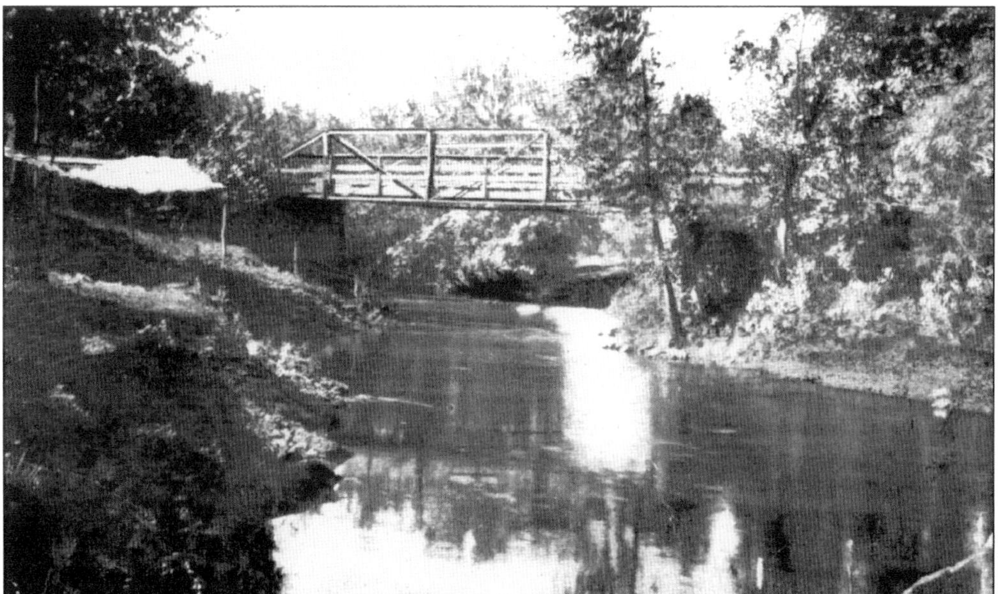

As the glacial Lake Agassiz drained, the Root River system was developed. The Native Americans referred to the river as Hokah, meaning "root." The early French and British fur traders explored the region and depending on the translation said Racine. After the Lewis and Clark Expedition of 1804, it is referred to as the Root River on every map. The river served as transportation, waterpower, food source, and recreational resource over the years. (Courtesy of the Gray family.)

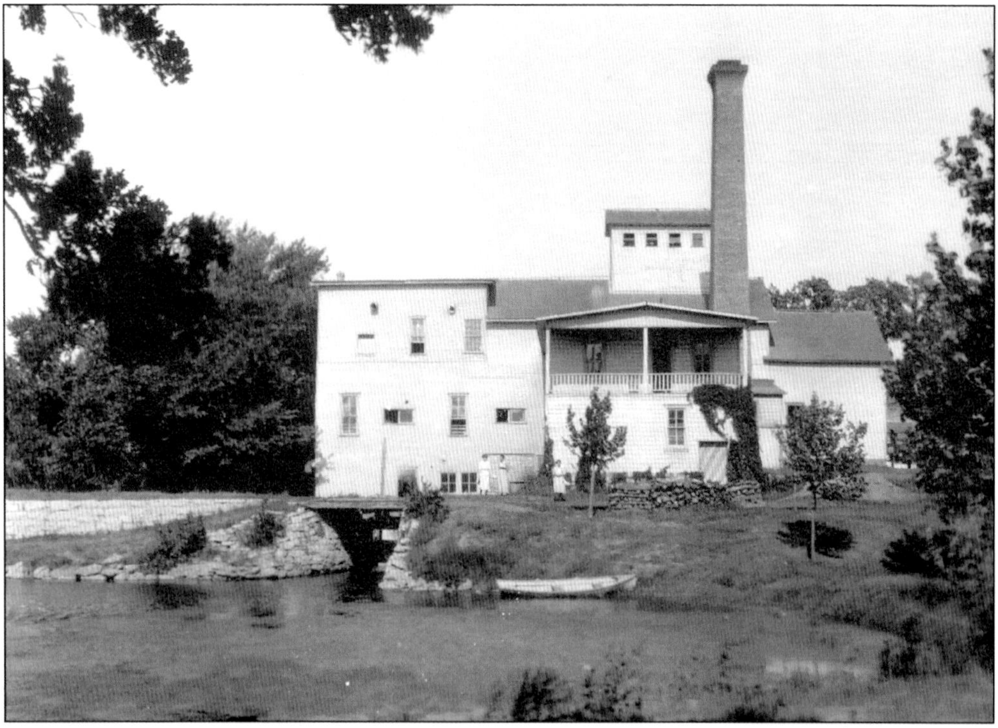

The Cussons Milling Company added a new engine and boiler room, a 30-by-50-foot addition, and also a new steam boiler to furnish power and heat in the winter months. Sleeping rooms were built in the second story of the engine room and an open porch was built facing the lake on the west. The limestone retaining wall and riprap was quarried right in the mill yard. (Courtesy of the OCHS.)

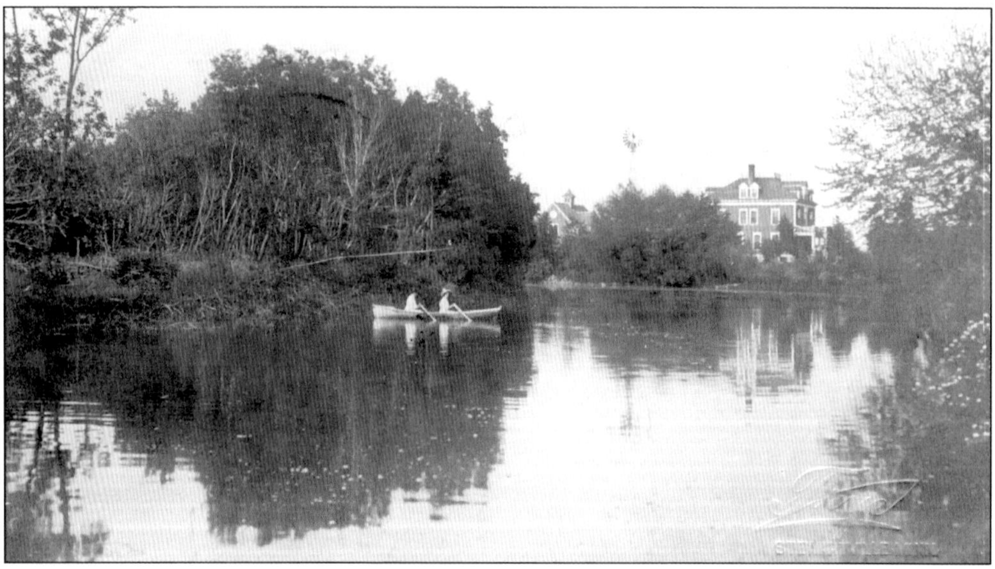

The Root River winds to the west around the Elmer Ginter place, built in 1890. It was the largest home in the city at that time, with 16 rooms housed in three stories. It has also served as a nursing home. (Courtesy of the OCHS.)

Six

AGRICULTURE

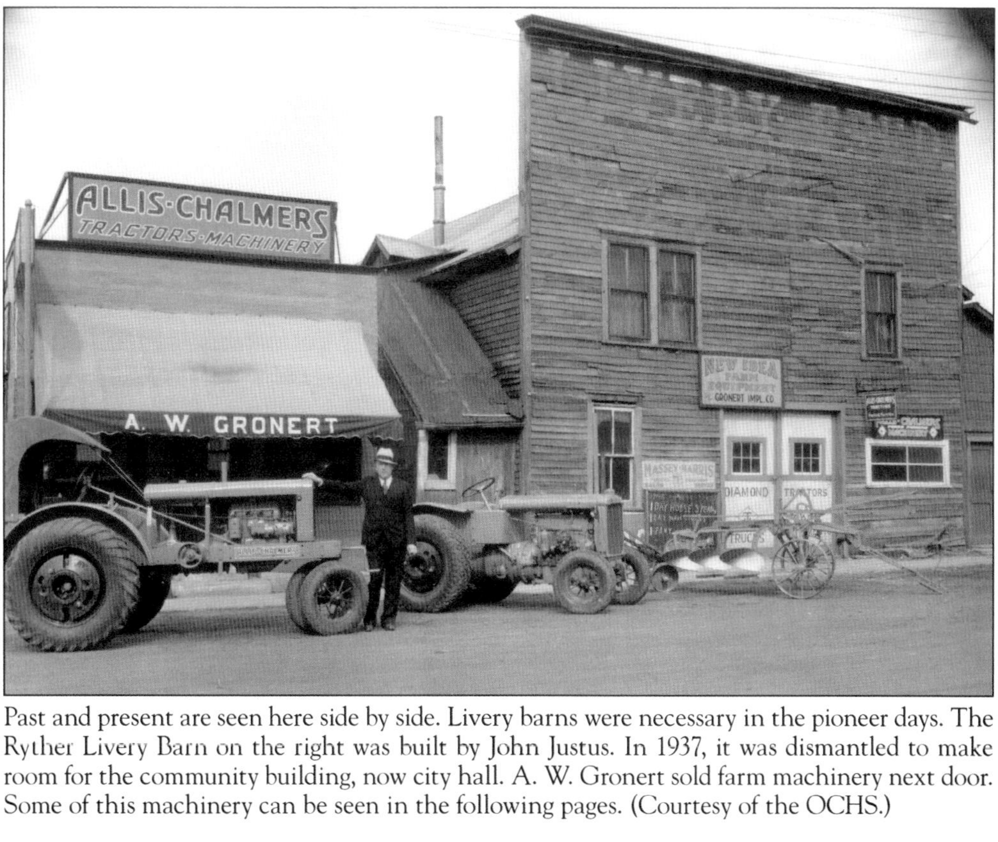

Past and present are seen here side by side. Livery barns were necessary in the pioneer days. The Ryther Livery Barn on the right was built by John Justus. In 1937, it was dismantled to make room for the community building, now city hall. A. W. Gronert sold farm machinery next door. Some of this machinery can be seen in the following pages. (Courtesy of the OCHS.)

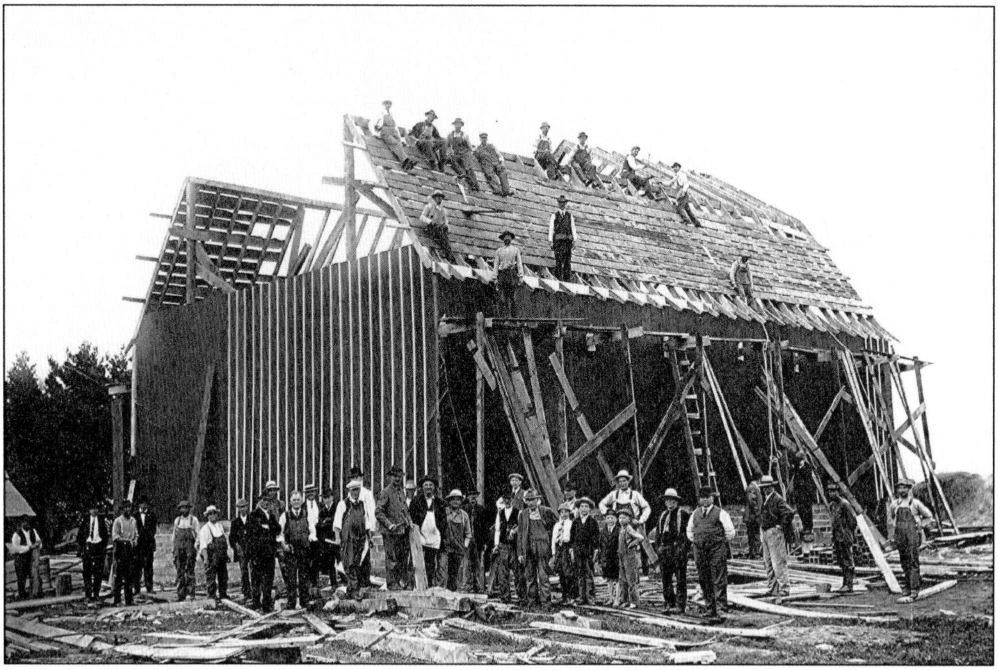

On a farm, the barn is one of the most important structures. It was built to protect the livestock from freezing temperatures during the winter months plus as a storage area for hay. A barn raising was a social event as well as a work event. Barns were erected quickly when neighbors gathered to build them. (Courtesy of the SAHS.)

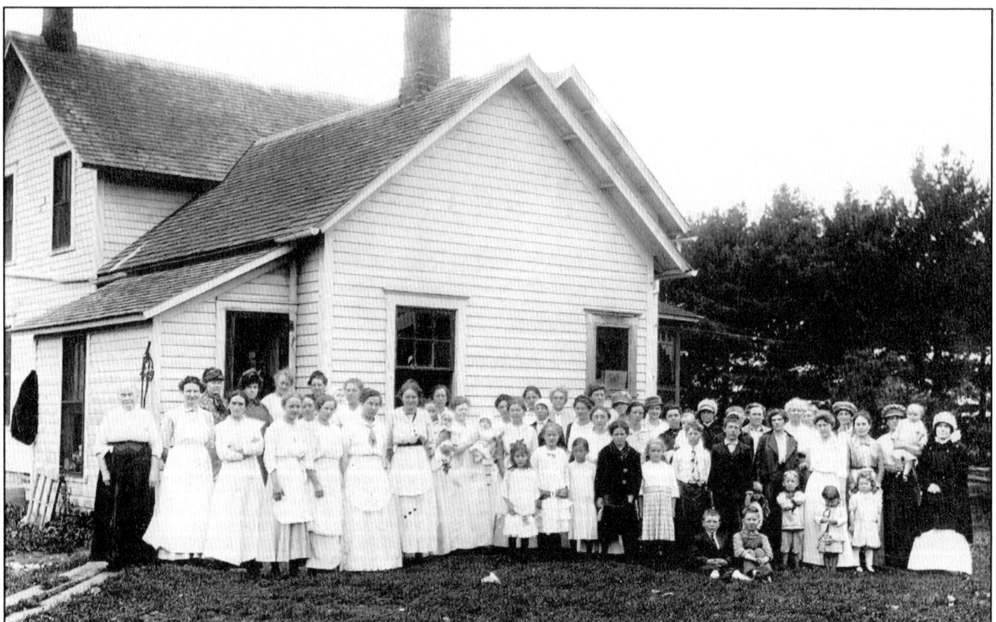

The women gathered to make the meals and socialize during barn raisings. The children would play games as the older ones supervised the youngsters. (Courtesy of the SAHS.)

A 1937 All-Crop Harvester was purchased by Joseph Warren in the fall of 1936 to combine oats. He was only able to use it one season because he passed away suddenly of a heart attack. The combine was then used by his niece's husband, Alfred Nicklay, who took over the farm until he retired from farming in 1966. It was kept in a shed until 2003 when it found a new home in the Allis Chalmers museum in Portage la Prairie, Manitoba, Canada. (Courtesy of Rosemary Oeltjen.)

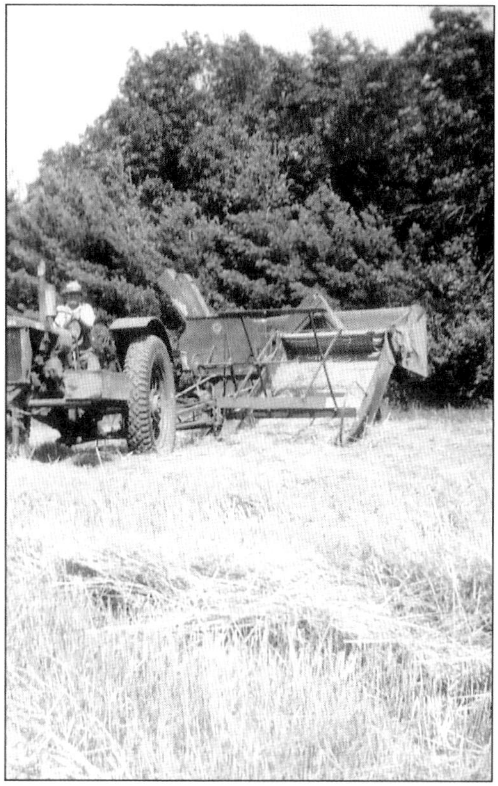

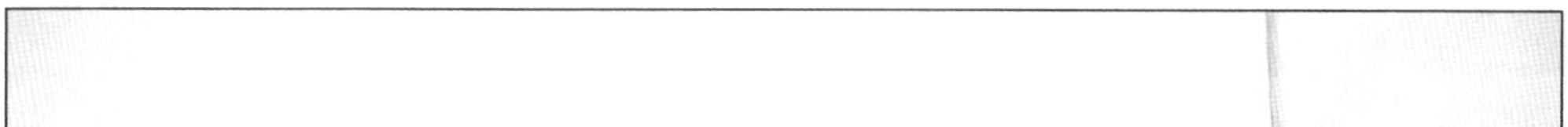

Joseph and Emma Warren are seen with their single-row corn picker, pulled by an Oliver Hart Parr tractor in 1933. Joseph and Emma Warren purchased their farm northeast of Pleasant Grove in 1917 and farmed until 1938 when Joseph died suddenly of a heart attack. The niece they raised, Garna King, and her new husband, Alfred Nicklay, took over the farming operation and the care of Emma and raised their family of six there. (Courtesy of Rosemary Oeltjen.)

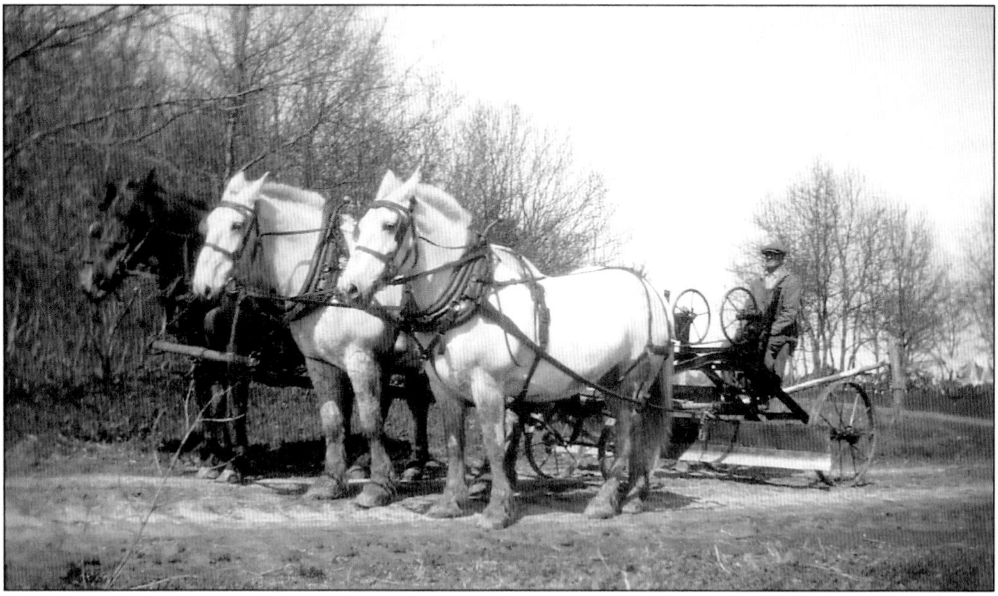

Joseph Warren is seen here with his team of horses and grader used to grade the farm yard and long driveway. (Courtesy of Rosemary Oeltjen.)

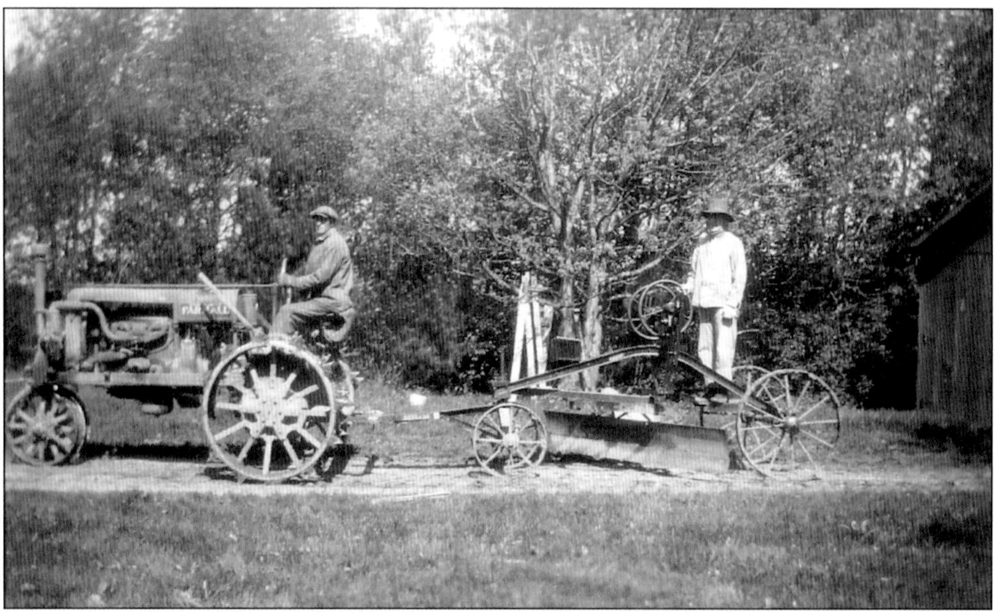

Warren is shown with his new Farmall steel-wheeled tractor pulling the grader in the early 1930s. (Courtesy of Rosemary Oeltjen.)

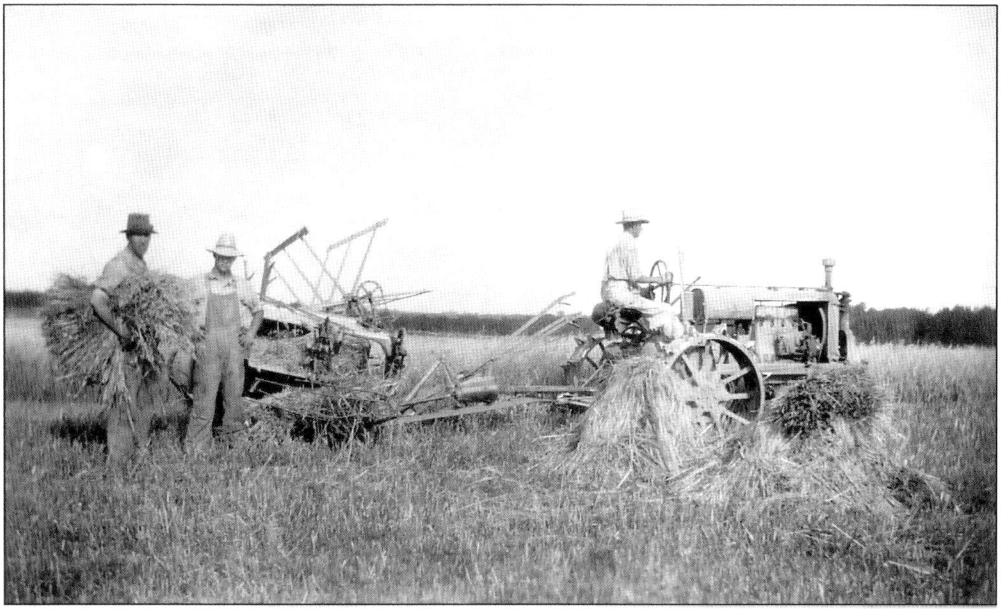

Warren is pulling the grain binder (used before the purchase of the All-Crop Harvester combine) with the Farmall steel-wheeled tractor in 1930. (Courtesy of Rosemary Oeltjen.)

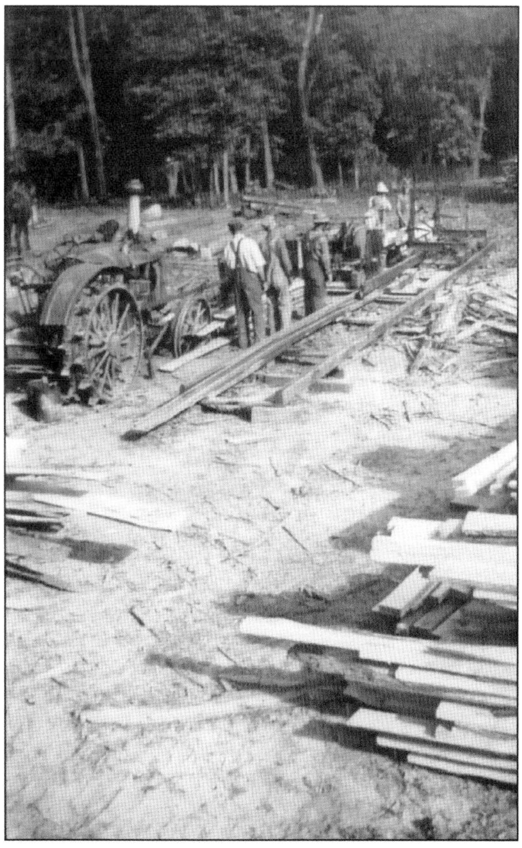

A portable sawmill was in use on the Joseph and Emma Warren farm in the early 1930s. Trees were cut down on the farm and put through the sawmill to make lumber for the construction of the barns. (Courtesy of Rosemary Oeltjen.)

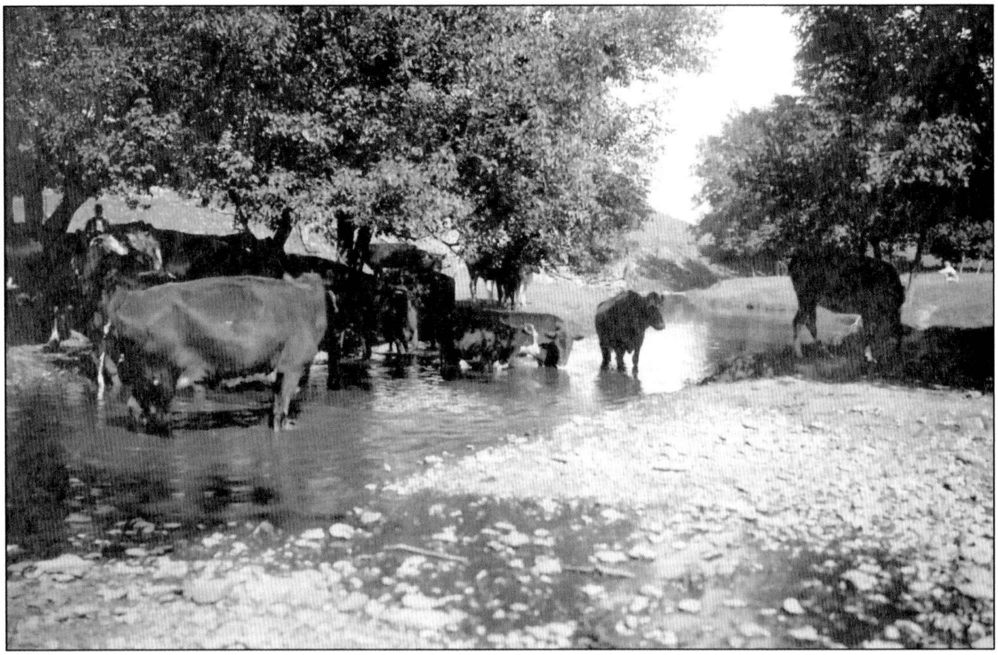

Herb Dodd drove his cows to pasture every morning and brought them back down Main Street to his barn near the community building in the center of town in the evening. The cows would go up the middle of the road, leaving ample room on either side for cars. (Courtesy of the SAHS.)

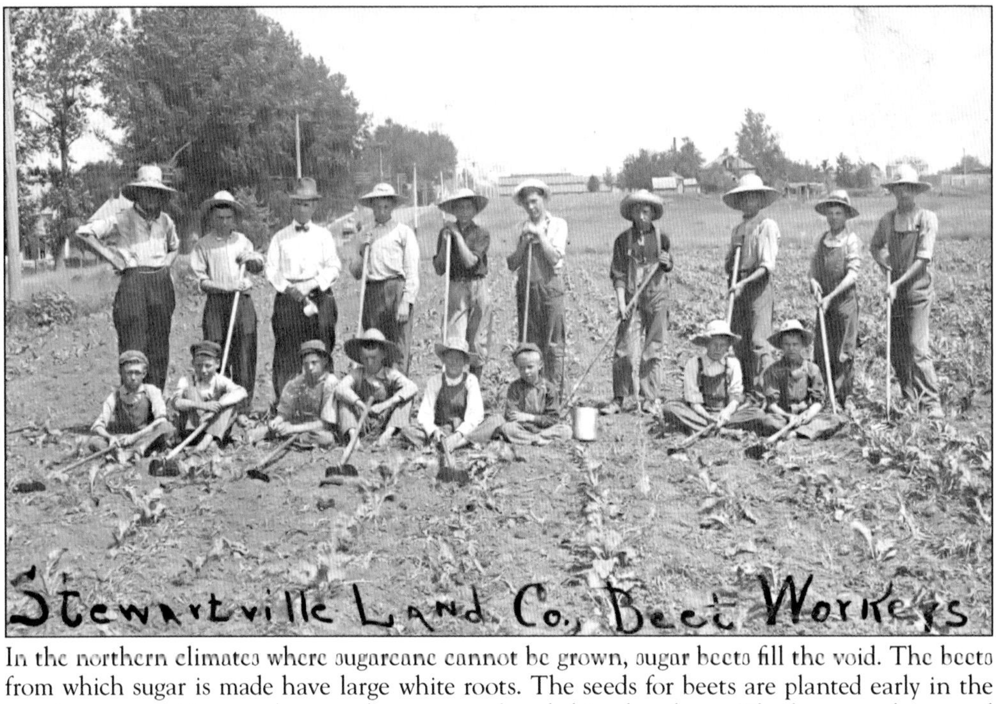

In the northern climates where sugarcane cannot be grown, sugar beets fill the void. The beets from which sugar is made have large white roots. The seeds for beets are planted early in the growing season. Here workers use hoes to weed and thin the plants. The beets are harvested when the sugar content is high, usually very late in the growing season. (Courtesy of the Gray family.)

The manager and board of directors for the elevator are seen in the 1940s. From left to right are W. A. Betcher, Martin Thompson, Henry Wood, Frank Fieck, and Harry Carothers. Not pictured is John Stewart. (Courtesy of All American Co-op.)

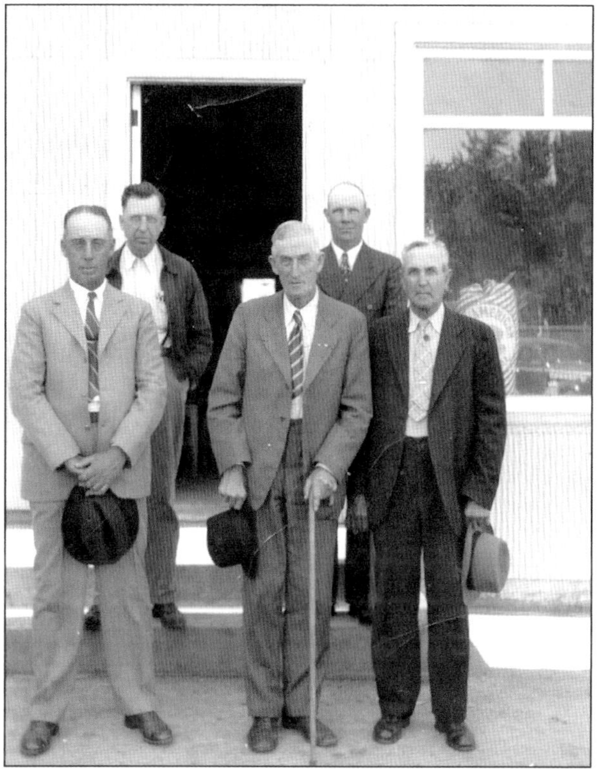

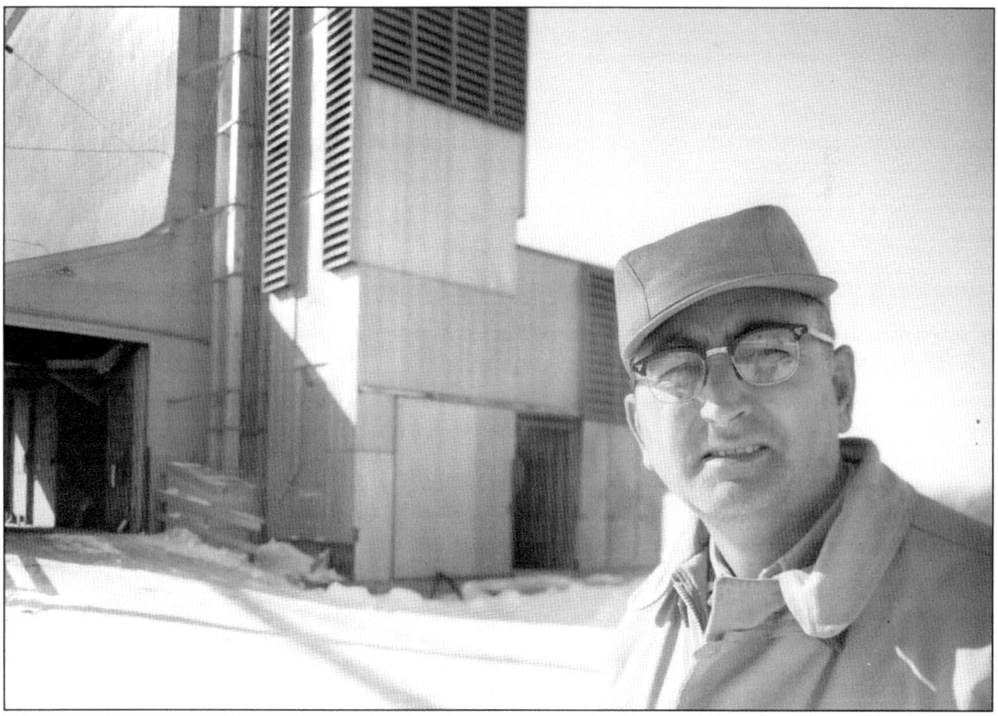

Wendell Lenton took over as manager of the elevator in 1945 and retired in October 1988. (Courtesy of All American Co-op.)

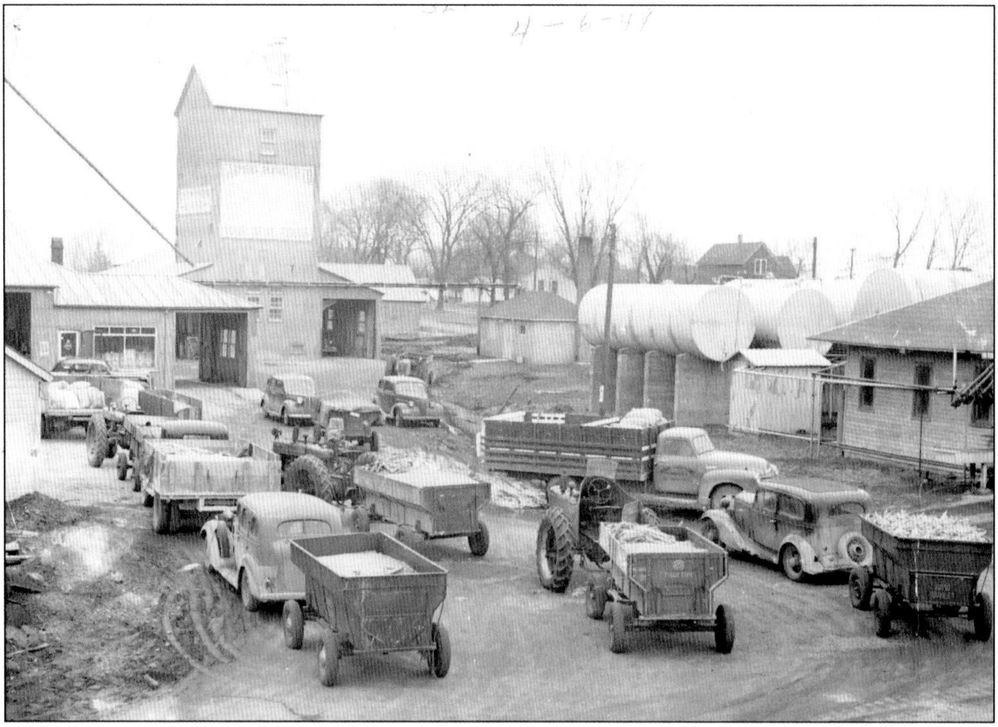

Seed cleaning at the elevator takes place on April 6, 1949. (Courtesy of All American Co-op.)

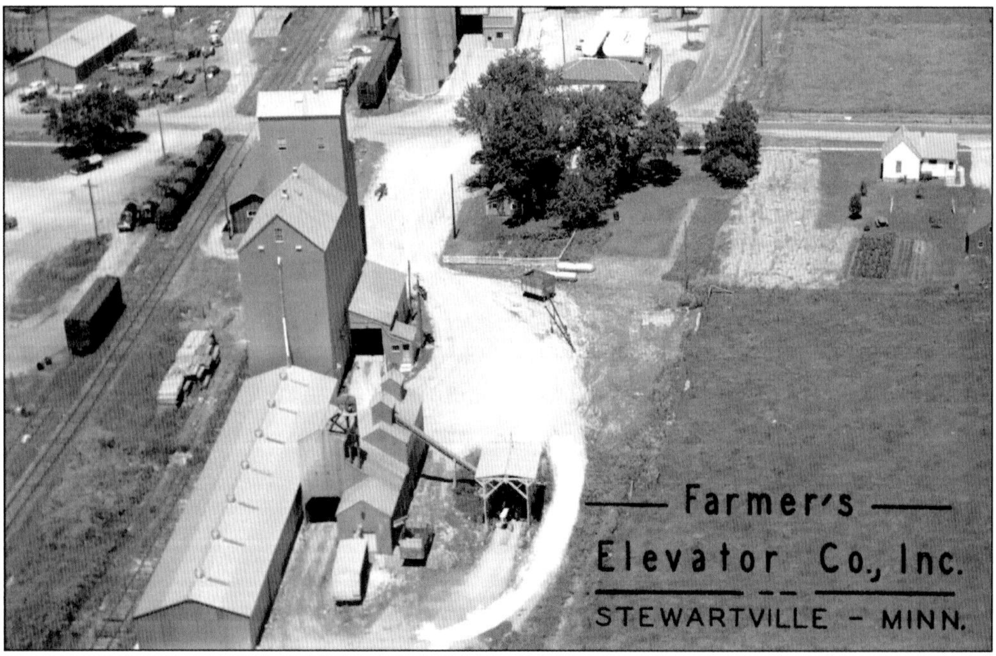

The Farmer's Elevator Company was founded and incorporated on October 15, 1908. The first manager was H. W. Schultze. Considerable building and remodeling has been done over the years. This firm manufactures feed under the trade name All American Feed and has modern machinery for the processing of feed, grains, and field seed. (Courtesy of All American Co-op.)

Seven

Historic Places

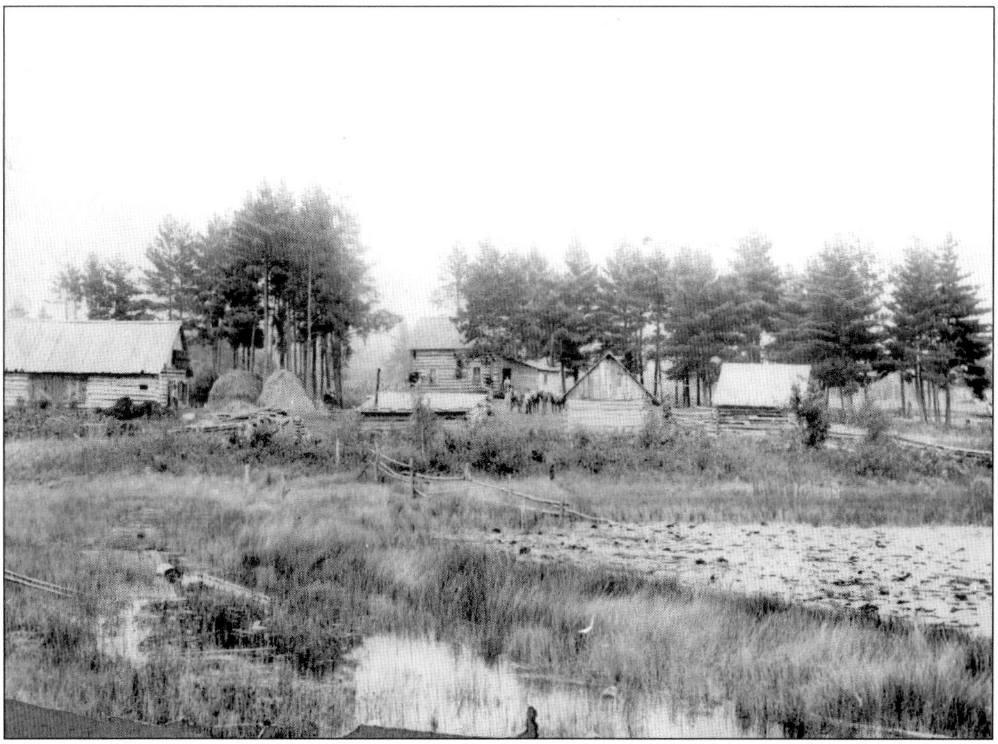

Eugene Wooldridge, son of one of the first five settlers of Stewartville, built the family home in 1878 at the corner of County Road 6 and Sixth Street SW. He married the youngest daughter of another early settler, Jabez Clemens. Current owners Ron and Shirley Carlson have faithfully restored the house to its original design. The house won the 2008 restoration/preservation award. (Courtesy of Shirley Carlson.)

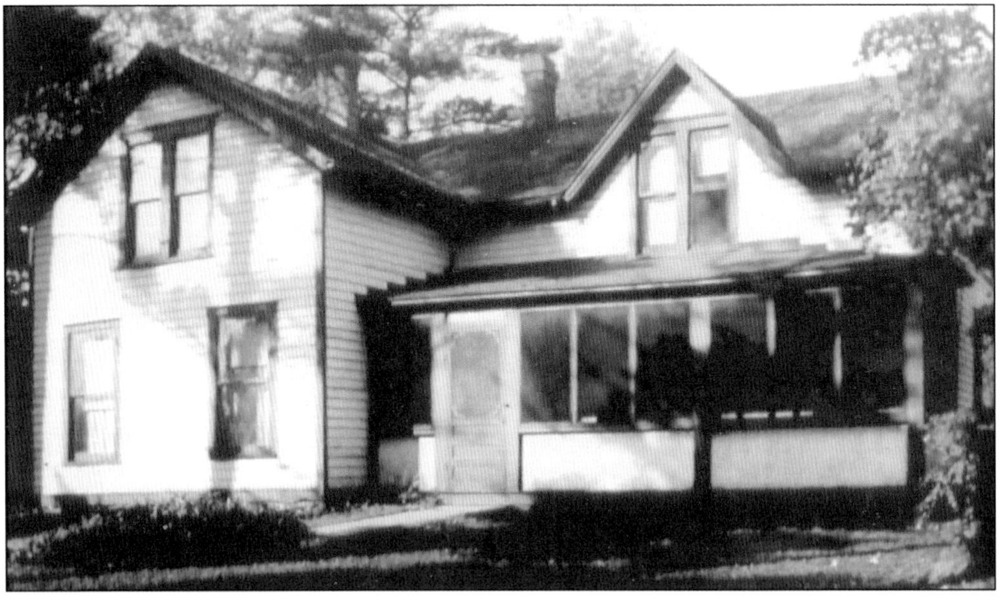

In 1863, Richard W. Sears was born in this house at 305 North Main Street. The last residents of the home were the Lins family. It has been the headquarters of the Stewartville Area Historical Society since 1993. The house museum holds treasures from the local area. (Courtesy of Dorothy Lins-Hanson.)

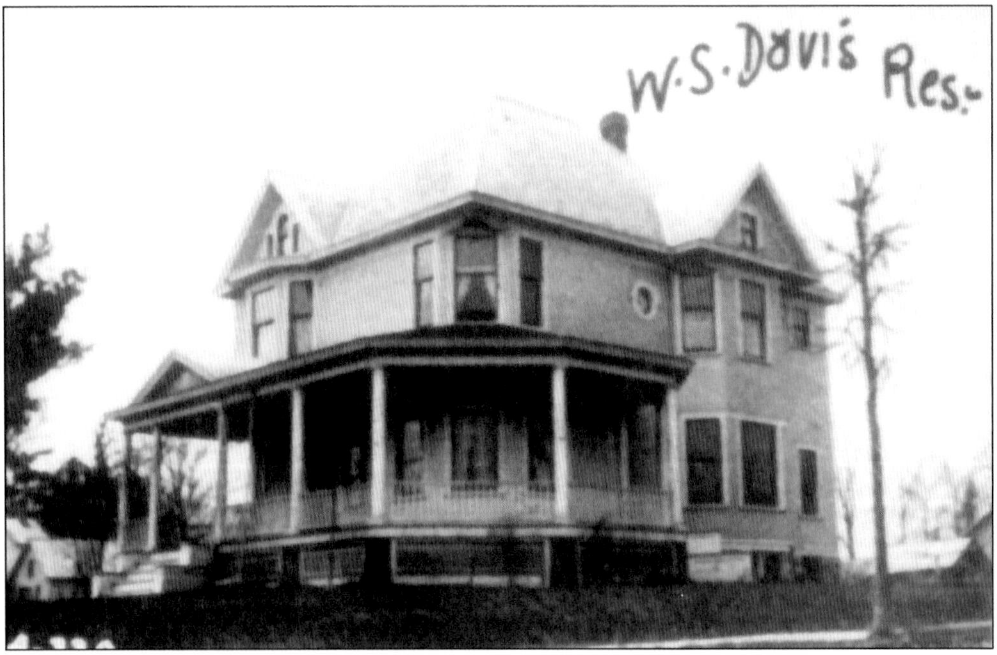

Built in 1905 by local merchant W. S. Davis, the former Winkels home at 309 North Main Street is a classic example of pre–World War I architecture that was favored by the affluent of that era. Its unusual house plan and beautiful interior suited large families, who liked to entertain. Current owners Joe and Jane Himmer use its interior as a perfect backdrop for their nifty gift shop, Home Sweet Home. The house won the 2002 restoration/preservation award. (Courtesy of the SAHS.)

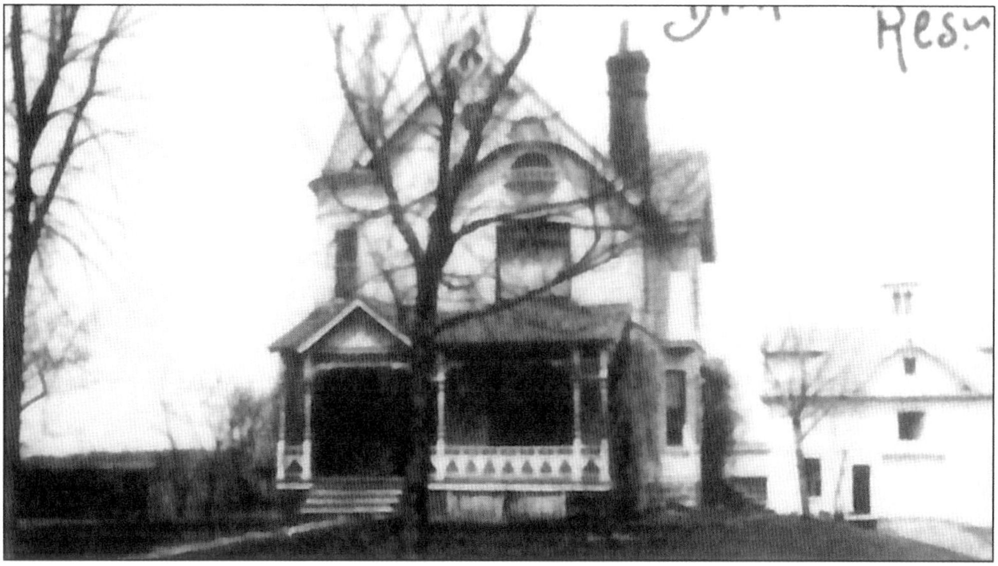

The first resident doctor of Stewartville was Dr. Edward Stoddard, who built this stately home in 1890 at 103 Lakeshore Drive, or the beginning of what is called Silk Stocking Road—if one could afford to buy silk stockings, one could afford a home along this street. The foundation stone was quarried from the Donahue quarry near Rochester. The total cost came to $6,000. It was of frame construction, 28 by 60 feet, and four stories including the basement. The next owner was Dr. Herman Russell, who began his local practice in 1899. He was a physician and surgeon for 24 years. (Courtesy of the SAHS.)

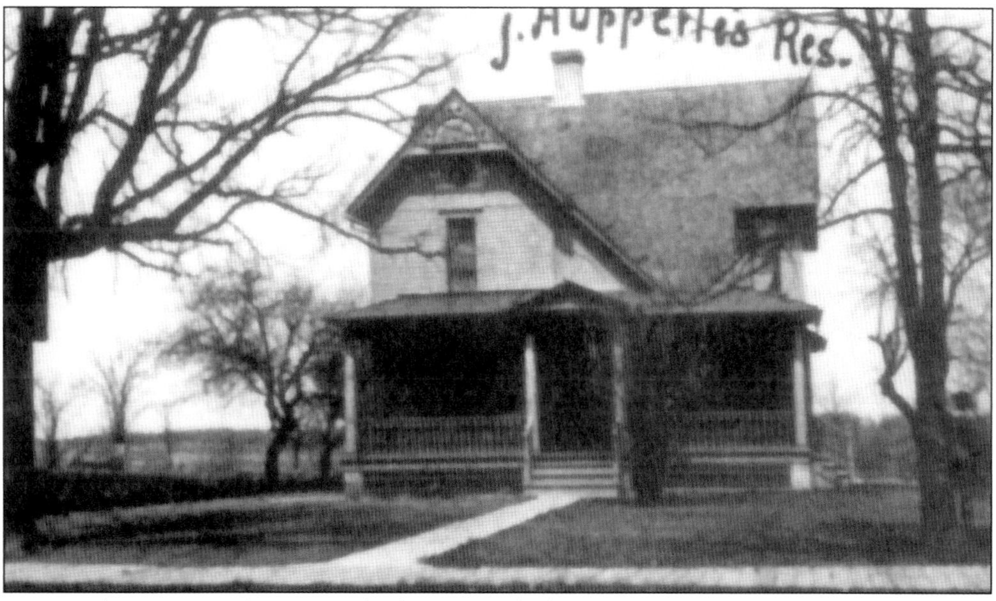

In 1888, this Victorian beauty was built at 105 Lakeshore Drive on land once owned by Charles Stewart. Its most recent owners purchased it in 1998 and shortly afterward began a major renovation of the house structure. The interior hardwood floors, plaster walls, woodwork, and beveled windows are conscientiously restored to the original state. It has beautiful scrollwork on the fan-shaped area above the windows plus an old hitching post out front. (Courtesy of the SAHS.)

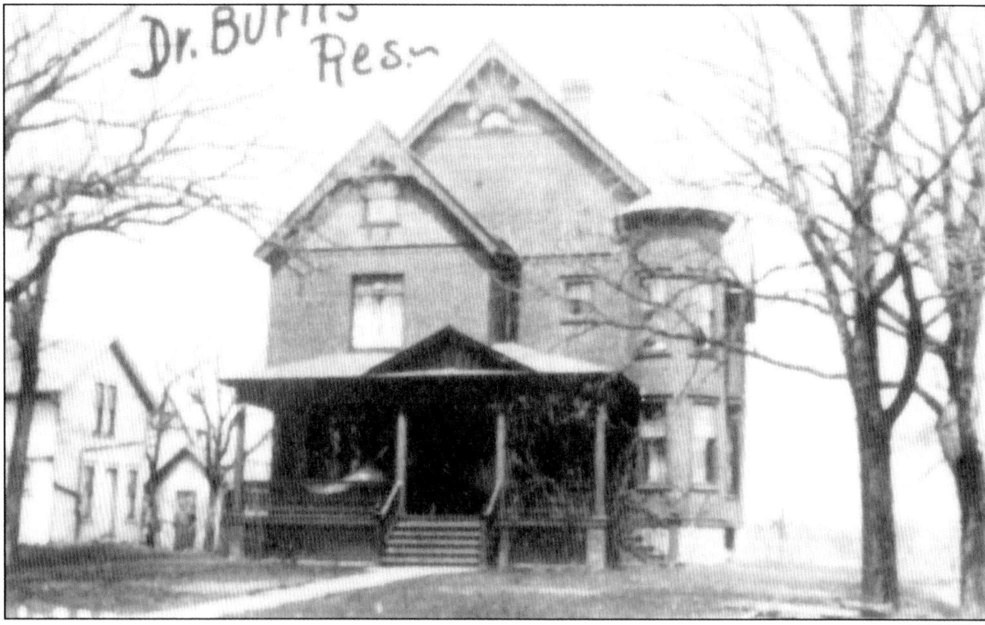

In 1901–1902, local physician Francis Burns and his wife, Mabel, built this home at 107 Lakeshore Drive. The present owner has lovingly preserved much of its original oak woodwork, brass hardware, and beveled glass. Exterior fishtail shingles, latticework, and molding define this residence as Queen Anne style. The home won the 1998 restoration/preservation award. (Courtesy of the SAHS.)

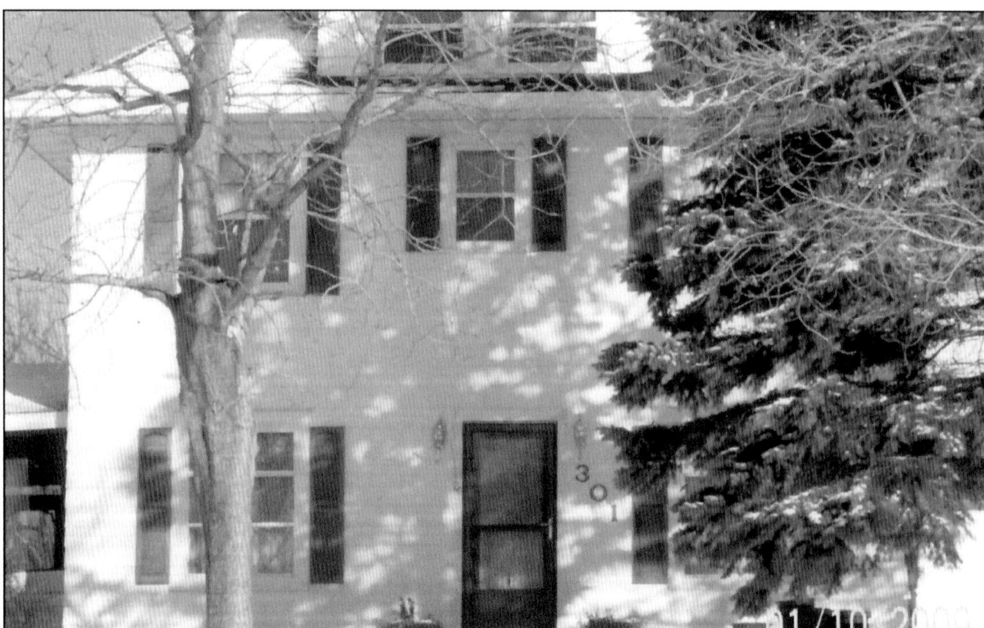

This historic home at 301 Lakeshore Drive was likely was built in 1909 by Truman and Luella Horton. The original land grant was acquired in 1859 by Stewartville's namesake and founder, Charles Stewart. (Courtesy of the SAHS.)

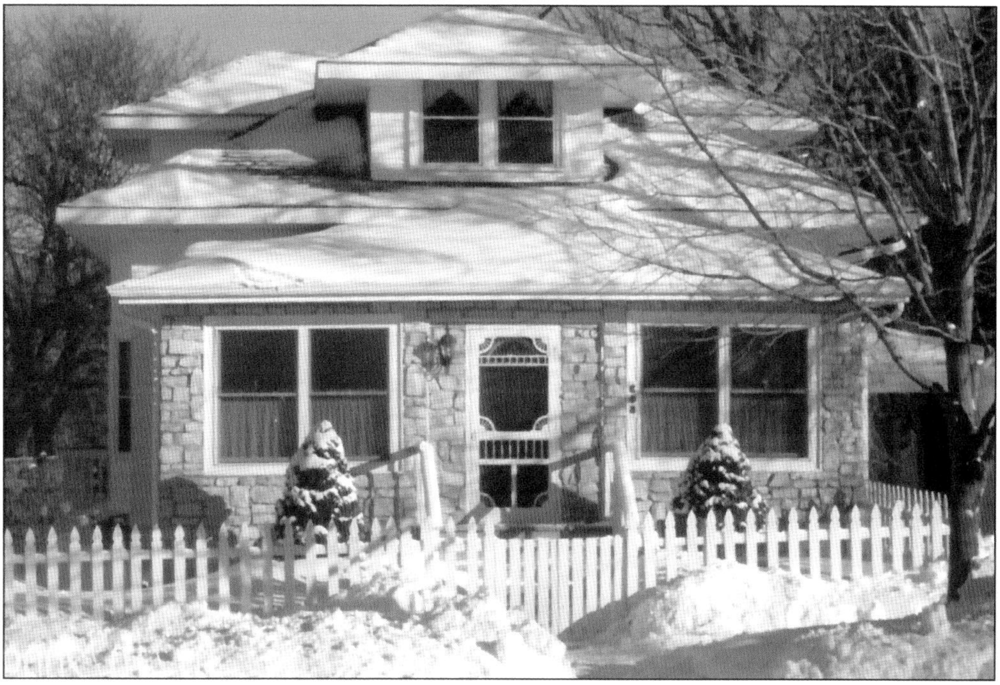

This cozy, prairie-style home at 305 Third Street NW was built in 1907 by Jackson Cussons on land purchased from city founder Charles Stewart. The house interior features birch woodwork and maple floors and leaded-glass windows that sparkle in the sunlight with a view of the old Cussons mill, formerly the Stewart mill, site across the street. (Courtesy of the SAHS.)

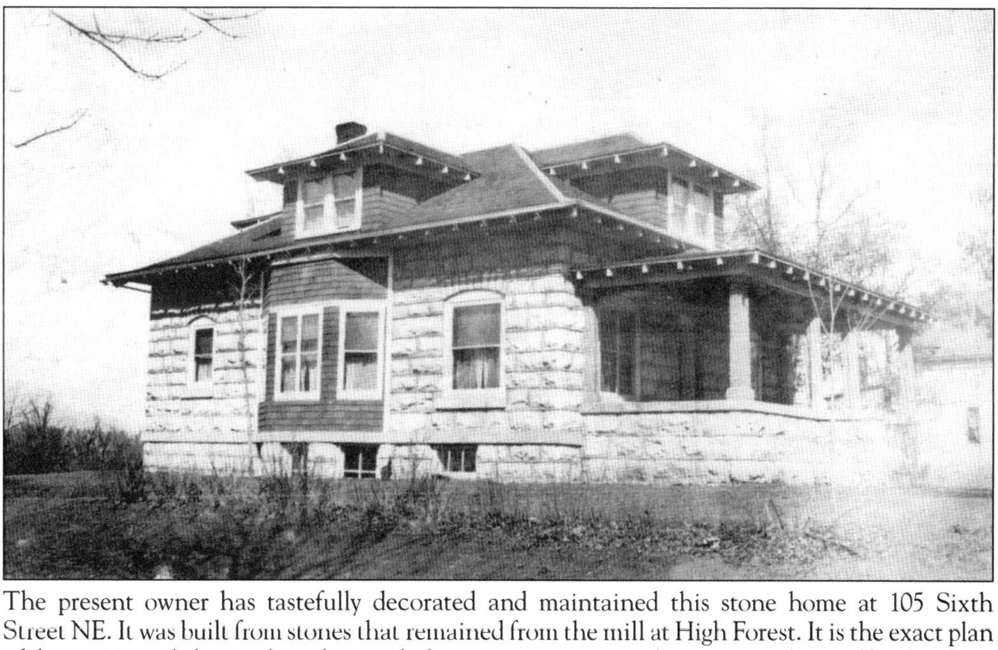

The present owner has tastefully decorated and maintained this stone home at 105 Sixth Street NE. It was built from stones that remained from the mill at High Forest. It is the exact plan of the prairie-style home above but made from stone versus wood. Mary Hoaglan and her husband were the original owners of the home, built in 1919. (Courtesy of the Hersch Hoaglan family.)

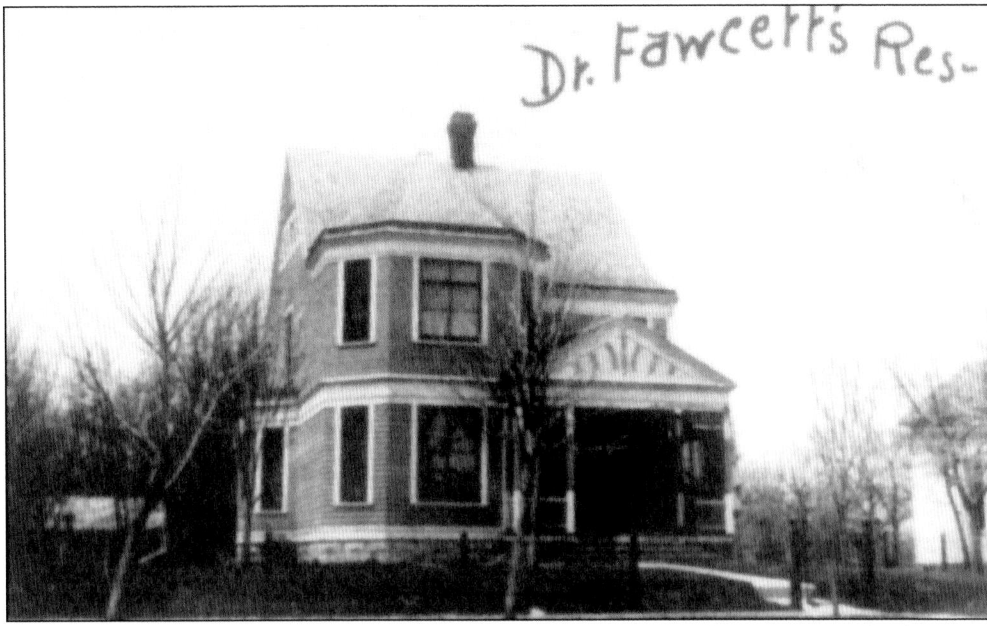

Built in 1898 by prominent physician C. E. Fawcett, this Victorian house at 301 Third Avenue NW stands on the site of Stewartville's oldest businesses—a mercantile store and post office established by W. E. Smith in 1878. It was restored by Rusty and Cheri Korte in 2000 and now is undergoing repairs by its present owner. The home won the 2001 restoration/preservation award. (Courtesy of the SAHS.)

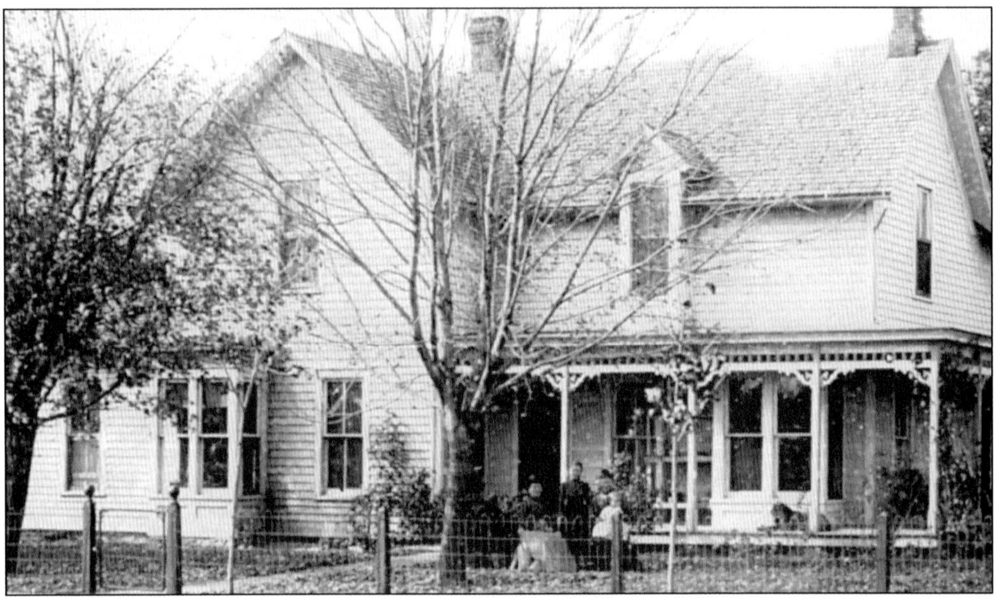

W. E. Smith, one of Stewartville's first merchants and postmaster, built the residence at 201 Third Avenue NW, the original spacious main street of the town. It was the residence of P. H. Griffin along with the Griffin Funeral Home. Additions and changes accommodated the growing family of P H. Griffin's daughter and her husband. A love of antiques and gardening make this a beautiful home. The home won the 2007 restoration/preservation award. (Courtesy of the Gray family.)

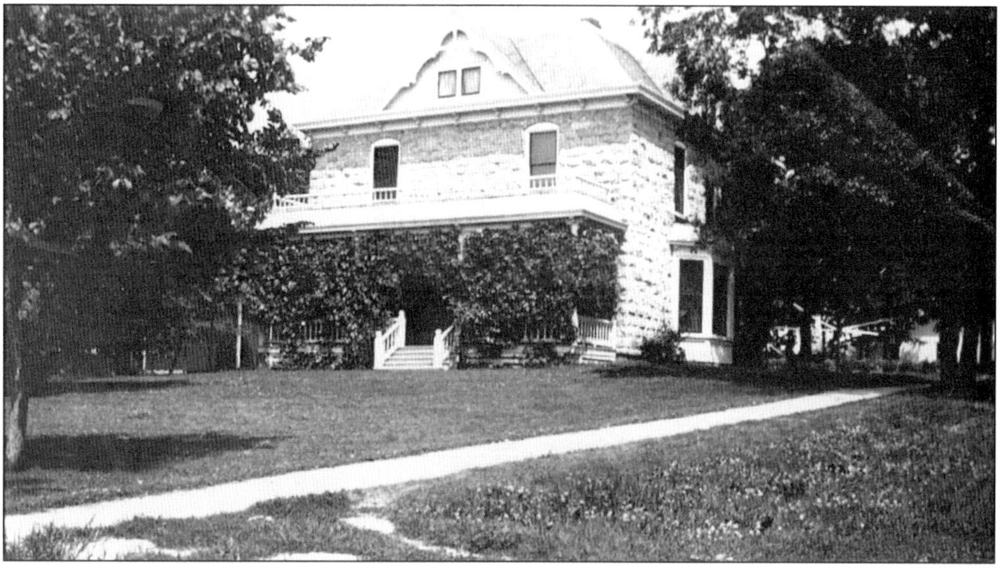

In 1898, Herb Robbins built this stately stone home at 600 North Main Street, the first house built in his Riverside Addition. It was part of the northeast Stewartville quarter section purchased by Reuben Austin, one of the original settlers. Fred Birum did a major restoration in the 1990s. The home won the 1999 restoration/preservation award. (Courtesy of the Hersh Hoaglan family.)

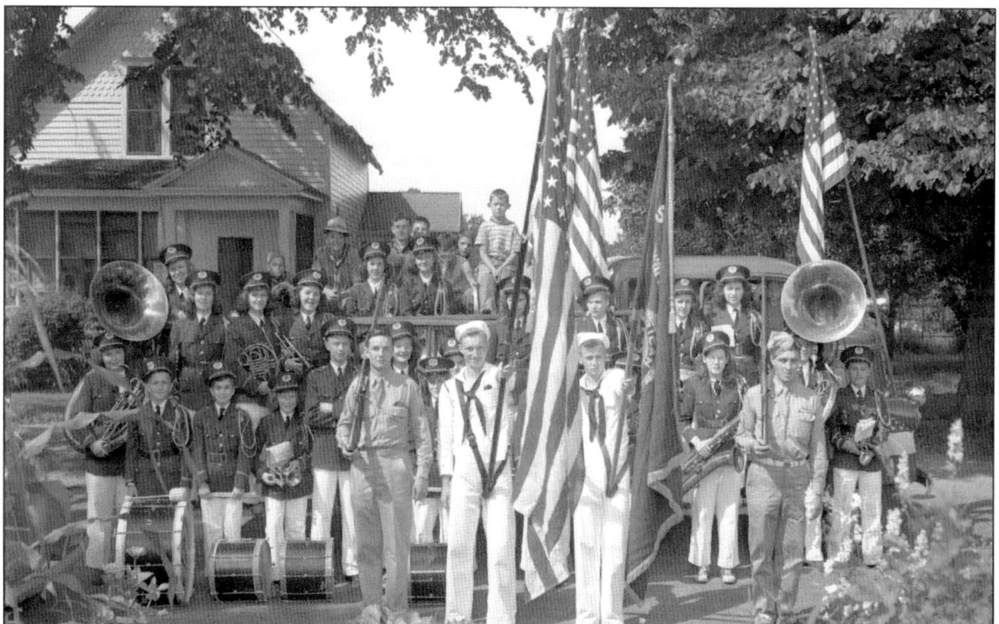

Mrs. Sullivan was dying, and her three sons, who were in the service, were able to come home for a visit. This photograph was taken celebrating the end of World War II, on August 15, 1945. The Stewartville High School band stands in front of the house. Pictured are Edward Egen, Philip Chamberlain, Thomas Kennedy, Leo Hanf, William Mundstock, Donald House, Phyllis Currier, Gerald Kennedy, Janet Beach, Marty McNeal, Mary Lee Wilson, Robert Dixon, Gerri Griffin, Kate McNeal, Phyllis House, Gwendolyn Vrieze, Mary Ann Johnson, Marilyn Lyman, Richard Sullivan, LeRoy Swigman, Mary Ann Kerich, and Patricia Griffin. (Courtesy of the OCHS.)

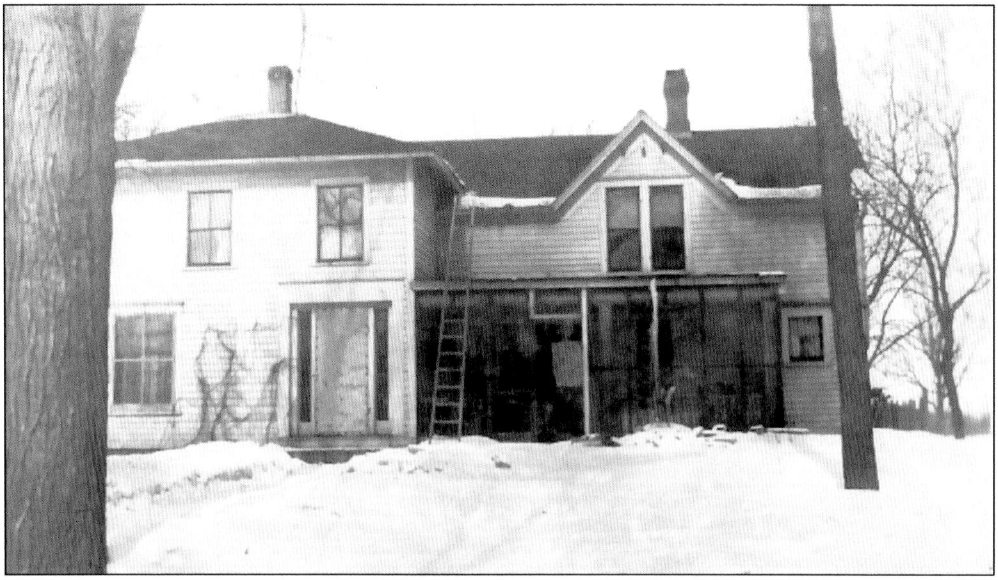

Charles Stewart built a house for his family a short distance from the end of the first main street, which is now Third Street NW. This was close by the Stewart mill site, which was at the head of the thoroughfare. Not long after, Stewart had the misfortune of losing his second wife. Daughter Helen, age 18, took over as head of a busy household. In 1878, Charles married for a third time to a widow named Annie Smith. (Courtesy of Katherine Skyhawk.)

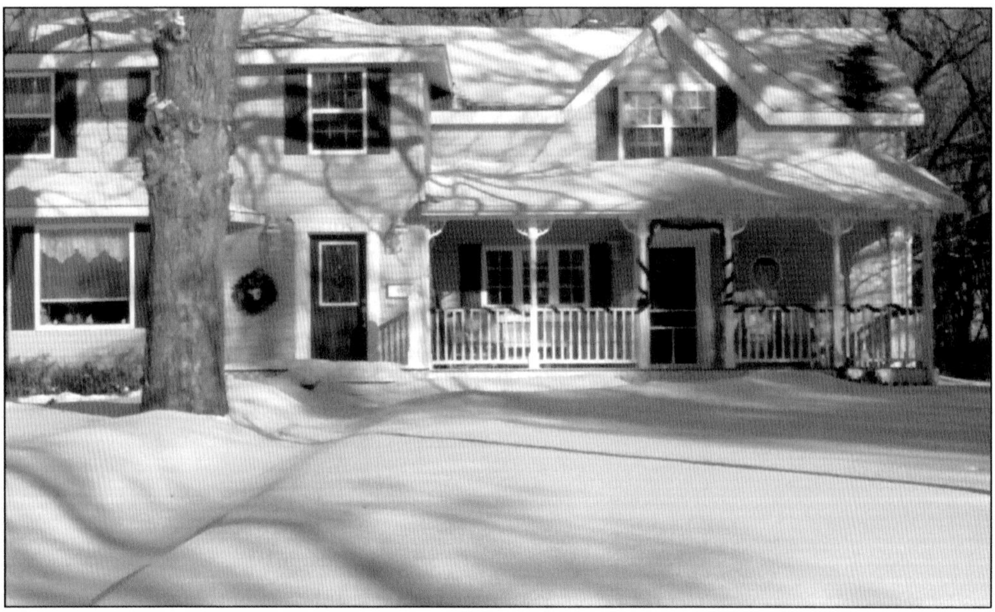

After many owners, various restructurings, and near demolition, the Stewart home was purchased and renovated by the Nelson family of rural Stewartville. Area residents were curious to see how the house they remembered as the Used Abit shop would look, so the Nelsons opened it for the public in May 2003. (Courtesy of the SAHS.)

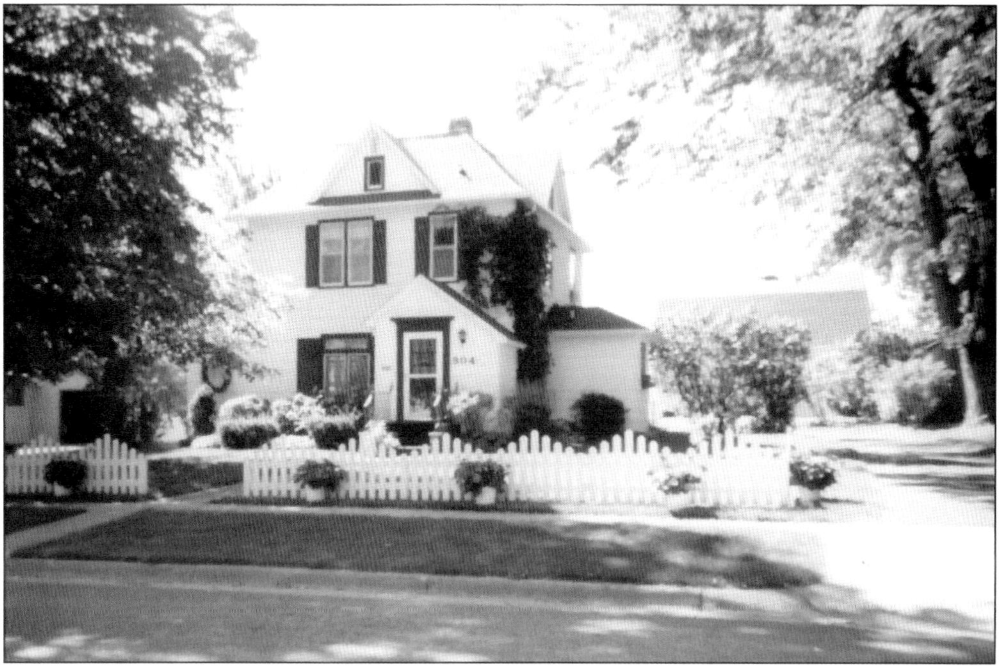

For almost 80 years, the Benedict house had stood as the home longest occupied by one family in Stewartville. Daughters Esther and Ida were its last family occupants. The home won the 2006 restoration/preservation award. (Courtesy of the SAHS.)

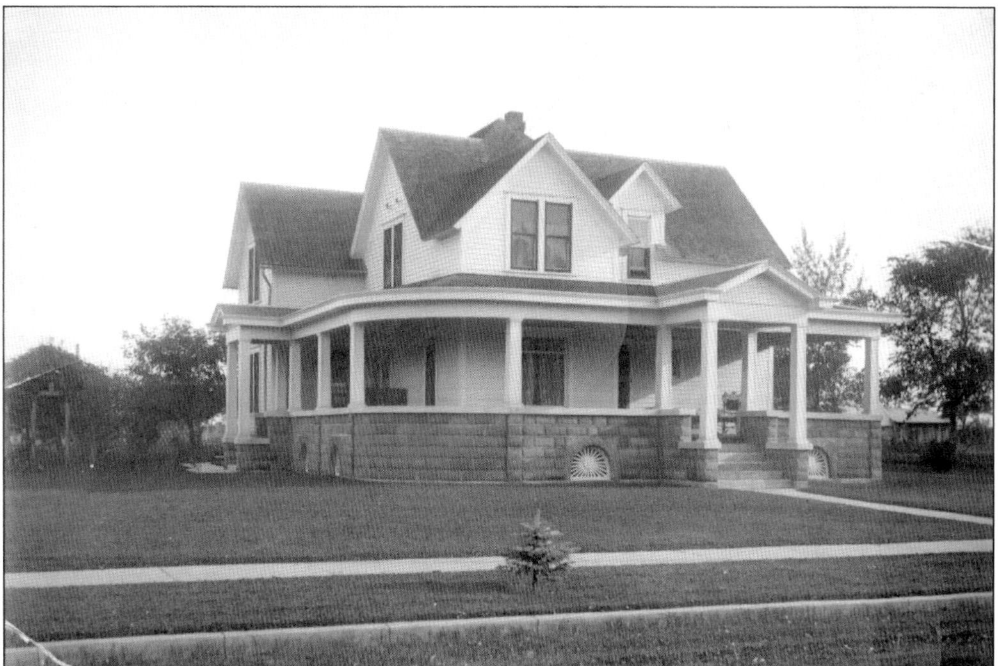

In 1908, Charles Cattle, owner of a local lumberyard and hardware store, built the house at his lumberyard and had it hauled to its location at 210 Third Street SW. Past and present owners have done major restoration to the home. (Courtesy of Judy Hanson.)

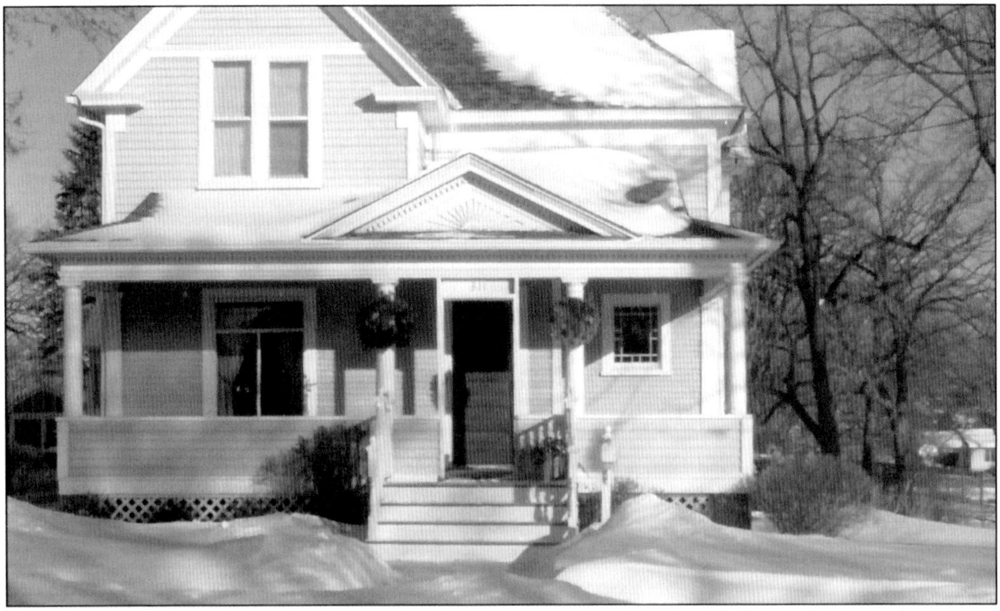

Built in 1894, the residence at 311 Second Street SW is one of the oldest residences in Stewartville and just west of Central Elementary School. The front porch is typical of that era and provides much comfort and shade during the hot summers, the Victorian equivalent of present-day air-conditioning. The oldest part of this home features the original woodwork, hard-pine flooring, and a fireplace in the foyer. (Courtesy of the SAHS.)

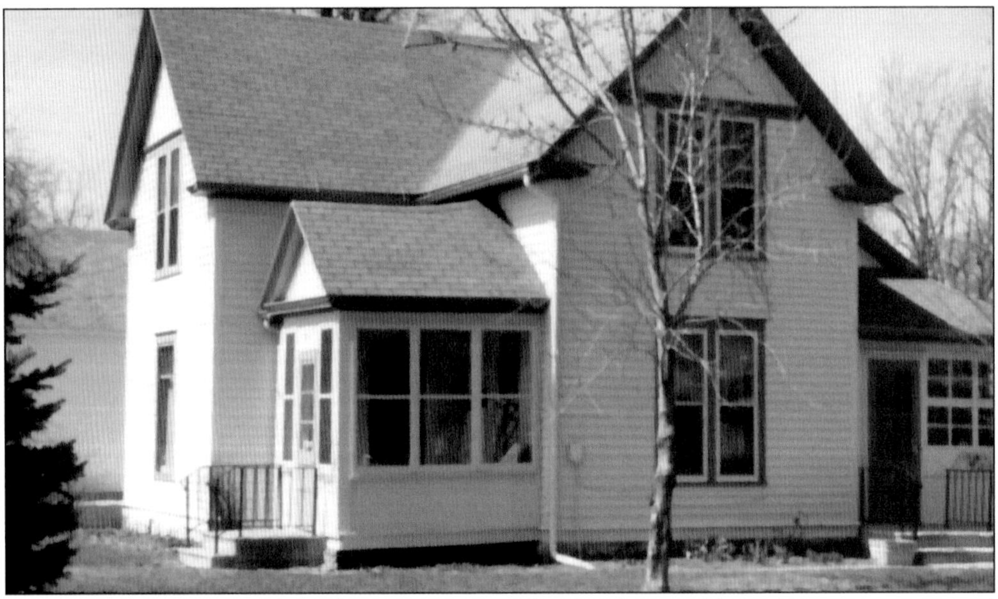

In 1914, this home was built by the Henry Bonner family. The wood framed house was occupied next by his daughter, LePearl Bonner, who was a former teacher and principal in Stewartville. After LePearl died, Carol King purchased the home and made extensive renovations. The home won the 1996 restoration/preservation award. This home was the start of the historical society's awarding a home owner or business owner a restoration/preservation award. (Courtesy of the SAHS.)

The Congregational church in Stewartville dates back to March 25, 1880, when Rev. E. P. Crane of High Forest assisted in organizing a Congregational society here. In 1895, the congregation purchased a lot from William R. Tubbs and a church building was erected. (Courtesy of the SAHS.)

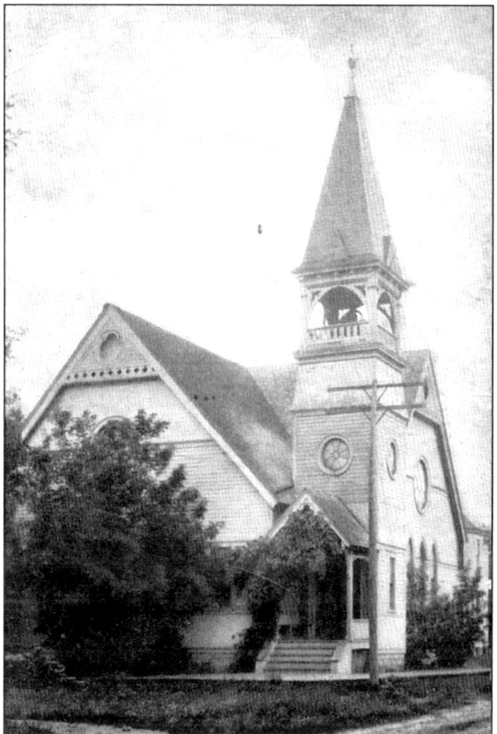

CONGREGATIONAL CHURCH, STEWARTVILLE, MINN.

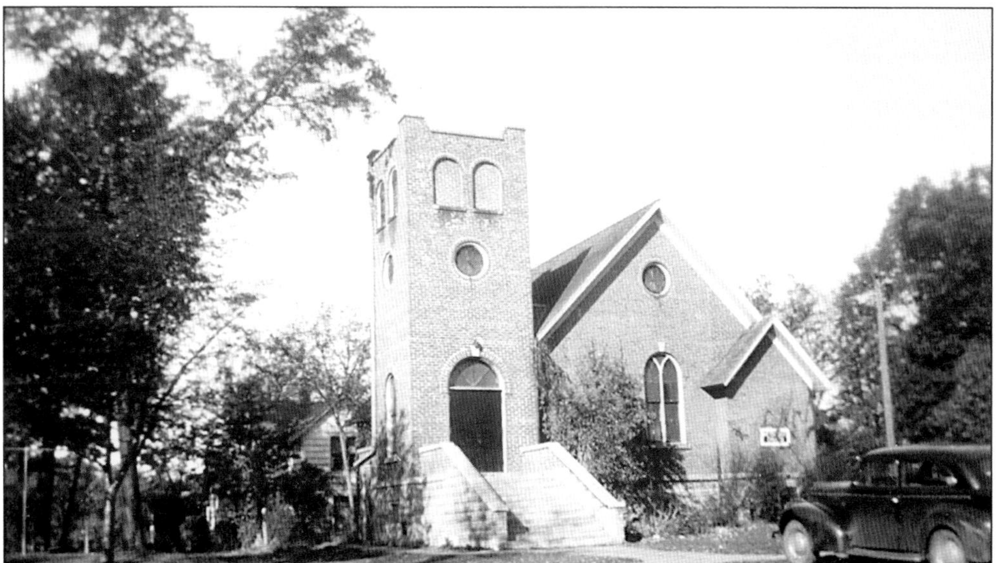

In 1870, Charles Stewart and Rev. George Ainsle, with the assistance of several others and the aid of missionary money, built the Presbyterian church. All the materials were brought from Rochester. Farmers hauling grain to market would bring back brick and lumber as the whole community helped to build the church. E. S. Wooldridge and Fred Robbins, two trustees of the Methodist church, bought the brick church from the Presbyterians. It was remodeled and a new entrance and belfry were built. (Courtesy of the SAHS.)

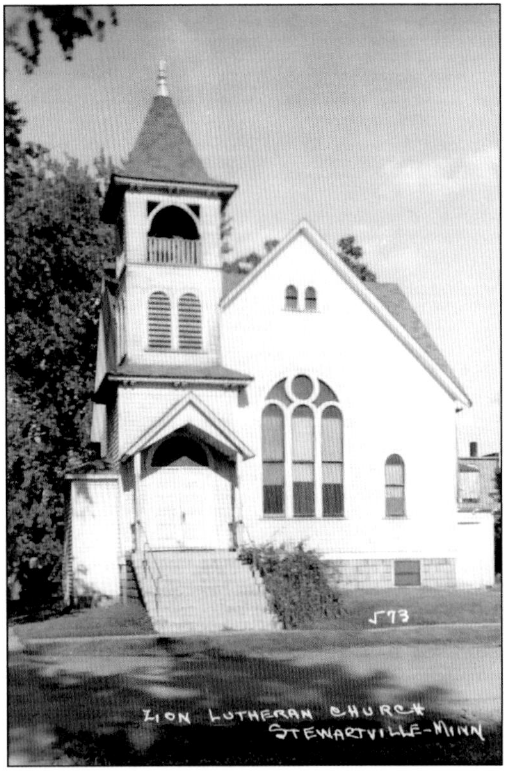

The Zion Evangelical Lutheran Church (locally referred to as the Norwegian church) originated in 1896 when Rev. J. A. Thorson of Rock Dell came to Stewartville twice a month on Sunday evenings. In 1915, funds were raised to build a church. It was dedicated on June 25, 1916. (Courtesy of the SAHS.)

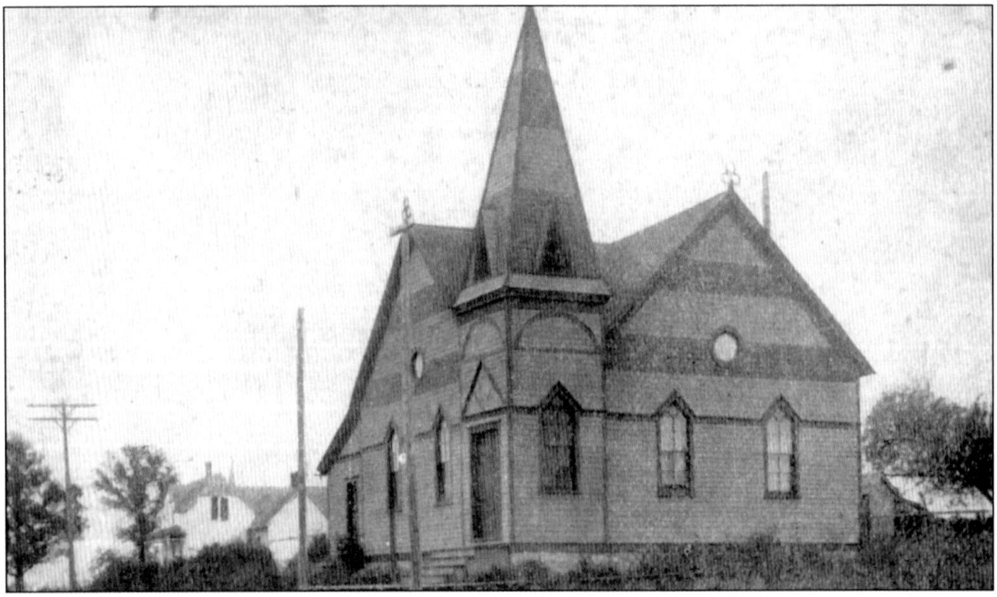

Early in the life of Stewartville, the first Methodist church was projected and built under great difficulties. The promoters of the plan were men not easily daunted by obstacles. On March 18, 1891, the church building was begun. The organizers were so anxious to occupy their church that it was dedicated without seats, and for several weeks rough board seats were used. The Methodists finally sold their church in the east part of town to St. John's Lutheran Church. (Courtesy of the SAHS.)

St. John's Lutheran Church was founded by Rev. J. C. S. Martin in 1892. In 1900, the congregation purchased the wood frame church on the east side of town. It was dedicated on July 1, 1900. Services were given in both German and English. (Courtesy of the SAHS.)

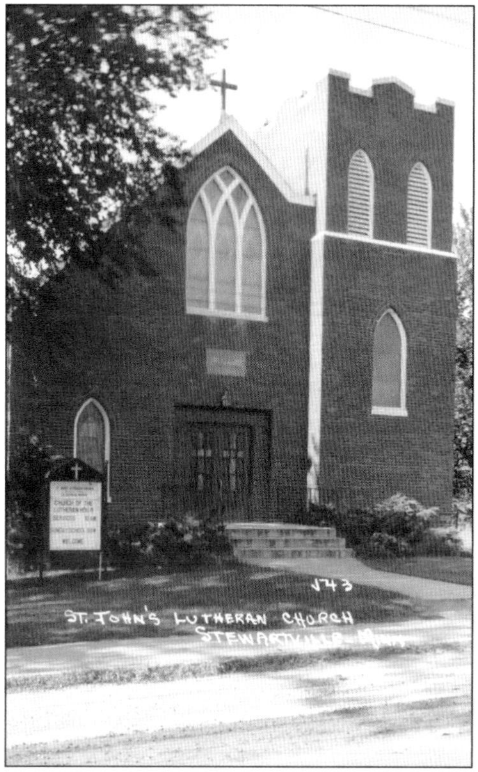

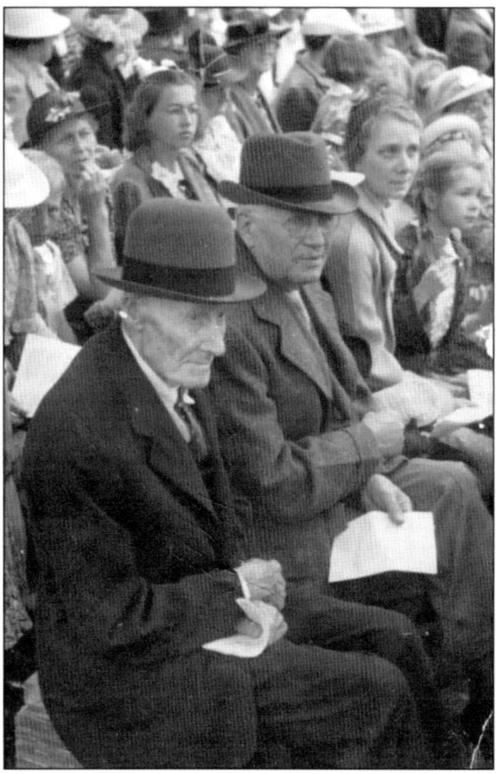

Grandpa Wegenke and Fred Stoltenberg, along with other families, donated the money for art glass windows in the church. (Courtesy of Ardis Copple.)

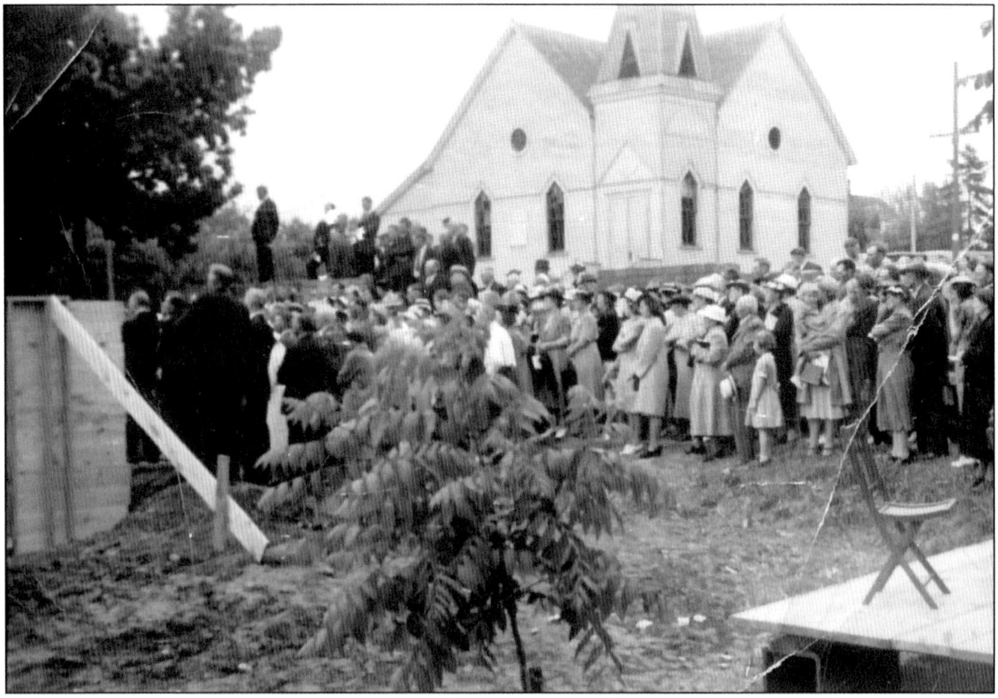

The cornerstone of the new church was laid on June 23, 1940. (Courtesy of Ardis Copple.)

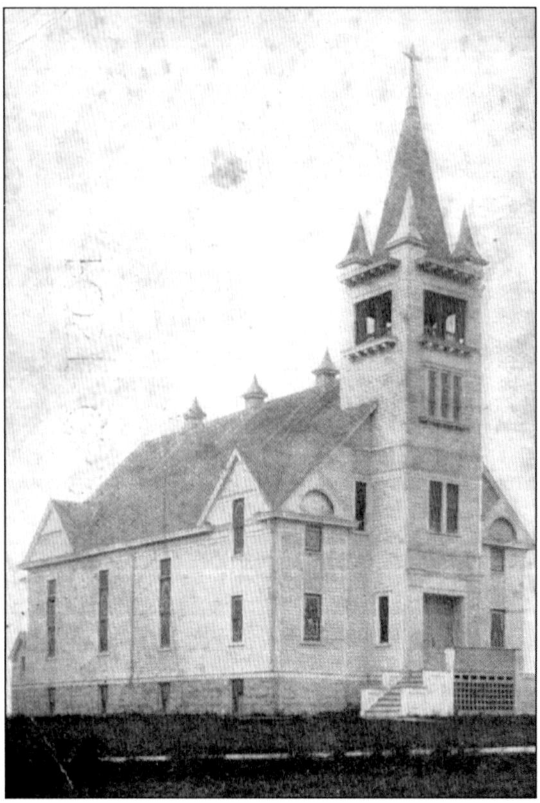

The beginning of the St. Bernard's congregation in Stewartville was closely associated with the formation and development of the St. Bridget's church at Simpson. On May 11, 1898, the church was dedicated. Fr. P. M. McTeague was the first resident priest and remained from 1916 to 1923. (Courtesy of the SAHS.)

Eight

PEOPLE

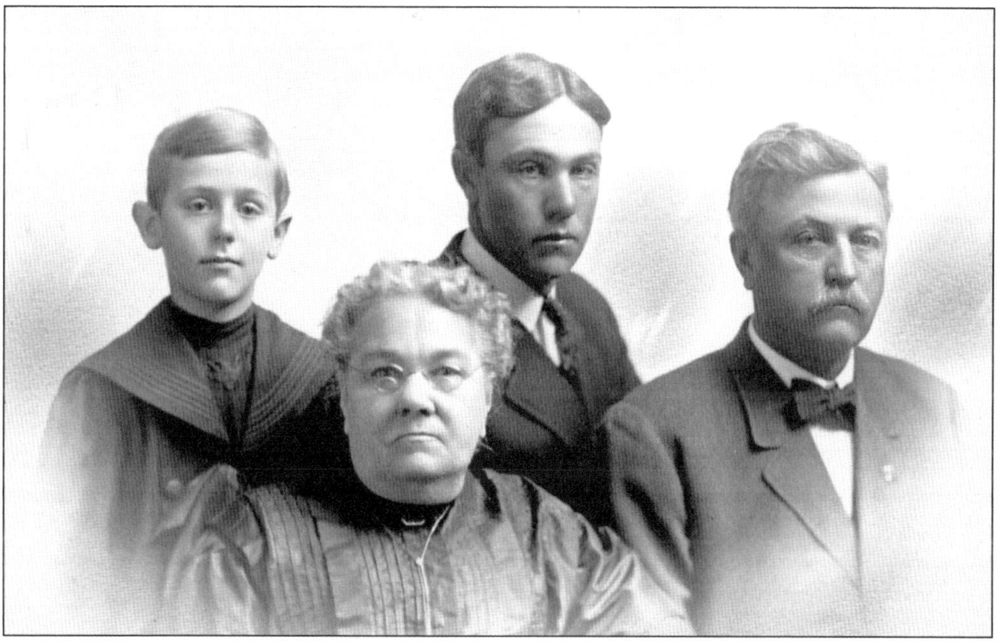

Seen here in 1912 is a four-generation photograph of the Siman family: Ann (Smart) Siman, F. Avery Tews (with bow tie), G. J. Thompson, and great-great-grandson Gersham Thompson. Ann (Smart) Siman, eldest in the four-generation picture, was born on January 20, 1839, at Waukesa, Wisconsin, to a family of nine children. She married John Siman in 1861. They left North Prairie, Wisconsin, with two pairs of horses and two schooners, heading for Fairmont where John had a homestead claim. After arriving, they found it had been jumped, so he traded two horses for oxen, one calf, and $100. John then received a 160-acre claim by Lone Tree Lake where they lived for the next five years. He then traded his farm for a saw- and gristmill near Winnebago, eventually coming to Stewartville in 1900. Ann owned one of the first sewing machines. She later became Stewartville's oldest resident. (Courtesy of the SAHS.)

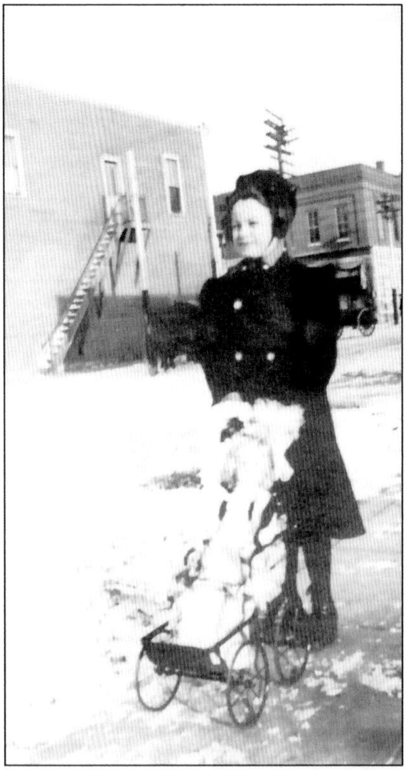

Helen (Tews) Hagen lived in Stewartville her entire life. Her parents owned and operated the Tews Hotel for 47 years. She is pictured with her 1930s Armand Marseilles doll, in the doll buggy, which is displayed at the Stewartville Area Historical Society museum. The doll is still in its original clothing. Hagen donated several thousand items to the society's archives. (Courtesy of the SAHS.)

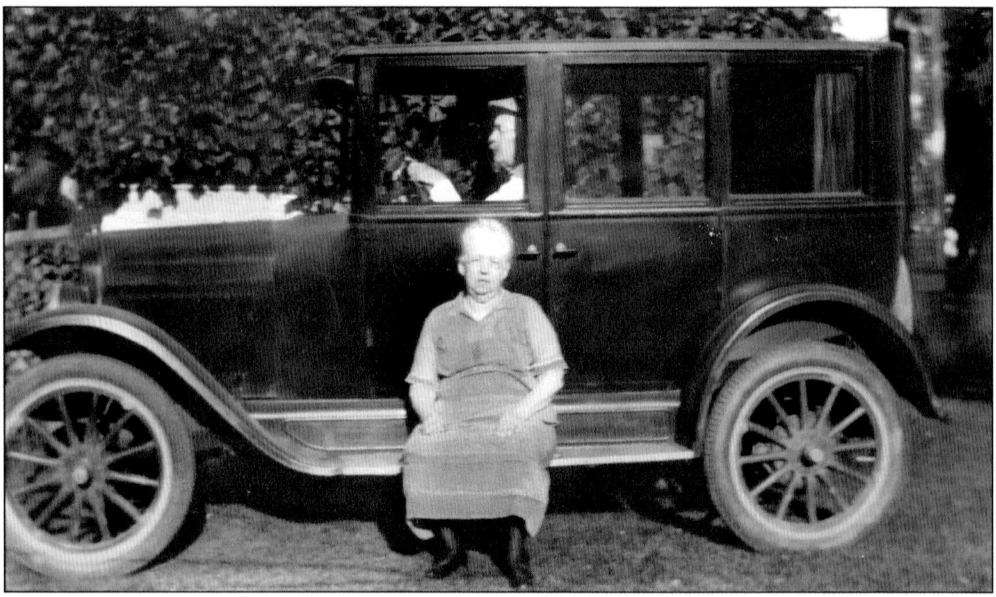

Henry Ringey's parents were of French descent, originally coming from Canada to Champlain, New York. Deciding to come west, they traveled by boat on the Great Lakes to Milwaukee, by train to Prairie du Chien, Wisconsin, and by boat to LaCrosse. They settled on a farm four miles northwest of Stewartville. A pair of twins, Henry and Hariett, were born. Henry was an area resident for 48 years. He is pictured seated at the wheel of his car with Anna Ringey seated on the running board. (Courtesy of the SAHS.)

Ruth Ringey is pictured in her graduation dress, which is on display at the Stewartville Area Historical Society museum. She lived next door to the Sears house and taught school from 1921 to 1924. She later married Dr. Halbert Christofferson from Racine. She was a member of the first library board appointed in 1938. (Courtesy of the SAHS.)

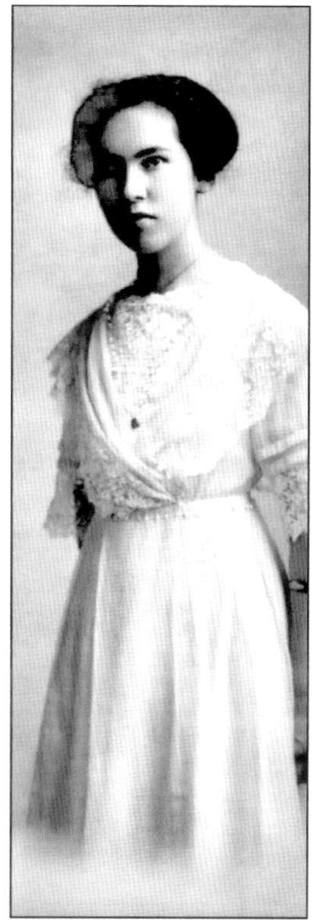

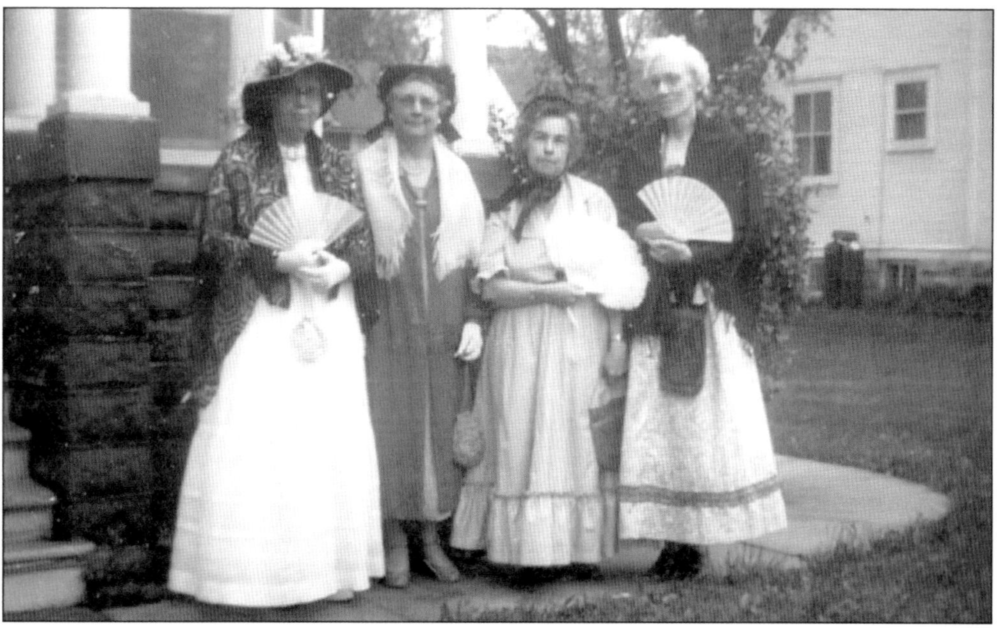

On January 10, 1957, a group of citizens interested in the civic, social, and community welfare of Stewartville met at the community building to lay the groundwork for the celebration of the community's centennial year of continued growth and prosperity. Pictured are, from left to right, LePearl Bonner, unidentified, Ruth (Ringey) Christofferson, and Gladys Owen at the 1957 centennial tea. (Courtesy of the SAHS.)

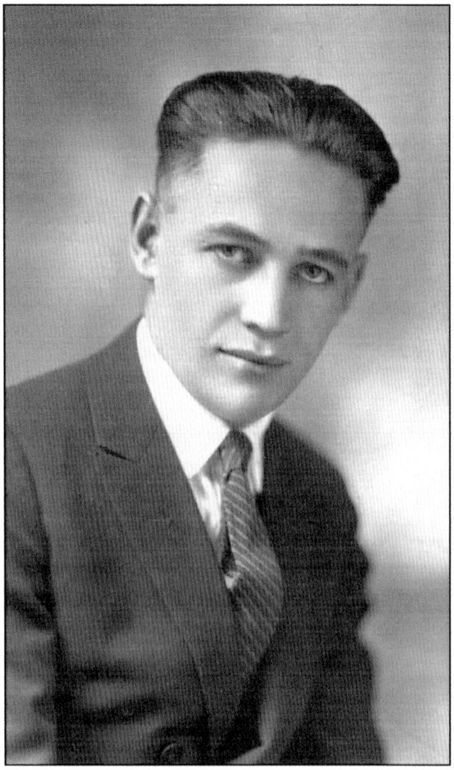

A. O. Hagen was born in Kasson on August 14, 1900, the son of Christian and Carrie Hagen. He obtained his early education in the schools of Kasson and graduated from high school in 1918. He entered the dental college of the University of Minnesota, from which he received his degree in dentistry on June 20, 1923. He opened his practice in Stewartville the same year. Hagen married Helen Tews on August 10, 1929. (Courtesy of the SAHS.)

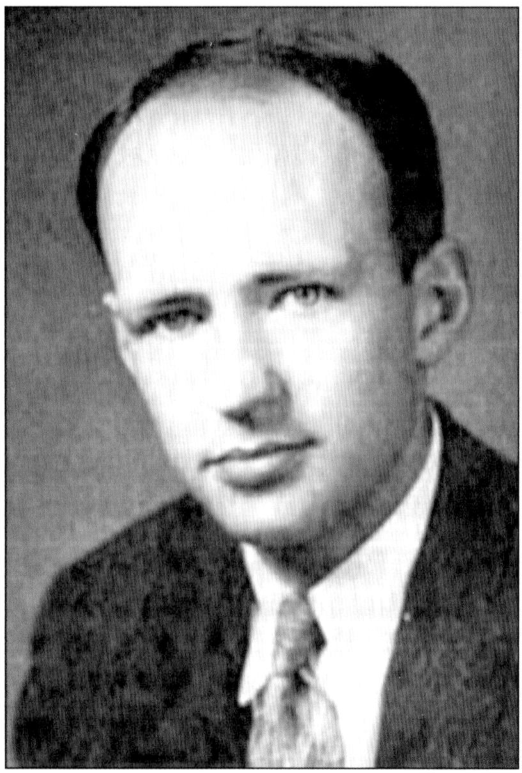

Dr. Alden Risser was born in St. Paul on May 14, 1912, the son of Gustave and Alice Risser. From 1929 to 1931, he received premedical training at the University of Minnesota and in 1935 graduated from the medical school. He served his internship at Miller Hospital in St. Paul. On October 9, 1937, Risser married Marion E. Evans of Minneapolis, and they raised a family of four children: Marjorie, Larry, Daniel, and David. (Courtesy of the SAHS.)

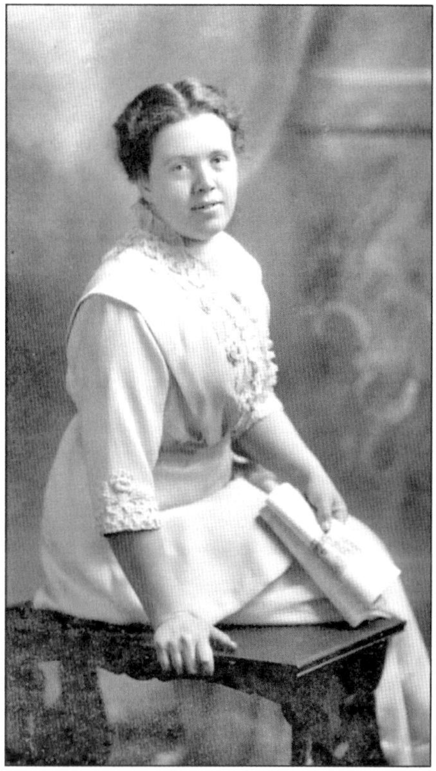

LePearl Bonner, a native of the area, was born on July 13, 1891, and graduated from Stewartville High School in June 1909 with the highest rank in her class. She taught in the rural schools of the Stewartville area from 1909 to 1913 and then attended college for a year, resuming her teaching in 1914. Another summer session of education took her to Winona Normal School, graduating in August 1919. Bonner went on to graduate from the University of Minnesota summer session with a bachelor's of science degree with distinction on July 28, 1927. She then became a high school principal in that year and was an educator in the Stewartville schools for 43 years. She was honored at a special recognition day ceremony on October 24, 1953. A great many of her loyal friends and former students gave her special honors for her long and faithful service as a teacher in local schools. Bonner died on December 16, 1986. She had an elementary school named after her. (Courtesy of the SAHS.)

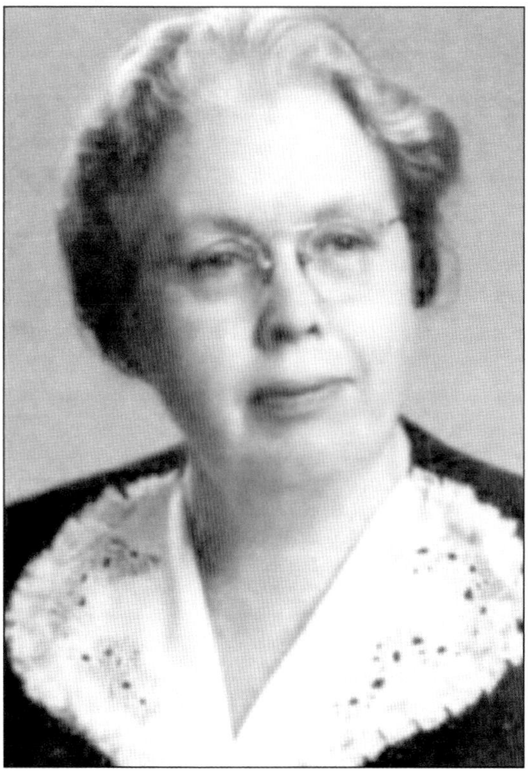

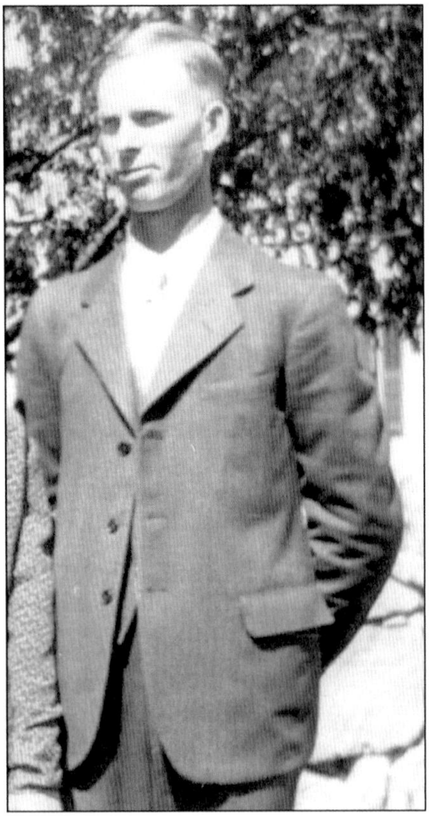

For more than 20 years, Herb Dodd herded his cattle down Main Street in Stewartville to and from the pasture on the south edge of town. This continued during the time of busy traffic on Highway 63 in the mid-1950s. In 1936, Dodd was seriously gored by an enraged bull and was saved from possible death by his two pet dogs who drove the animal off. Dodd was married to Avis Tubbs, who was born on November 21, 1904, and died on May 9, 1972. Herb died on June 17, 1968. (Courtesy of George Beach.)

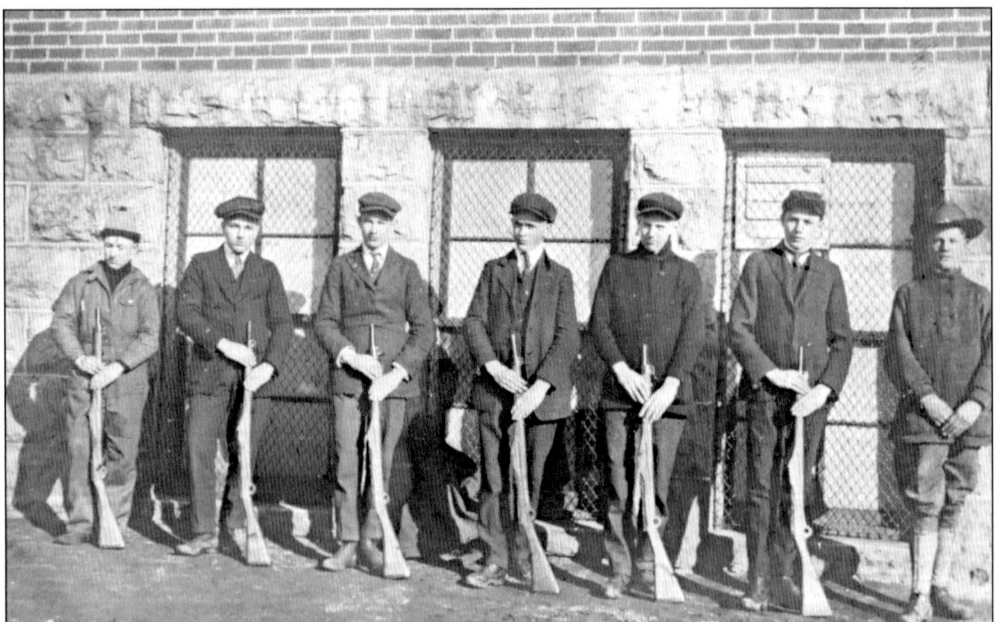

From left to right, hunters Harvey Rabine, Don Fawcell, Howard Joyce, John Burton, Lloyd Benedict, Ralph Towey, and Lyle Russell are seen here. Burton became a doctor and was later killed in an automobile accident. (Courtesy of the Gray family.)

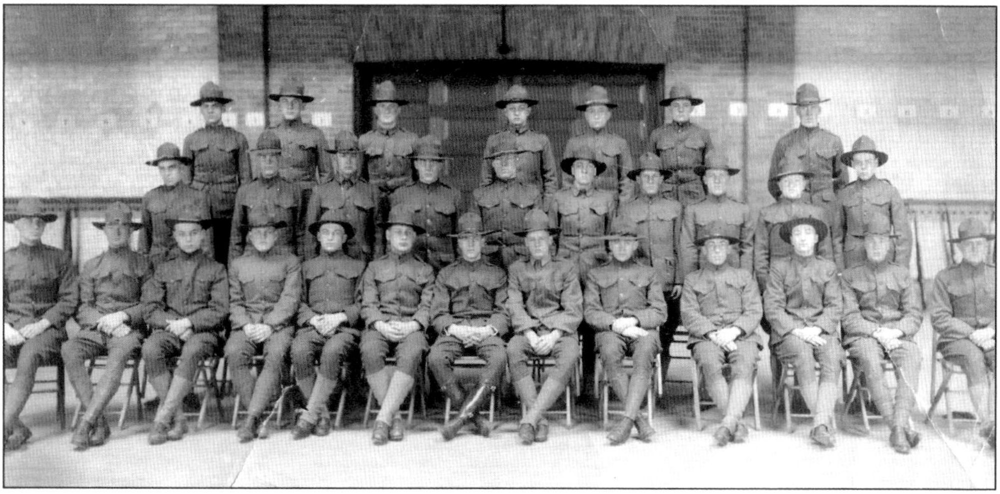

On April 6, 1917, the United States entered World War I. Fifteen days later, on April 21, 1917, seven young men from Stewartville answered the call of their country. The American Legion is a national organization of the American veterans of world wars. The local post was named in honor of Ivan Stringer, the first Stewartville boy to die on a World War I battlefield. (Courtesy of the SAHS.)

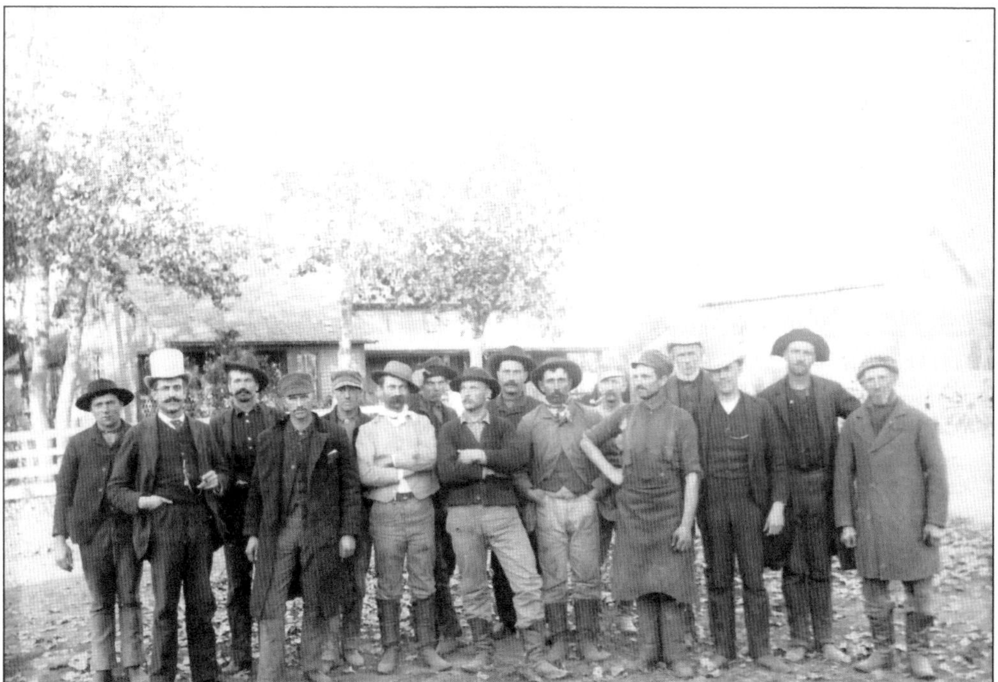

The above is a photograph of a company of Stewartville citizens taken in 1888. From left to right are Rolla Parks, W. E. Smith, Dick O'Connor, F. E. Dean, Gus Griesdale, Al Tichenor, Clad Munson, Al Howard, ? Kiester, Charles Lenton, T. B. Horton, James J. Kelly, ? Stevens, B. W. Tuttle, William O'Connor, and ? Grimm. (Courtesy of the SAHS.)

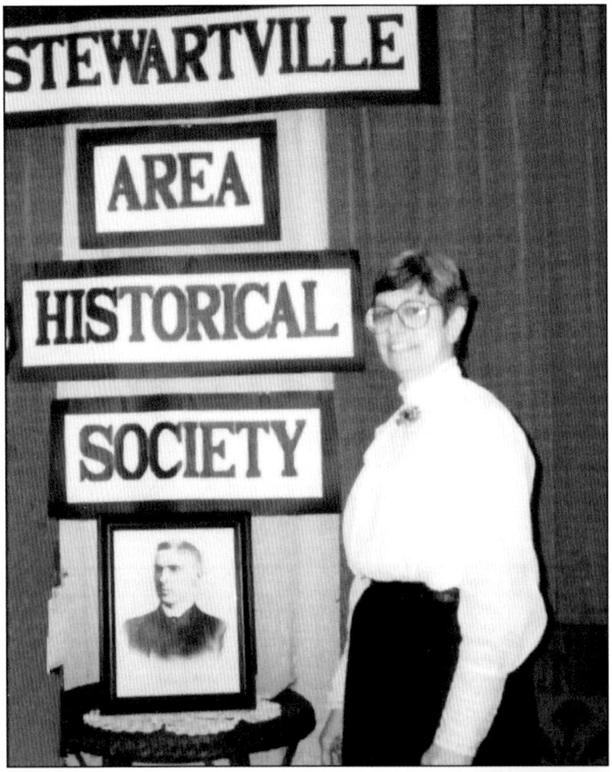

Carol King was born on December 19, 1933, in Fillmore County about a mile from the farm where her great-grandparents homesteaded in 1854. She was the fourth child of six. She attended college in Winona and was employed as a teacher in several states, including Hawaii. She was married and had two daughters. Eventually she found her way back to Stewartville and was instrumental in getting the historical society organized here. King was a very determined person, and through hard work, networking in the community, and sweat equity, her dream became a reality. She served as president of the historical society until her death at age 65. She had battled cancer for years and was an inspiration to all who knew her. (Courtesy of the SAHS.)

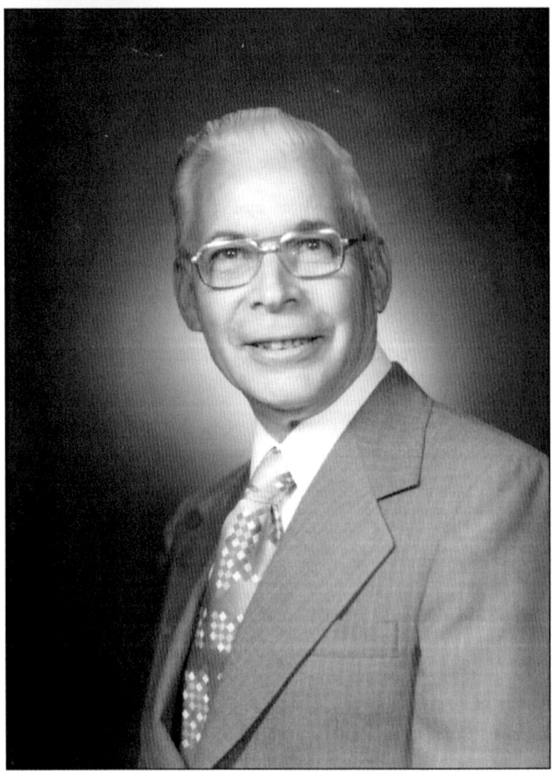

Mearl Raygor, a local historian, kept the area's history alive through his writings. His books include *Indians of Southeastern Minnesota*, *Early Days of Stewartville*, *Rochester Story*, and *Merchant to Millions*. He also helped spearhead efforts to save Richard W. Sears's birthplace home. (Courtesy of the Raygor family.)

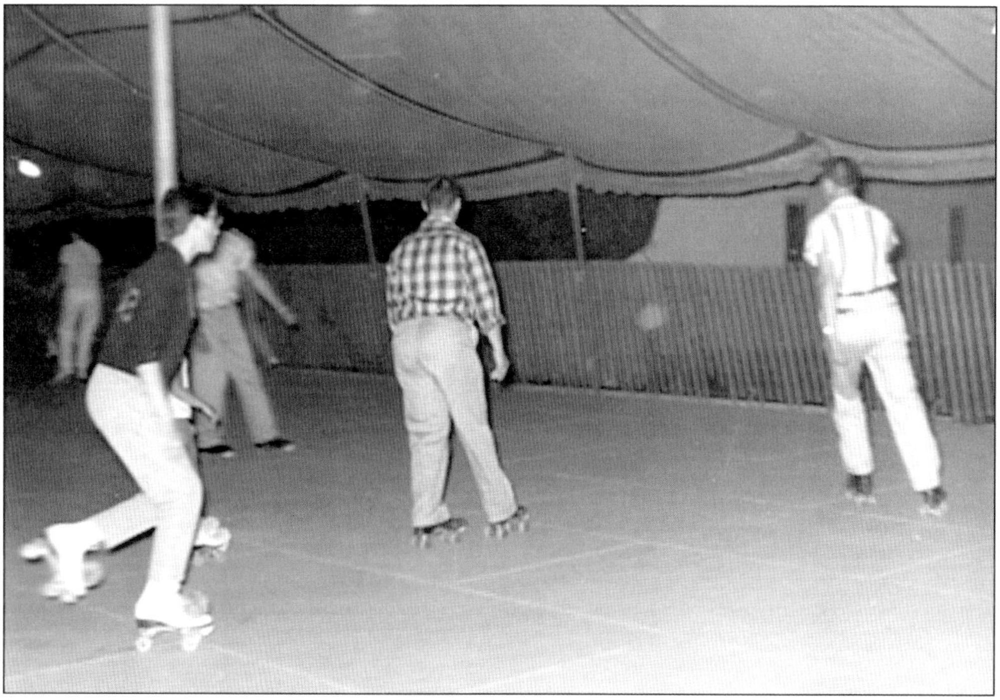

Glover's Roller Rink opened in Stewartville in 1956. For two years, Marian and Franklin "Buddy" Glover operated the rink under a big tent. (Courtesy of Sue Runkle.)

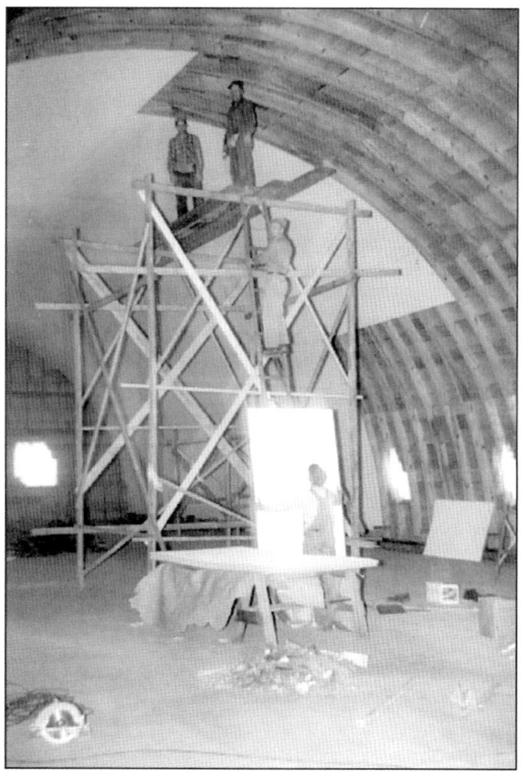

In 1958, the Glovers built a permanent year-around rink on the southeast end of Highway 63 South and Main Street. (Courtesy of Sue Runkle.)

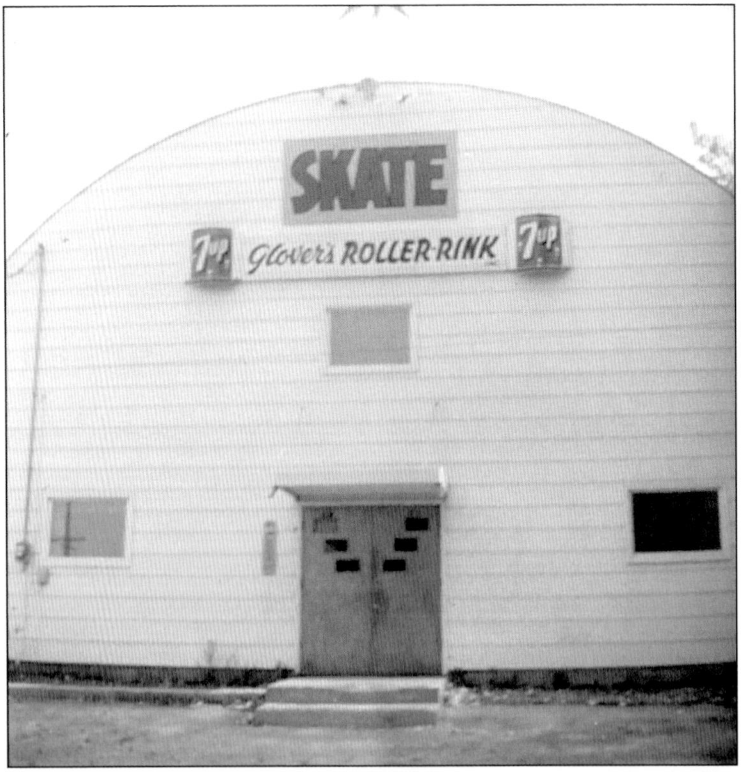

In addition to the rink, the Glovers operated a school bus line in 1948 with one route and one bus. It increased to eight routes in 1976. (Courtesy of Sue Runkle.)

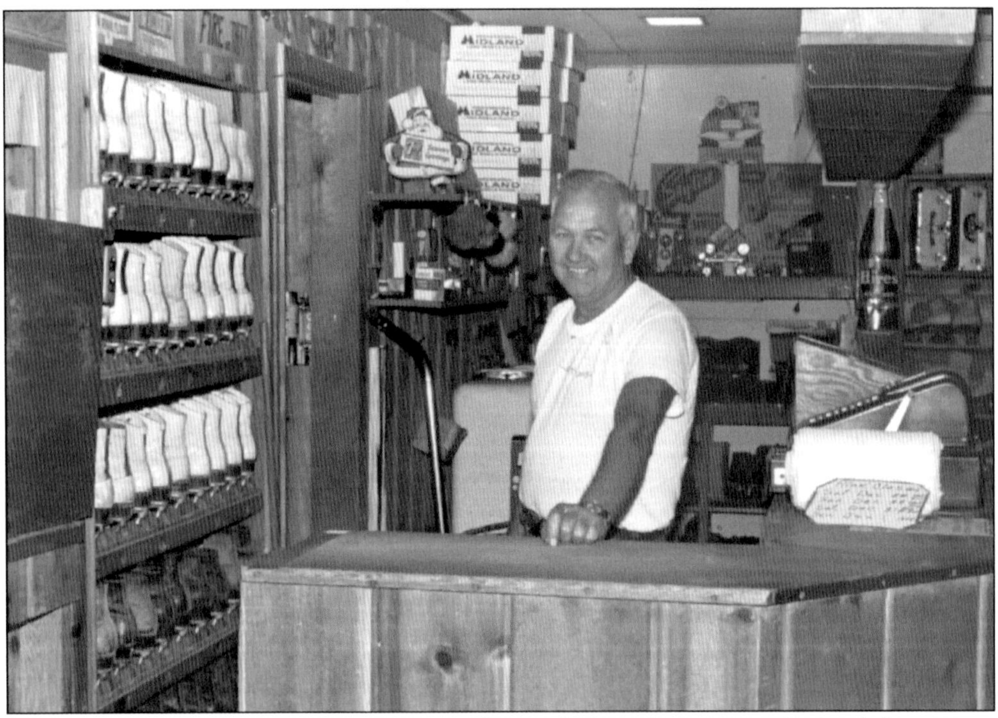

Franklin "Buddy" Glover greeted everyone with a smile. Here he is pictured behind the counter of the roller rink waiting for the lineup of kids to get their skates. (Courtesy of Sue Runkle.)

Nine

IMPORTANT EVENTS

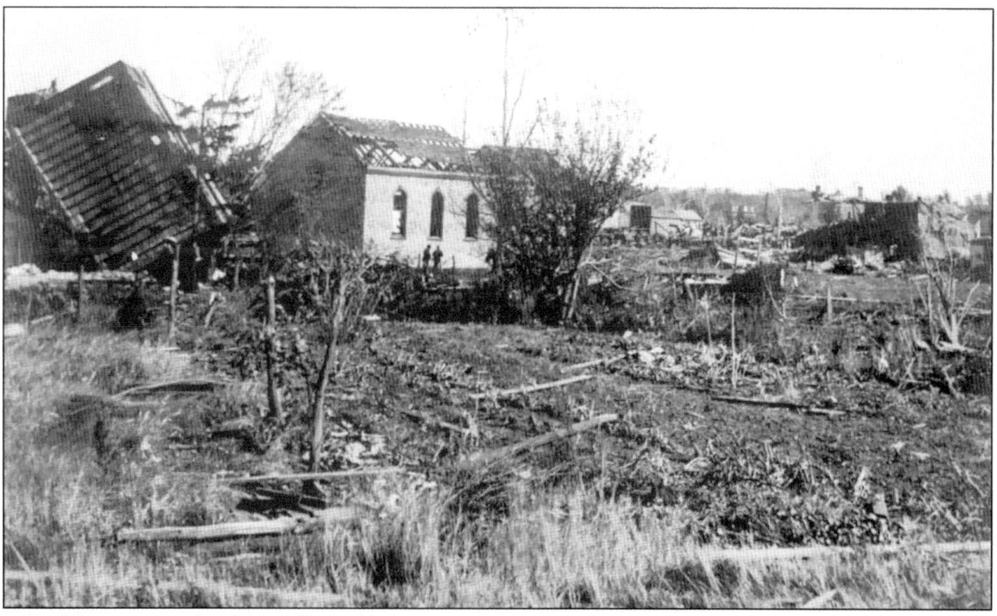

It had been a week of hot, humid weather with many storms going through the countryside. Tornadoes had hit Hamilton and Pleasant Grove before the sad news of a disastrous cyclone in Rochester on August 21, 1883, had been received. About 30 people lost their lives, and many were badly injured. The Stewartville area communities were served by the doctors who resided in Rochester—Dr. W. W. Mayo made the professional calls by horse and buggy or horse and cutter. (Courtesy of Madelyn Betcher.)

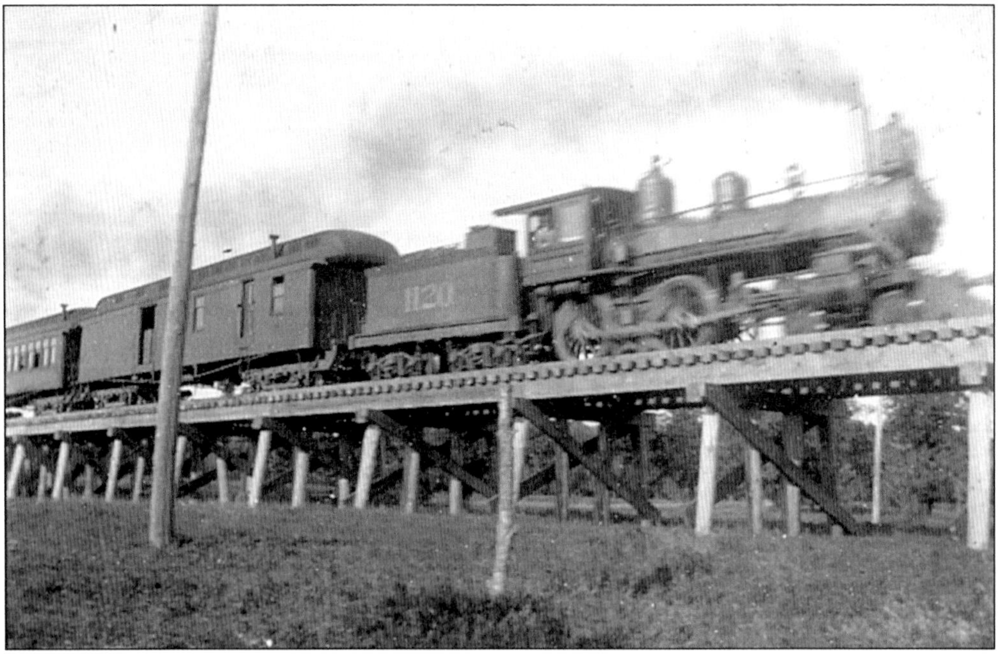

The railroad came to Stewartville in 1890 with the building by the Winona and Southwestern Railway of a line from Osage, Iowa, to Winona. One of the most important factors of building this rail line was the rapid development of Stewartville, which was centered in a rich farming area and had a flourishing mill as its main enterprise. (Courtesy of the Gray family.)

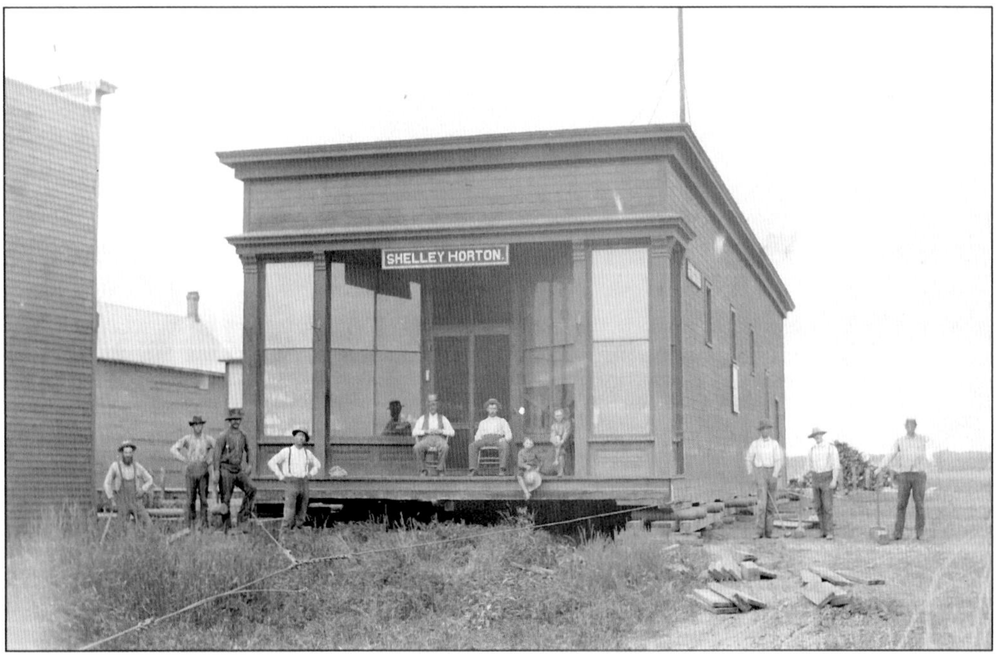

In 1891, the business houses in the Railroad Addition are being moved to the west side of the tracks. Shelley Horton made the start, and his large general store was put up on rollers. A month was required to perform the job of moving all. Old settlers tell about John Voltz, who was an expert in moving buildings with four horses and a yoke of oxen. (Courtesy of the SAHS.)

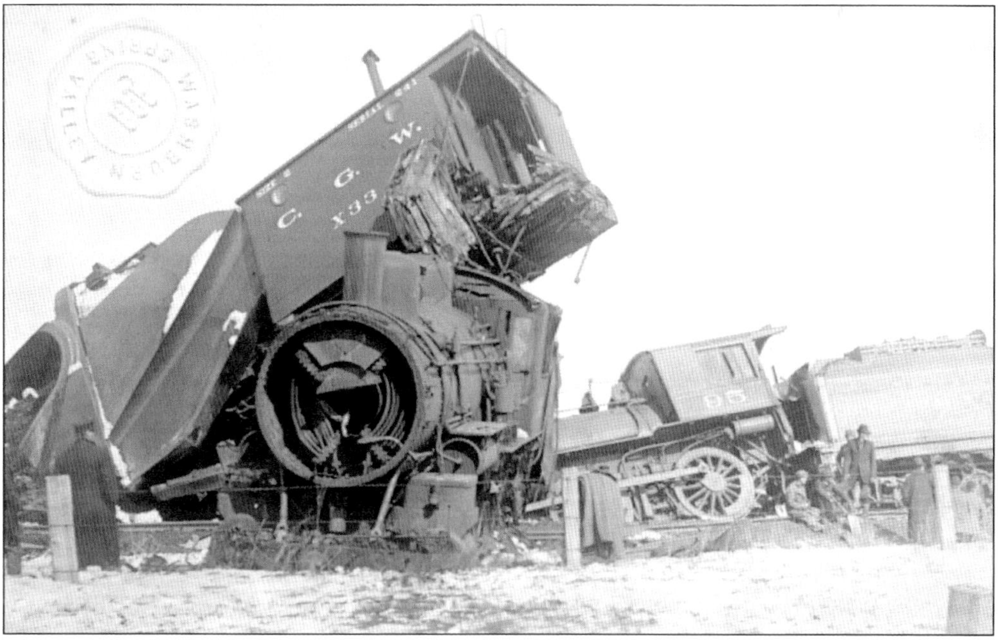

The grim result of a head-on collision, such calamities were frequent on the single-track lines of the era with basic signaling systems. (Courtesy of the Gray family.)

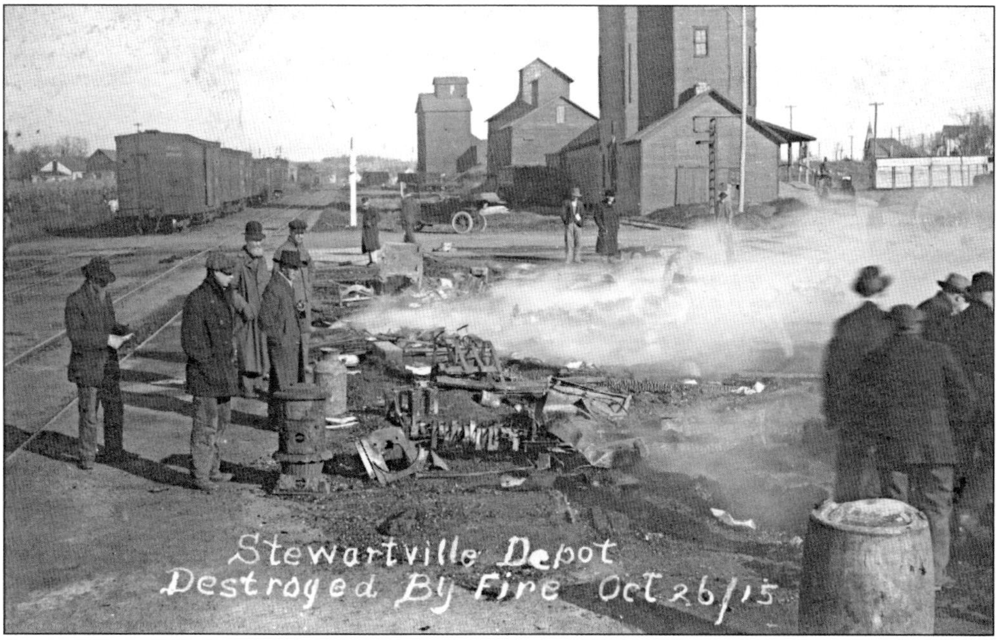

Fire destroyed the building and contents of the Chicago Great Western Railroad depot on October 26, 1915. (Courtesy of the Gray family.)

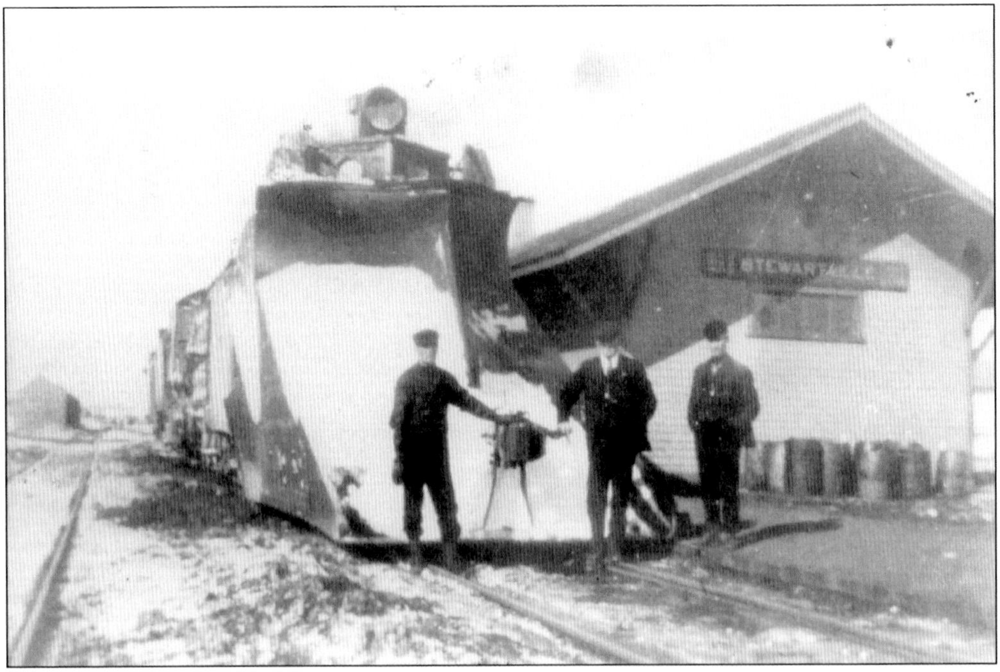

In order to keep the tracks open in winter, it often took three engines to push the plow through the drifts. (Courtesy of the Gray family.)

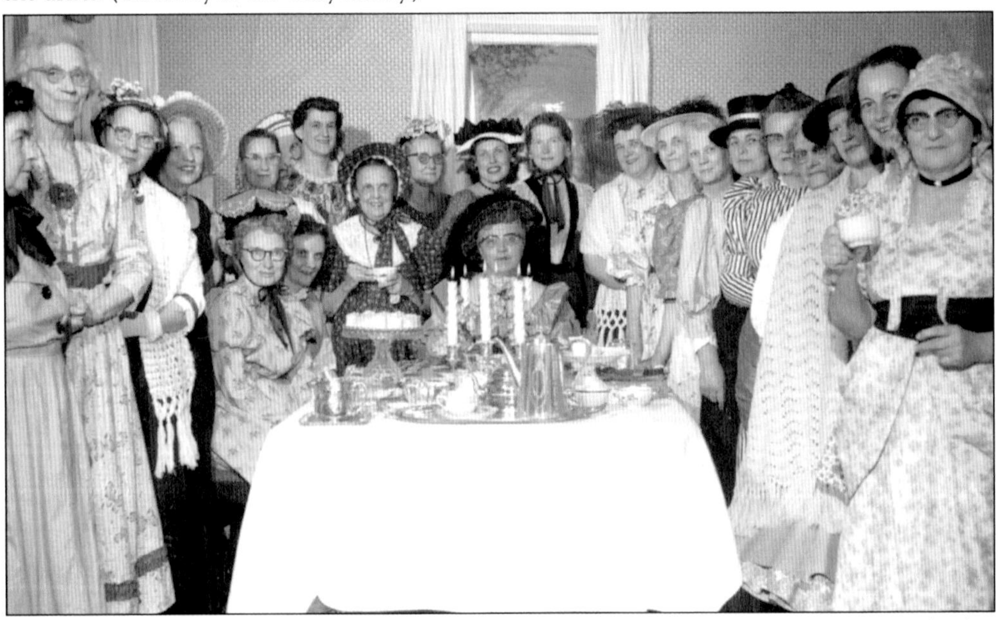

Marcia Tysseling was known for her many years of service as a postmaster and civic leader. Tysseling organized the 1957 centennial tea and served angel food cake with lemon sauce, which was her favorite dessert. Pictured here are (first row) Bea Foote, Altie Schaefer, Midge Brown, and Marion Lenton; (second row) Ruth Ringey, Gladys Owen, Alice Smidt, Edna Light, Dolly Carr, Dorothy Robinson, Marion Light, Gerri Gray, Margaret Engel, Florence Born, Elmedia Bentley, Marcia Tysseling, Marion King, Kay Hoeft, Lena Jensen, Jean Hillesland, Helen Hagen, and Esther Lenton. (Courtesy of the Gray family.)

INDEX

Big Elm, 85
Bonner, LePearl, 115, 117
centennial tea, 124
Central Elementary School, 45, 47, 50
Cussons Milling Company, 81, 90
Dodd, Herb, 118
Farmer's Elevator, 97, 98
Fugle mill, 37
Glover's Roller Rink, 125, 126
Gray, Cecelia, 18
Hagen, A. O., 116
High Forest, 23, 25
Hoaglan, Hersh 18
Idle Hour, 81, 82
King, Carol, 120
Lake Florence, 83–88
Lake Florence dam, 79, 80
Light, Marion, 19
Moore Block, 65
opera house, 64
Pleasant Grove, 39
Raygor, Mearl, 120
Risser, Dr. Alden, 116
Root River, 89, 90
Sears, Richard W., 14
Smith, Edna (Staples), 15
Stewart, Charles, 13
Stewartville Fire Department, 78
Stewartville High School, 56
Sumner Center, 44
Sutherland, J. E., 46
Tattersall House, 24
Tews Hotel, 67–69
tornado, 121

ACROSS AMERICA, PEOPLE ARE DISCOVERING SOMETHING WONDERFUL. *THEIR HERITAGE.*

Arcadia Publishing is the leading local history publisher in the United States. With more than 3,000 titles in print and hundreds of new titles released every year, Arcadia has extensive specialized experience chronicling the history of communities and celebrating America's hidden stories, bringing to life the people, places, and events from the past. To discover the history of other communities across the nation, please visit:

www.arcadiapublishing.com

Customized search tools allow you to find regional history books about the town where you grew up, the cities where your friends and family live, the town where your parents met, or even that retirement spot you've been dreaming about.

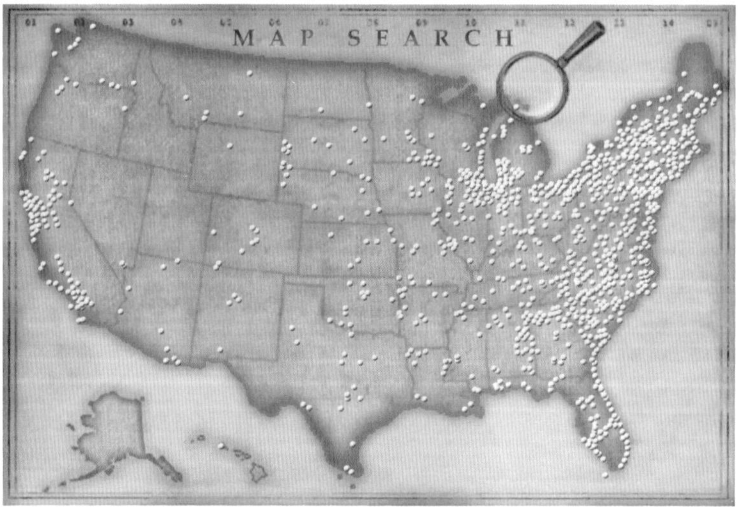